Yale Studies in English, 178

THE DREAM THOUGHT OF

Piers Plowman

by Elizabeth D. Kirk

New Haven and London   Yale University Press

1972

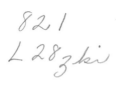

821
L28₃kᵢ

Copyright © 1972 by Yale University.
Library of Congress catalog card number: 72–75198
International standard book number: 0–300–01545–3

Designed by John O. C. McCrillis
and set in Granjon type.
Printed in the United States of America by
The Colonial Press, Inc., Clinton, Massachusetts.

Published in Great Britain, Europe, and Africa by
Yale University Press, Ltd., London.
Distributed in Canada by McGill-Queen's University Press, Montreal;
in Latin America by Kaiman & Polon, Inc., New York City;
in Australasia and Southeast Asia by
John Wiley & Sons Australasia Pty. Ltd., Sydney;
in India by UBS Publishers' Distributors Pvt., Ltd., Delhi;
in Japan by John Weatherhill, Inc., Tokyo.

Am

For
Helen G. Hole

On a huge hill,
Cragged, and steep, Truth stands, and hee that will
Reach her, about must, and about must goe.

JOHN DONNE

and every attempt
Is a wholly new start, and a different kind of failure
. . . .
There is only the fight to recover what has been lost
And found and lost again and again: and now, under conditions
That seem unpropitious.

T. S. ELIOT

Nasce per quello, a guisa di rampollo,
  a pie del vero il dubbio; ed è natura
  ch'al sommo pinge noi di collo in collo.

DANTE

Contents

Acknowledgments

Completing a work like the present study is a time for awareness of how much it owes to others. I must thank Yale University and Brown University for summer stipends that freed time for writing and the Fulbright Program for a year in England that permitted me to spend a memorable morning on Malvern Hills. To my friends Joan Grenthot Whitehead, Elizabeth Bassett Keiser, Anne Case, and Alice-Augusta Miskimin, who have been involved in the project from the beginning, belong ideas I can no longer distinguish from my own. I am grateful to my Brown colleagues Barbara Lewalski, Rosalie Colie, Henry Zerner, and George Anderson for generous help and advice and to Melvin Keiser for guidance on many theological points. To Alvina P. Wheeler I owe special gratitude for indispensable help in the final preparation of the manuscript. And I must thank my students at Brown not only for many specific insights but for the perspective they helped me gain on the problems of *Piers Plowman.*

At this time I feel acutely how much I owe to the teachers in whom I have been so fortunate; I am especially conscious of my debt to Professor John C. Pope and Professor Wayne C. Booth. But above all, I must thank Professor E. Talbot Donaldson, who directed the dissertation on the A text which marked the beginning of my interest in *Piers Plowman,* who has allowed me to use readings from his and Professor Kane's forthcoming edition of the B text, and who has read the manuscript more than once. Without his judicious irony, it would have been twice as long.

I also wish to acknowledge here my gratitude to Jacques Plasse le Caisne, weaver and lecturer on medieval art, who once gave a teen-aged tourist the great arch in the crypt of the Mont-Saint-Michel.

This book belongs to all these people, but it belongs most fundamentally to my husband, who has believed in it more than I have, and without whose comments and suggestions on draft after draft it would never have become intelligible. Nevertheless, it is dedicated to my

mother, from whose example comes the commitment to literature and
to teaching which I hope this book enacts in the area of criticism.

                                                                      E. D. K.

Rehoboth, Massachusetts
1971

Introduction

It is a cliché of literary handbooks that *Piers Plowman* is more "medieval" than Chaucer, and like most clichés this one has its truth. No work of art could be more intimately bound up with the social life and the thought of its own culture—not the *Divine Comedy* or *The Dunciad* or *Catch-22*. Yet the poem also suggests dangerously anachronistic comparisons with the later course of Western civilization—with the Reformation, the romantic movement, existentialism, modern social and economic theory, recent Catholic theology, surrealism, and the fiction and drama of the absurd. Perhaps *Piers Plowman,* for all its archaic idiom, is *less* "medieval" than Chaucer, and where Chaucer's least medieval qualities suggest the Renaissance, *Piers Plowman* suggests post-Enlightenment attempts to deal with the crumbling of the medieval and Renaissance synthesis, not that the synthesis has already broken down, but because the poem reflects a consciousness capable of facing, from within, what others did not recognize until they were looking at it from without. That *Piers Plowman* exists in three puzzlingly different versions is no coincidence but is a reflection of this quality.

The very existence of these distinct yet similar poems, which we call the A, B, and C texts, defies our ordinary understanding of how an artist works and evolves yet corresponds even less with what we know of revisers and continuators. Taken together, their successive attempts to resolve problems fundamental to man's position vis-à-vis objective truth form three stages in a drama as powerful as it is enigmatic. The structure of *Piers Plowman* is accretive; yet it is genuinely a structure. Many medieval works have been compared to Gothic cathedrals: some to cathedrals built all in one style, some to cathedrals built in a series of styles, some to unfinished cathedrals. Others suggest a tapestry or a kaleidoscope or a series of mutually reflecting mirrors. *Piers Plowman* suggests a mobile. Whatever version we read first is like a finished mobile, a complete and structured whole, yet one which is complex and flexible enough to invite the viewer to watch it from a variety of angles and perspectives and to see its parts respond to each other in new and developing patterns. When we turn to another version, we think of the process by which a mobile is built. As each new part is added, the previous network of connected parts remains, but it adjusts, altering the relative position and total effect of the parts. The parts of the *Piers Plowman* mobile are not, like Chaucer's tales, separate, self-contained structures that can be viewed either in isolation or in an infinite variety of combinations with other parts. They are pieces of all sizes and degrees of complexity whose nature admits of multiple kinds of suggestiveness but whose meaning is determined by the particular context in which each is fixed—which is precisely what changes from version to version.

The poem's early commentators, while aware of how difficult much of its intellectual content was, did not seem to think there was anything abstruse about the poet's purpose. They seem to have found the poem eccentric, amateurish, or even incompetent on the surface and preferred the least puzzling, most "sociological" passages, but they assumed it had a straightforward purpose like that of any spiritual autobiography. The successive revisions seemed understandable, if not always successful, attempts to do the same thing a little better by a poet constitutionally incapable of carrying out any purpose smoothly and rationally. His incapacity was a childlike quality characteristic of all medieval minds, except for those occasional geniuses like Chaucer who are not very "medieval" (except when they are writing passages we happen not to like); or, his "puritan" attitude to his own artistic temperament left him incapable of applying artistic or intellectual discipline consistently; or, the genres he was working in were intrinsically formless and digressive.

These theories all seemed to receive considerable support from the style. In the available texts—the Skeat editions on which, for the B and C versions, we are still largely dependent even today—line after line is fuzzy and peculiar in a way that looks more and more mindless the more carefully it is studied, and hosts of purely scribal differences between the versions seriously obscure the relation among them. If Avarice's wife "spak to the spynnesteres to spynnen it *oute*" as she does in Skeat's B text (5. 216), the meaninglessness or redundancy not only weakens the line but weakens one's attention to the lines afterwards.

Yet the B text must originally have had, as Skeat's A text does, "spak to the spynstere to spynnen it *softe*," so that the cloth woven from the resulting thread can more easily be stretched by the process Avarice describes. And if Robyn the Roper, in the well-known Skeat line, arises "bi the southe" to umpire the game in Glutton's tavern, the text becomes not merely mindless but riddling, whereas the original B-text line, as Chambers and Grattan establish, had "Robyn þe ropere arise þey be-souȝte," by analogy with the A text's "Robyn þe ropere was red to arisen." [1] A poem systematically weakened by this superficial meaning-lessness, especially when its craftsmanship is somewhat uneven at best, will necessarily seem the work of a simple-minded and petulant indi-vidual, whose strategies scarcely invite our serious attention and whose difficulties seem gratuitous and at best quaint.

Three major developments in *Piers Plowman* studies separate us from such an attitude. The first and most important has been editorial. The *Piers Plowman* manuscripts combine all the factors which most compli-cate the editor's task: careless and poorly disciplined scribes; contami-nation among manuscript traditions and between versions of the poem; subject matter so immediate to the scribes' experience that it tempted them sometimes to add to their original and sometimes to censor it, and a verse form flexible enough to encourage them to do so; and, above all, a text diverse and uneven enough that identification of the characteristics of a genuine line becomes peculiarly difficult. Since the work of Thomas Wright and W. W. Skeat, the collation of immensely complex material and a revolution in the assumptions of editing have been necessary. Now, definitive texts of all three versions are within reach, and our understanding of the poem, and of the special character of each version, has been transformed. This has been a gradual process. For the A text, George Kane's edition[2] permits the reader to see the

1. See R. W. Chambers and J. H. C. Grattan's articles on the text of *Piers Plowman,* in *Modern Language Review* 4 (1908): 357–89, 11 (1916): 257–75, and 26 (1931): 1–51; Chambers, "Incoherencies in the A- and B-Texts of Piers Plowman and Their Bearing on the Authorship," *London Mediaeval Studies* 1 (1937): 27–39; and Elsie Blackman, "Notes on the B-Text MSS of *Piers Plowman,*" *Journal of English and Germanic Philology* 17 (1918): 489–545.
2. *Piers Plowman: The A Version* (London, 1960).

effects of this restoration work on the whole texture of the poem. For the other two texts, we must still read the old editions, while attempting to correct our impressions in terms of new understanding and of those new readings which have found their way into critical discussion of key scenes or passages.

The second development, the authorship controversy, has dominated *Piers Plowman* studies during most of this century. Except for the impetus it gave to work on the text and to study of the poem's intellectual background, it now seems in retrospect a contentious and short-sighted argument which too long distracted scholars from the real issues. Not only was much of the controversy based on a misunderstanding of the texual situation, but the multiple-authorship theory turned out merely to restate the problem, not to solve it, since it left us with three poets at least as odd as the one from whom it tried to extricate us. Defenders of single authorship, on the other hand, have generally minimized the differences between versions and failed to confront seriously enough what an extraordinary artistic and psychological process they were postulating. Perhaps nothing that has appeared in the past decade has done more to restore clarity, relevance, and objectivity to discussion of *Piers Plowman* than a short and unpretentious study whose conclusions are, in a sense, only negative: George Kane's masterly analysis of the authorship question, which evaluates the extent to which the various arguments rest on valid evidence, establish any verifiable conclusion, or have any real bearing on the questions at issue. Kane shows that no argument yet presented invalidates the traditional view that one "William Langland" wrote all three versions.[3] In the saner atmosphere which resulted, our attention can now be reoriented toward concern with the context of these poems and their distinctive characteristics, instead of toward extrapolating their difficulties into a biographical question for the consideration of which we lack, at least at present, any valid basis.[4]

3. *Piers Plowman: The Evidence for Authorship* (London, 1965).
4. Nevertheless, in dealing with passages which played a crucial role in the authorship controversy, I have tried to indicate briefly how greater knowledge of medieval thought and convention, as well as wider grasp of the poem's structure, have thrown a completely new light on what they imply about authorship: see especially chapter 1, pp. 25–28, and chapter 2, pp. 64–70. I deal with very few of the C poet's

One result of Kane's study has been a strong reaction against the subjectivity of "version umpiring," manifested in an increasing emphasis on the once despised C text,[5] whose more systematic and intelligible structure is most accessible to theological and philosophical analysis and whose more objective mode of narration and decreased emphasis on an individualized dreamer provide a useful corrective to the critic tempted by superficially modern interpretations.[6]

Nevertheless, the multiple-authorship theory advanced by J. M. Manly[7] still lies behind the major advances in our understanding of the poem, since it was his realization of how striking the differences among the three versions really are that opened the eyes of single- and multiple-authorship critics alike to how drastically *Piers Plowman* challenges any conception, medieval or modern, of how artists work. What we are groping for when we argue about authorship is not really the source of the versions but their nature and relationship. Knowledge of the first will not of itself tell us the second, but the second can be grasped without the first and may indeed supply it: "If you know how, you know who," as Dorothy L. Sayers wrote in quite a different connection. The authorship controversy rested on highly simplistic assumptions about the Middle Ages and about the applicability of modern stylistic

changes, but none of them seems to me incompatible with the evolution of a single man's ideas or with a perfectly understandable, if not always judicious, attempt to devise solutions to what are serious artistic problems about the B text.

5. See, for instance, Elizabeth Salter and Derek Pearsall, eds., *Piers Plowman,* York Medieval Text Series (Evanston, Ill., 1967), p. 1; and Edward Vasta, *The Spiritual Basis of Piers Plowman* (The Hague, 1965), pp. 24–25.

6. The reinstating of the C text, which began with E. Talbot Donaldson's major study, *Piers Plowman: The C-Text and Its Poet* (New Haven, 1949), has been of crucial importance in recent progress. But in the long run C's artistic stature, relative to that of A and B, will have to be faced, not in order to argue about who wrote C, but in order to appreciate what is involved in writing a long poem on the subject that we might call, by analogy with the subdivisions of medieval romance, the "matter of Christianity." To this problem, many of the aspects of *Piers Plowman* that are liabilities (or at best irrelevancies) when we are trying to work out the poem's intellectual argument prove the most important; such aspects of *Piers Plowman,* for better or worse, are much less prominent in the C version.

7. *"Piers the Plowman* and Its Sequence," *The Cambridge History of English Literature* 2 (Cambridge, 1908): 1–48.

criteria to earlier poetry and on even more simplistic ideas about artists. Increasing knowledge of how the creative process takes place, especially in artists for whom ideas and ideologies are a matter of deep concern, has destroyed the argument that an artist will not "spoil" his own work as his ideas evolve. The real problem, which is a problem under either theory of authorship, is why an artist should not break loose from existing poems and do something fresh. We expect an artist to feel like the young Keats, whose dissatisfaction with *Endymion* led him, not to revise it, but to put it behind him: "the foundations are too sandy." [8] This is a problem that goes far beyond the question of why artists as diverse as Wordsworth and Yeats should have gone on continually tinkering with their earlier works, with controversial results, and it involves the question of "privileged subject matter." Whether or not such subjects exist in any absolute sense, they certainly do in practice, and they can be of two types. There is subject matter to which artists continually return because it is both rich and communal and thus lends itself, both in the artists' own development and in their relationships with their audiences, to richer and richer permutations and combinations, as Michelangelo's *Pietàs* or the history of Arthurian romance illustrate. A completely different kind of privileged subject matter is that which is personally essential to the artist himself, so that he keeps returning to it as if his power as a creator, his very development, even his own identity were tied up with the problem of dealing adequately with that situation. This is most common in the form of the recurrent theme or plot; the one-book artist is obviously an extreme case, although by no means unknown. There is obviously all the difference in the world between Henry James writing again and again about the American in Europe and extensively revising *The American* itself for the New York edition—a dubious "improvement"—and a hypothetical Henry James who did nothing but rewrite *The American* each time his work entered a new phase. That would have been ludicrous, because *The American* was not worth it. The particular grasp it has on its subject is not rich enough, nor could James possibly have felt that its inadequacies were crucial ones, intrinsically bound up with the solution of

8. John Keats, preface to *Endymion*.

all his problems, a riddle that somehow held the clew to everything else. But it is not ludicrous to imagine that some other subject could be worth it, because it was privileged in both the public and the private sense and because it lent itself to extensive addition as well as to revision. The relationship between the A and B texts with which the present study will be concerned defines *Piers Plowman* as precisely this sort of poem.[9]

The third major development that has rendered the old view of *Piers Plowman* obsolete has come through intellectual history. Not only is *Piers Plowman retardataire* in its verse form; its idiom and dramatic techniques, its intellectual methods, its sources and assumptions are also highly traditional. Again and again, what has long seemed to be random or idiosyncratic association of ideas in *Piers Plowman* no longer appears so, as soon as we cease to approach the poem provincially. The more we learn about medieval art and thought, the more we create for ourselves a "glossary" of its arguments and motifs, which interprets them and their connotations just as a good dictionary's correlation of usage defines a poem's diction. The greater our knowledge of patterns of thinking current in the Middle Ages, especially the clusters of biblical texts, theological issues, similes, and illustrations which were handed on from thinker to thinker, the more we realize it is impossible to overstress the extent to which *Piers Plowman*'s images, allusions, quotations, and arguments are drawn from them. Again and again, no sooner do we identify one element from such a cluster than we begin to notice others in the immediate vicinity.

On the other hand, this very scholarship shows us that if the poem is conventional where we thought it eccentric, it is indeed eccentric where we thought it conventional. The integers of *Piers Plowman* may be the common property of medieval thinkers, but the structure built from them is anything but conventional, as the B poet's treatment of

9. Since an understanding of this relationship depends on appreciating the strikingly different artistic strategies and psychological emphases of the A and B versions before going on to a consideration of their complementary nature, I have generally referred to "the A poet" and "the B poet" rather than to "Langland," a mode of reference that also serves to emphasize the fact that the present study is an analysis of structure rather than an argument about authorship, though its conclusions would constitute an argument for single authorship (if one is still needed).

the personification Imagination and his defenses of poetry illustrate most dramatically. To relate the motifs and citations of the three poems to medieval preaching and theology is essential, but it is quite another thing to assume that their rationale and structure can be defined as Alain de Lille defined the sermon: "Praedicatio est manifesta et publica instructio morum et fidei, informatione hominum deserviens, ex rationum semita et auctoritatum fonte proveniens." [10] To do so is to render the poems unintelligible as drastically as ignorance itself can do, since it forces us to discard too much of the poem as essentially irrelevant, when the textual critic and the scholar both tell us that the old image of a wooly-minded poet has to be abandoned.

Daunting complexity, frequent clumsiness, and apparently contradictory changes made in successive revisions are inherent in the poems' central purpose. They are a function of the poet's attempt to use the verbal, dramatic, and theological givens of his day from a perspective and for a purpose sometimes as incongruous with ordinary usage as a pun. The poem is dealing with human experience at a level to which its intellectual and artistic vocabulary can be adapted only at the price of constant tension. In this sense, *Piers Plowman* is, as has long been recognized of its political theory, both radical and conservative. Its difficulties and its spiraling mode of argument are part of the poet's attempt to view radical hopes for the future as a return to the sanctions of the past. In this respect, *Piers Plowman* reminds us, not of the great artists who were its contemporaries, Chaucer and the Gawain poet, but of a figure like Roger Bacon. Both the poem and the thinker have been badly served by partisan critics who have tried to divorce Langland and Bacon from their contexts and to turn them into forerunners of later movements. Admittedly, both have affinities with much that happens later and that is already beginning to happen in the later Middle Ages. Nevertheless, to see them primarily in this perspective is to distort their very nature as irascible, often inaccurate, unfulfilled critics of their milieu who are nevertheless an integral part of it and who work within

10. "A sermon is a clear and public teaching of morals and faith, devoted to the instruction of men, issuing from the path of reasonings and the fountain of the authorities." Quoted in Etienne Gilson, *Les idées et les lettres* (Paris, 1932), p. 97, n. 1.

it as "radical conservatives." The terms in which David Knowles has described Bacon are surprisingly apt for *Piers Plowman*:

[he undertook] a pursuit foredoomed to frustration in that age, and what with his own sense of inferiority, his constant financial stringency, his conflict with authority and his own temperament, he passed from one period of distress to another. He was to all appearances, irresponsible and neurotic and as such, perhaps, unmanageable and friendless. Yet he had great intuitive genius and rare critical power. He seized with precision the basic faults of later scholasticism. . . . He deplored the divorce of pure thought from life and experience. . . . Yet the ultimate aims, the philosophical prepossessions and the outward form of his writings are purely traditional.[11]

The problem of the relationship between *Piers Plowman*'s intellectual content and its manner is part of a larger question, with which students of the Middle Ages, and of the Renaissance as well, have lately been much concerned: the relationship of art to explicitly formulated theology, and whether this relationship may be taken to be axiomatically different in the Middle Ages from later times. To answer it, we must rethink what didactic poetry is instead of treating the term automatically as pejorative. *Piers Plowman,* like all medieval art, requires that we learn how to tell when a poem means what it says directly and when what it says directly is only a means of saying something else, by rhetorical techniques that range from allegory to irony, two modes that medieval rhetoricians considered to be related. In fact, even the literal level itself raises similar problems. We are dealing with a poem full of long, expository, doctrinal, and argumentative passages: do these constitute the main current of its movement? Or are they one means, among others, to an end not fully intellectual, part of a process symbiotic with, but in a very real sense merely symptomatic of, some quite different development? The poem is bound together by continuities that inhere in just those factors that complicate our understanding of its argument and make it hard to follow, the features that seem at first sight irrelevant

11. *The Evolution of Medieval Thought* (New York, 1962), p. 286.

to its dramatic and thematic continuity and that some readers dismiss as mere artistic flaws—the signs of an incompetent craftsman. Some of this can be traced to medieval conventions and habits different from those of the theologian and philosopher. Some of them are built up, step by step, within the poem through its cumulative treatment of the Dreamer, the apparent circularity and digressiveness of many sections, their shifting tone and emphases.

This view of the poem depends on seeing it linearly; that is, such features constitute a pattern, or a structure, only if the order in which they appear is taken seriously. This is precisely the aspect of *Piers Plowman* that the parallel-text reader and the theological commentator most obscure in the very act of illuminating the integers of the poem. What sets off the allegorical controversy, as regards *Piers Plowman,* from that which most other medieval poetry has provoked is precisely this matter of order. The controversy over whether the Prologue is "allegorical" is not really, as it would be in comparable discussion of Chaucer, between critics who say that plowmen are plowmen and others who say they are anything but plowmen: both agree that, in the poem, the plowman becomes a metaphor for spiritual leadership. The question is how soon this happens. Is the poem saying something about real plowmen, too? Is what it eventually says about bishops dependent on its having first dealt with plowmen as such? An allegorical text, designed to deflect our awareness from its apparent content into an enriched perception of some other, must have properties that *cause* the deflection process to take place and that determine its direction.

Order is the key to the poem's intellectual argument as well. Recent analysis has been invaluable in moving out sideways, as it were, from each unit of the poem's discourse, to demonstrate that, far from being a discrete unit in a series, it is part of a cluster of ideas that are not only communal but inherently related to every major element of Christian doctrine. That is the kind of structure Christianity is. In the Christian universe, every key doctrine, every crucial problem, is integral to every other; the beginning is related to the end and participates typologically in it; the means are organic to the purpose, the past to the future, the concrete to the abstract, the personal to the communal, the social to the theological. Within the medieval frame of reference, the principles governing the macrocosm are those that govern the microcosm, and those that govern the psyche govern the political and economic structure as well. At some fundamental level, it may have been impossible for a medieval writer to deal with any subject without suggesting truths of wider applicability.

Even outside the medieval world, it is the property of any great work of art from the smallest lyric to the greatest epic, to be, in some sense, about all human experience. Yet none of these historical and aesthetic truisms is of any use in criticism if it obscures the practical distinction between one subject matter and another or between one rhetorical technique and another. Nor can an intellectual argument work like a reversible equation in chemistry, no matter how closely related any two ideas may be. If, in the larger perspective of the Christian theologian, the revelation of Law is the precursor and, in that sense, an image of the revelation of Love, that very fact is dependent on the difference between the law of Law and the law of Love; and the existence of the connection between them is a function of the sequential, historical process by which the human race moved from the one to the other. As finite minds, we must necessarily experience sequentially what in an eternal dimension coexists. And if it is true that Christianity is a religion of simultaneous pattern, it is also the most strictly and progressively historical of all religions and one which sees the eternal God interacting with men in a sequential process in which everything hangs on the quality of the particular moment and the identity of the particular creature. What corresponds to this historical dimension in the created universe is the order of the parts in a poem or argument. The key to almost every enigma of *Piers Plowman* is a sense of its sequence. The spiraling character of the poem, in which the same issues and problems recur and are repeatedly reexamined, may at first sight obscure this but in the long run makes it all the more important, as Albert Descamp points out in explaining the comparable progression that Paul follows in the argument of the Epistle to the Romans:

Paul procède par approches successives, ou, si l'on préfere une autre image, il trace autour d'un seul point central divers cercles concentriques. C'est moins une argumentation linéaire, procédent par adjonction d'éléments nouveaux, qu'une dialectique par répétitions amplifiées, le nouvel exposé enveloppant en quelque sorte le précédent.[12]

Perhaps the ideal commentator on *Piers Plowman* would bring to the poem total, simultaneous awareness of the timeless structure that is Christian theology. But he would be drawn by the poem, not into contemplation of this simultaneity, but into rediscovery through order. He, like every other reader, will be made to see some things first and others later, to understand the later in terms of what the first looked like, and to reinterpret the first in terms of the later. He will find arguments that begin by confronting one issue and not others, in a process which cannot advance to new issues until a perspective on the first has been achieved, either through intellectual lucidity or through despair. We tend to think of such reexamination of Christianity as a function for art only in a post-Christian era. It is also properly a role of art in a securely Christian one, where the dangers are not hostility, incomprehension, or alternative hypotheses but apathy, habituation, ignorance, conflict between the ideal and the actual, the insidious degeneration of religious language and thought into dead metaphor and intellectual or cultural convention. In the Christian as in the non-Christian society, the problem is to find experience that will make what the mind constructs and assents to synthesize with what actuality shows; correlate the intellectual with the experiential; and, in artistic terms, fuse the structural with the dramatic. These are, in a very special sense, the functions of those diverse art forms we group under the term "allegory." To respond to allegory is to respond to its power to make connections *in the order* and *in the terms* in which it presents them. To respond in this way is a skill in which the modern consciousness is grievously awkward; we have prejudice and historical ignorance to overcome, although our age, which characteristically expresses itself in terms of the ironic, the absurd, the surrealistic, the abstract, and the allusive, is much less alien to it than the age of Victoria, which found medieval thought childlike. But the interpretation of allegory is not, in the last analysis, different from the appre-

12. *Studiorum Paulinorum Congressus Internationalis Catholicus* 1961 (*Analecta Biblica* 17–18) Rome, 1963, p. 12.

ciation of the larger category to which it belongs, art. Rigidity in defining
how art may convey meaning and lack of flexibility in recognizing what
means are being used in any given case are as severely limiting as
historical ignorance. Which of these dangers a particular critic will stress
will depend a great deal on which of the possible errors and distortions
he considers most likely and least appreciated. Great indeed are the
dangers of not knowing medieval thought and of not taking it seriously
or of searching through it, like pack rats, for bits and pieces that please
us in our own perspective. Perhaps even greater is the danger of ignoring
the extent to which the poem is its own demonstration and assumes the
authenticity of its own subject matter, not as any sort of sugarcoating
of its meaning—little enough of *Piers Plowman* "delights" in the
Horatian sense—but as the very situation in which God and man meet.

In view of all these developments in twentieth-century *Piers Plowman*
scholarship, a study like the present one, which not only concentrates
on A and B but takes them more or less literally and compares them,
may seem perhaps regressive. It is not so intended. We have reached a
point when it has become possible to refocus our attention, not on
authorship, but on those aspects of *Piers Plowman* that the authorship
controversy obscured in the very process of attempting to illuminate
them and that have since benefited more from neglect than from
polemics. It should now be possible to address ourselves to how extraordinarily, vividly, and excitingly different the three poems are from
each other, without inevitably becoming parallel-text readers; to ask
ourselves how one text grows out of another, without becoming em-
broiled in the problem of authorship; and to face the fact that these
poems are poems and not treatises, without ceasing to learn from medieval theology, philosophy, and pulpit oratory and without allowing a
concern with aesthetic problems to reduce the whole argument to acrimonious subjectivity.

Any discussion of *Piers Plowman* must necessarily be selective. My
concern will be "dramatic structure," a feature many feel no characteristically medieval work contains (Dante and Chaucer being, as usual,
"not medieval"). Certainly Aristotle would not accept *Piers Plowman*
as having a "plot" that is its "soul." These episodic poems, full of
riddling scenes whose relationship with others is largely implicit, lack

almost all the features in terms of which we are used to finding coherence, intelligibility, and cumulative force in works of art. Yet, if we focus on the elements *Piers Plowman* has instead of on those it omits, a dramatic structure does emerge that gives a new meaning to Aristotle's terms, one fully applicable to medieval artistry at its best. In its uneven execution, *Piers Plowman* does not achieve the highest levels of medieval artistry; it is unquestionably more diffuse and sometimes more difficult than it needed to be, and its pacing, like Blake's, often works against its structure. On the other hand, the A-text *Visio* and the B text as a whole, when the relationship between scene and scene is appreciated, display an architecture that can only be called brilliant, substantial, coherent, and original, one of the great and underrated intellectual achievements of the Middle Ages. *Piers Plowman* has no claim to the particular splendor of the *Divine Comedy* or of *Troilus and Criseide*. What has drawn readers back to it in spite of manifest clumsiness, amateurishness, discursiveness, and every other "unpoetical" quality—and at the cost of more hard work than most "better" poets can induce their readers to invest—is its capacity to actualize in profoundly moving, if not always clear, dramatic terms the process of trying to be a human being and a Christian without jettisoning the essence of either. As such it enacts, as no other work of art does, the attempt of human nature both to think and to embody a pattern adequate to the universe.

I

A Fair Field Full of Folk

Like olives or anchovies or even coffee, most of *Piers Plowman,* for most people, is an acquired taste. But its Prologue is irresistible: brilliant and savage satire for the critic, sociological detail and cultural attitudes for the historian, and a gold mine of medieval "local color" for the literary tourist. Under its spell, one remains largely unconscious of how it is designed and why the poet chose to begin his poem this way. Yet the opening lines of any long poem are what focus the expectations and assumptions the reader brings with him, through which he will be drawn into it, and these natural reactions are precisely what is most vulnerable to the passage of time and readers' differing literary and cultural background. The first audience of *Piers Plowman* did not know, until the poem told them, that they were embarking on a long, controversial, eccentric mélange of satire, ethics, and theology. They were acquainted with a variety of specific kinds of poems, and their reaction to the opening of the A text came in great measure from the way in which it seemed to relate itself to recognized literary types, by resemblances or by divergence within a well-known idiom.

The charming first lines are full of contradictory suggestions:

> In a somer sesoun whanne softe was the sonne
> I shop me into a shroud as I a shep were;
> In abite as an Ermyte, vnholy of werkis,
> Wente wyde in þis world wondris to here.
> But on a may morwenyng on maluerne hilles
> Me befel a ferly, of fairie me þoughte:
> I was wery forwandrit & wente me to reste

Vndir a brood bank be a bourne side,
And as I lay & lenide & lokide on þe watris
I slomeride into a slepyng, it swiȝed so merye.
Þanne gan I mete a merueillous swevene.

[A Pro. 1–11][1]

One group of features includes the lovely setting "in a somer sesoun" and the dreamer whose aim is to hear "wondris." The dream is "a ferly, of fairie" and "a merueillous swevene," and a psychological excuse for it is provided, in the hypnotism of the brook and the exhaustion of the Dreamer. These features belong, not to the realm of true faerie or vision literature, but to the tradition of courtly French dream visions, from which Chaucer took them. They suggest that the poem will provide an aristocratic and gracious entertainment, a sophisticated love allegory, or a graceful turn on court news, set in a subtly contrived "never-never land." Descendants of *The Roman de la Rose* used the dream to create a consciously mannered, self-contained world that exists, not for its own sake, even as what Tolkien calls a "secondary creation," but to point outside itself to the equally mannered and artificial world of court life where, too, art and ritual were invoked to turn real life into a pageant. Within the artificial framework of the "dream," a pattern is set up to be appreciated with judicious connoisseurship in terms of the world outside. The dreamworld is a vehicle for playing upon—and, in the hands of a great enough artist, for exploring—relationships between entities and modes of experience whose existence outside must be taken as a given.

Yet if we turn to the archetype, the *Roman* itself, the contrast with *Piers Plowman* is striking.[2] The *Roman* has a much longer exposition. It begins by arguing the validity of dreams, on the authority of Macrobius, to remind us that this dream is to parallel reality, and then explains for some twenty lines the name, motive, purpose, and subject

1. All A text quotations and any citations of variants follow George Kane, *Piers Plowman: The A Version,* unless otherwise noted; I reproduce spelling, punctuation, and so on, but not such editorial apparatus as brackets and italics.
2. Whether or not the poet knew the *Roman* itself is difficult to discern and is of no practical importance, since it is certain that his world was full of its offspring.

of the ensuing poem, eliminating all uncertainty about the object of the poetic journey and the status of the dreamworld. The *Roman* introduction also reminds us that the setting, with its river, meadow, and month of May so characteristic of this genre, contains the standard properties, not of "waking" introductions, but of the "dreams" themselves.

Other details of the A text suggest quite a different type of dream vision. The explicit and unassuming nature description, along with the sociological associations of "unholy" hermits and searches "in þis world," brings to mind the provincial school of poetry which survives in *Winner and Waster* and *The Parlement of the Three Ages*.[3] These poems use the dream form to address themselves to man's social actuality rather than his love, art, and ceremony, and, like their earlier and more facetious cousin, *The Owl and the Nightingale,* they are examples of the "genre" of the inconclusive social debate. A poem like *Winner and Waster* is serious in its satire and social concern; yet the role of the dreamworld in relation to reality is essentially the same as that of the *Roman*. It is not delicate and allusive, but it is nonetheless a highly artificial setting in which are presented variations on a theme from the world outside. Even today, the debate is a gratuitous form engaged in for pleasure or education but not for intellectual inquiry. In the medieval debate poem, two incompatible aspects or poles of a problem or situation are set against each other in the form of debating personages, whose witty and artificial duel leaves the question before the reader. The issues have been put through their paces but not resolved. The realism made possible by the poet's sharp eye for detail and the seriousness of the issues for ordinary people may obscure the fact that the debate itself remains a conscious execution of feats of mental agility for a discriminating audience; it is the "play" of a quite different sort of cultivated circle, for whom the shrewdness and exhilaration of good satire take the place of the charm and allusiveness of the French *dits*. Whatever

3. The dating of *Winner and Waster,* at least, seems to establish the existence of this type before the A text. In any case, the presence in both these slighter, clumsier, and less original poems of many conventions and phrases better known and better used in *Piers Plowman* (and in *Gawain and the Green Knight*) is most readily explained by assuming that *Winner and Waster* and *The Parlement of the Three Ages* are the survivors of a body of work of this type.

unsolved mysteries surround the Middle English "alliterative tradition," it cannot be thought of as the rough, unmannered outpourings of the relatively uneducated. No one is ever tempted to make this error about the poems of the *Pearl* group; we recognize that they are consciously formal and cultivated, seeking elaborate vocabulary and verse forms, playing on the contrast between traditional and nontraditional diction and between conventional and nonconventional motifs in a way that requires high sophistication in both poet and audience. They are artful in the most overt sense. But the difference between the *Pearl* group and the rest of the alliterative tradition is a difference of degree—a difference of relative excellence—rather than of pretension. These poems address an audience whose appreciation is based on recognizing the archetype on which any given phrase, line, or story is a variation. And here, too, the comparison brings out the terseness and economy of the A poet and the fact that he has omitted all overt explanations of his poem. He avoids even indirect hints like the minstrel's plaint on the corruptions of the present age in *Winner and Waster,* which focuses our attention on the aspects of "real life" to which the "dream" is to be related. Combining two sets of divergent dream conventions and omitting all overt exposition make the reader expect the dreamworld to be an artifice, pointing outside itself to reality for an explanation, and yet puzzle him as to the kind of artificial world and the kind of reality involved. He will thus bring to the poem curiosity and detached appreciation of the dreamworld as a microcosm, without any fixed attitude toward its status.

Two further elements in the opening lines complicate this effect. One is the highly unusual introduction of a specific and uncommon place name. Quite apart from the implication of the particular place involved, to which we will return later, this counteracts the remoteness of court or faerie with suggestions of the local and idiosyncratic, as does the mention of rough clothing and bad hermits. The second element is the uneasy atmosphere that surrounds the Dreamer himself and is not accounted for by the stock dreamers of evoked convention: the would-be lover and courtier or the often irascible spokesman of satire. He is marked by his strange garb, "as I a shep were." Even if this merely means "I dressed up as a shepherd," the Dreamer's search is undertaken in a mode not his own, if not actually in disguise, and

the suggestion of the proverbial "wolf in sheep's clothing" seems inten-
tional, especially when the next line explicitly associates this garment
with *un*holy hermits.[4] Thus the Dreamer's search is undertaken under
a sign of contradiction and is associated with both good and evil by
specifically religious standards. The Dreamer is by his own choice both
pilgrim and pariah, and in his case, unlike that of Dante the Pilgrim
for all his limitations, the two seem interdependent.

As the dream itself begins, we leave the charming springtime setting
and enter a far more realistic one:

> Þanne gan I mete a meruecillous swevene,
> Þat I was in a wildernesse, wiste I neuere where;
> Ac as I beheld into the Est on heiʒ to þe sonne
> I saiʒ a tour on a toft, triʒely Imakid;
> A dep dale beneþe, a dungeoun þerinne
> With depe dikes & derke & dredful of siʒt.
> A fair feld ful of folk fand I þere betwene
> Of alle maner of men, þe mene & þe riche,
> Worching and wandringe as þe world askiþ.

                                                   [A Pro. 11–19]

We are given in practical and dramatic terms (the gesture implied in
"on heiʒ to þe sonne" is largely responsible for this effect) the geography
within which the action is to take place. Two towers, such as real or
painted medieval landscape might have, are distinguished concretely
by their contrasting position and architecture, not by ethical labels,
though the position of the folk "þer between," revolving in the shadow

---

4. Both the verb "shop . . . into" and the noun "shep" as applied to a human
being are surprising usages; even if they are rare idioms or nonce words, their
presence in the second line still requires explanation, and the parallels cited for this
meaning are not conclusive. See Walter W. Skeat, *The Vision of William Concerning
Piers the Plowman in Three Parallel Texts* (Oxford, 1886), vol. 2, note to C 1. 2;
B Pro. 2; and A Pro. 2. (All B and C text quotations and any citations of Skeat's
notes or glossary follow this edition unless otherwise noted, except that Skeat's
medial dot has been eliminated. The occasional readings in square brackets were
supplied by E. Talbot Donaldson from his and George Kane's forthcoming edition
of the B text, but I have avoided arguing questions in which the difference beween
these editions is a major issue.)

of both, makes it clear these towers are the poles of the dreamworld. Both towers, however, are silhouetted against the sun to the east of the Dreamer, who is still clearly outside the landscape he is describing. In fact, this scene is precisely the landscape one still sees looking east from any point along the heights above Malvern and its Abbey Church. The eastern slope drops sharply to a flat plain that runs east until it disappears into haze, interrupted only by the requisite "toft," Bredon Hill. As one stands there, feeling one is on the western marches looking across the body of England toward London and beyond to the sea, all Middle Earth seems spread out like a pageant. The effect is unusual and striking; it has received only minimal heightening in the poem, and its appropriateness to the poet's purpose is great enough to account for his tying the vision to this particular spot, though his doing so obviously tells us something about his biography. The poet's eccentricity in putting a "dream" landscape into the introduction is thus complemented by his putting a real, though symbolic, one into the "dream."

But the Dreamer does not remain in Olympian detachment, looking down at the field and its scurrying antlike figures. As he begins to enumerate the folk before him, he seems to move down toward them, and as the descriptions become more and more vivid and detailed, the figures finally seem to surround him. At the same time, we become more and more aware of a colorful and idiosyncratic voice selecting and commenting. The first groups the Dreamer mentions are described in syntactically parallel three-line units; with the third, the syntax shifts, and the Dreamer adds that these hermits, unlike some he could name,

> Coueite not in cuntre to cairen aboute
> For no likerous liflode here likam to plese.
>
> [A Pro. 29–30]

In a few more lines we come to his first personal attack, directed against friars:

> Siþen charite hath ben chapman & chief to shryue lordis
> Manye ferlis han fallen in a fewe ʒeris.
> But holy chirche & hy holden bet togidere
> Þe moste meschief on molde is mountyng vp faste.
>
> [A Pro. 61–64]

Such a remark no longer pretends to be bound to what is to be observed before our eyes, and the last pretensions to strict realism are abandoned when the Dreamer shows the Pardoner striking the people who crowd around him and snatching their jewelry with his "brevet." As Charles Muscatine observed of Langland's style in general, this development "produces a hallucinatory effect, in which the distinctions between abstract and concrete, moral and physical have all but been lost." [5] At this point, the narrator addresses us directly for the first time, demolishing the distinction between the folk on the field, who are inside the poem, and the folk in the audience, who are supposedly outside:

> Þus ȝe gyuen ȝoure gold glotonis to helpe
> And leniþ it loselis þat leccherie haunten.
>
> [A Pro. 73–74]

This combination of direct address and personal tirade continues through the section on lawyers, which ends, again, in the second person:

> Thou miȝtest betere mete myst on maluerne hilles
> Þanne gete a mom of here mouþ til mony be shewid.
>
> [A Pro. 88–89]

The vibrancy of so justly famous a descriptive set piece comes in large measure from precisely this personal immediacy of narration and from the sheer shrewdness with which realistic details are chosen, the element the nineteenth-century critics of the poem, as of the Chaucer general prologue, valued so disproportionately. But the tight control the poet exerts over his realism and colloquialism is as important as their presence. The details, unlike Chaucer's, are largely restricted to clothes and to an occasional emblematic object carried in the hand, like a saint's iconographic symbol on a medieval facade; this gradually imparts to man's "cuntenaunce of clothing" the cumulative force of a primary metaphor, which it is to retain throughout the poem. An almost Popean wit exploits the alliterative pattern to yoke two words together, whose juxtaposition puts the precise fallacy or distortion of the person satirized in a nutshell: "Ermytes on an hep"; "siþen charite haþ ben chapman"; "Pleten for penis and poundide þe lawe." A different kind of heighten-

5. *Chaucer and the French Tradition* (Berkeley, 1957), p. 101.

ing comes from the satirist's controlled exaggeration. He may affect to believe that the hidden motive is one openly admitted by society, as when he pictures parsons appealing for permission "To synge for symonye, for siluer is swete," or describes pilgrims who, after a trip "to seke seint Iame" or to Rome, "hadde leue to leiȝe al here life after" (A Pro. 49). Or he may portray an emblematic action epitomizing the effect of a corruption on society as if it were a literally visible action like the others, as in the case of the Pardoner and his brevet. The tendency toward stasis and inertia in an enumeration of professions is counteracted by portraying each group, again in marked contrast to Chaucer's Pilgrims, as in vigorous movement:

> Bidderis & beggeris faste aboute ȝede
> Til here bely & here bagge were bratful ycrammid;
> Flite þanne for here foode, fouȝten at þe ale.
>
> [A Pro. 40–42]

Active verbs are found even where a "still life" would seem inevitable:

> Þere *houide* an hundrit in houuis of silk,
> Seriauntis it semide þat *seruide* at þe barre.
>
> [A Pro. 84–85; italics mine]

The resulting kaleidoscopic effect is intensified by the fact that the order in which the figures appear does not provide any systematic, cumulative analysis of the social fabric; indeed, the lack of emphasis on the power structure itself or on the key administrative figures, lay or clerical, focuses the reader squarely on the variety of forms in which the general population adapt their individual existences to the corporate one. The passage begins, of course, with the plowmen on whose productivity the whole population depends, but the only consistent movement is from larger and more basic groups to more specialized and colorful ones.[6] The immediate principle seems to be juxtaposition of

6. The order is: plowmen (with a reference to wasters); the proud; good monks and hermits (with a reference to bad); merchants; minstrels (with a reference to japers and janglers); beggars; pilgrims; bad hermits again; friars; a pardoner; renegade parish priests; lawyers; clerics who take government posts; six lines of miscellaneous professions like butchers and weavers; diggers and delvers; cooks and taverners.

contrasting groups who are associated by economic effect (plowmen, wasters, the proud), by superficially similar movements in the landscape of the "fair field" (minstrels, beggars, pilgrims, bad hermits), or by obviously parallel functions in society (bad hermits, friars, pardoners, renegade priests); but the pattern is no easier to rationalize than that of the Canterbury Pilgrims. Above all, the reader feels the cumulative pressure of human nature's ethical complexity and sheer magnetism drawing him further and further into the variegated patterns of life itself.

This results not simply from the order but from a gradual modification of the traditional satirist's persona assumed by the Dreamer, the sardonic, irascible voice of one who stands outside the abuses he attacks and views them with righteous wrath. This humanization results partly, of course, from the gusto with which he, like Chaucer, describes whatever is energetically and wholeheartedly itself, even when it is clearly a moral evil; one thinks of Keats's "The Creature has a purpose and his eyes are bright with it. . . . Though a quarrel in the streets is a thing to be hated, the energies displayed in it are fine." [7]

Another humanizing element, much more closely related to the order in which groups are mentioned, is the disproportionate amount of space devoted to the disreputable, wandering professions and the confused violence of the comments about them.[8] The passage on minstrels first calls this to our attention.

> And somme merþis to make as mynstralis conne,
> And get gold wiþ here gle giltles, I trowe.
> Ac Iaperis & iangleris, Iudas children,
> Fonden hem fantasies & foolis hem make,
> And haue wyt at wille to wirche ʒif hem list.
> Þat poule prechiþ of hem I dar not proue it here:
> *Qui loquitur turpiloquium* is luciferis hyne.

[A Pro. 34–39]

7. Journal letter to George and Georgiana Keats, 19 March 1819, *The Letters of John Keats,* ed. Hyder Rollins (Cambridge, Mass., 1958), 2: 80.
8. For a discussion of the attitudes to these professions in the three texts and their relevance to the portrayal of the Dreamer, see Donaldson, *Piers Plowman: The C-Text and Its Poet,* chap. 5 (hereafter cited as *C-Text*).

"Judas's children" and "Lucifer's servant" seem disproportionately violent terms, especially since the difference between "making mirths" and
"devising fantasies" is hardly clear. The proportion of criticism to approval—five lines of attack to two of acceptance, and rather dubious
acceptance at that, with its grudging "giltes, I trowe"—is typical. The
treatment of beggars, hermits, and other kinds of irresponsible, peri-
patetic clerics is equally belligerent. All this must necessarily associate
itself in the reader's mind with the ambiguous opening portrait of the
Dreamer as an unholy hermit, a disguised and impoverished seeker after
wonders. Thus the "saeva indignatio" of the satirist is modified as the
speaker himself seems goaded into it, at least in part, by his awareness
of apparent complicity in the very parasitism and instability he sees before him. This is a very different matter from the convenient "stupidity"
of Chaucer's narrators and equally different from the out-and-out hypocrisy to which it bears a certain uncomfortable resemblance.

But the increasing vivacity of the scene portrayed, the increasing immediacy of the Dreamer and his comments to the reader, and the increasing complexity of the catalogue of professions are manifestations
of a more fundamental structural development. As the professions the
Dreamer enumerates become more and more specific, he begins to name
actual institutions (including the Court of King's Bench and the Clerks
of Accounts), specific places (like Walsingham and the City of London), topical events like the plague, and finally the king himself (A Pro.
91). Then we realize that the fair field between the towers has widened
until it is revealed to be literally, not metaphorically, the poet's own
world of medieval England in all its color, vitality, and concreteness:

> . . . dikeris & delueris þat doþ here dede ille
> And driueþ forþ þe longe day wiþ *dieu saue dame emme;*
> Cookis & here knaues crieþ "hote pyes, hote!
> Goode gees & gris; go we dyne, go we!"
> Tauerners to hem tolde þe same:
> "Whit wyn of ossay, & wyn of gascoyne,
> Of þe ryn & of þe rochel, þe rost to defie!"
>
> [A Pro. 102–8]

As the narrator closes with the formal phrase, "al þis I sauȝ slepyng & seue siþes more," the essential alteration of the audience's perspective on their own experience, which began when a dream wilderness proved to be a known landscape, has been achieved. The self-contained dream-world, that artifact accessible and intelligible only in terms of the greater reality beyond on which it is dependent, has turned out to be "real life"; it is human society in all its concreteness, human existence susceptible of the pattern and significance characteristic of art or of religious and philosophical systems but with the pattern suspended until we have been immersed in the reality.[9]

THE B OPENING

The *Piers Plowman* Prologue is best known, not in this basic form of the A poet's, but in B's version, which contains two of the passages most discussed by critics and historians and most often remembered by readers: the procession of personifications portraying the role of king-ship in society, and the brilliant vignette of the rat parliament. It is not always appreciated that the B poet took over the whole of A's complex structure and simply inserted one major block of new material. But to add a passage as long as all of A, and quite different in emphasis and dramatic level, has a drastic effect on A's spare and vivid image of the human situation. The result is that B incorporates A's strictly visual and spatial model of man's condition in Middle Earth into a more complex one in which time has become an essential dimension.

After an introductory passage on clerics in office, B continues:

> I parceyued of the power that Peter had to kepe,
> To bynden and [vnbynden] as the boke telleth,
> How he it left with loue as owre lorde hight,
> Amonges foure vertues [most vertuous of alle],
> That cardinales ben called and closyng ȝatis,

9. For an appreciation of the opposite kind of introduction from that of A and B, see D. A. Traversi's analysis of the vividness and economy with which the C text sets up complete clarity of purpose and values, in "The Vision of Piers Plowman," *Scrutiny* 5 (1936–37): 276–91.

> There crist is in kyngdome to close and to shutte,
> And to opne it to hem and heuene blisse shewe.
> As of the cardinales atte Courte that cauȝt of that name,
> And power presumed in hem a pope to make,
> To han [þe] power that Peter hadde impugnen I nelle;
> For in loue and lettrure the eleccioun bilongeth,
> For-thi I can and can nauȝte of courte speke more.
>
> [B Pro. 100–11]

This consciously witty style, with its elaborate play on the office of cardinal, the cardinal virtues, and the Latin *cardo* (hinge), is essential to the poet's complicated point about the relationship between the divinely sanctioned vocation of the Church and the sociological realities of its temporal administration. From the point of view of the A Prologue, however, the striking thing is to find the Dreamer seeing anything as abstract as "the power Peter had to kepe." Such power does exist there on the field, of course, but the level on which we are "seeing" Middle Earth has clearly changed. And clearly to "see" a factor in society in this sense is to see it in the time dimension which links Peter to the contemporary papal elections, to see it evolving out of its origin and normative purpose into the manifestations we find before us. A's panorama suddenly seems like a scene painted on a curtain, which now parts to reveal a new vista of history, turning A's landscape into the foreground of a much more complex composition.[10]

At this point, in the intersection, as it were, of A's landscape and B's vista, there appears a group of figures set off from the crowd by their abstractness like the masquers at a court function. These figures perform an emblematic action that analyzes the structure of the society hitherto portrayed directly:

10. Compare the discussion by Xavier Leon Dufour, S.J. ("Juif et Gentile Selon Romains I–XI," *Studiorum Paulinorum Congressus Internationalis Catholicus* 1961 [*Analecta Biblica* 17–18], Rome, 1963, pp. 309–15) of the counterpoint between two perspectives on temporal experience in Paul. On the one hand, he presents the human condition as an absolute state, in its "essence." On the other, "il s'adresse à des hommes qui sont, comme lui, immergés dans un temps dont la totalité leur échappe; aussi doit-il reparcourir sans cesse le cheminement historique que Dieu a suivi dans sa révélation; il presente alors la réalité dans son 'devenir'" (p. 310). This second role of history becomes more and more marked throughout the B text.

> Thanne come there a kyng knyȝthod hym ladde,
> Miȝt of the comunes made hym to regne,
> And thanne cam kynde wytte and clerkes he made,
> For to conseille the kyng and the comune saue.
>   The kyng and kniȝthode and clergye bothe
> Casten that the comune shulde [hire comunes] finde.
> The comune contreued of kynde witte craftes,
> And for profit of alle the people plowmen ordeygned,
> To tilie and trauaile as trewe lif asketh.
> The kynge and the comune and kynde witte the thridde
> Shope lawe and lewte eche [lif] to knowe his owne.
>   [B Pro. 112–22]

The resulting situation is then commented on by three contrasting spokes-men—the lunatic, the angel, and the "chorus" of commons. If we re-member that the A poet used no allegorical figures at all in the Pro-logue, that he mentioned the actual king of England elsewhere, and that the actions were all going on continuously in the present, we will appreciate the drastic change in the level of dramatic action involved when the B poet introduces personifications who are involved in a single action, at a given moment in the time sequence. The passage thus superimposes on a literal portrayal of society an emblematic analysis of that society. The passage works perfectly within the A poet's frame-work, partly because the ideas complement the appearances he cap-tured and partly because his level of action, as his quasi-emblematic treatment of the Pardoner shows, is pitched at a point between realism and allegory that almost cries out for such a development.

Here again, with no transition but that of juxtaposition, the immedi-ate plane of action is rolled back to reveal a new "play within a play," exploring what such a political structure demands of the individual. The rat parliament, with its bitter humor and the ingenuity with which it inverts the old fable of belling the cat, mixes animal and human terminology to evoke an incongruous double image of mice and men and to point the application of the ideas at each step, as when the "biȝes" about the necks of "segges" in London, so graphically de-scribed by the "ratoun of renon most renable of tonge," are sometimes clearly burgesses' gold chains and sometimes clearly dog collars, or when the ringing of the proposed bell will sometimes let "men" run away and sometimes let mice "crope vnder benches," or when the rats dare not hang the bell "for alle the rewme of Fraunce." Equally pleasing is the satirist's persona of the disreputable and sarcastic outsider applied to the "mous that moche good couthe," who points out with such satisfaction that he never contributed toward buying the collar in the first place. These speeches of the rat and the mouse also show a remarkable ear for language as it is actually spoken and a gift for just the subtle heightening of it characteristic of a good comedy of manners. But the humor is bitter indeed. The mind which defines and affirms this radically conservative social structure with such clarity does not flinch from defining with equal clarity the price of such a structure or the shoddy characteristics of human nature that make it necessary. And not every satirist is so frank about recognizing that his Swiftian lucidity is a function of his having less at stake because he is less involved.

To read the Prologue in the B text is much more demanding as well as more rewarding, however greatly one admires the terse and vivid effect of A's brilliant structure when it is uncomplicated by further variations. The risk of overburdening the underlying drama with supplementary structures may seem a bad omen for the future of the poem, but here, at least, much is added and little is lost. Out of A emerges a structure so much more massive and inclusive as to be an adequate basis for a new kind of drama, a great pageant of the human race on a quest through time.

The Dream Guide: Lady Holy Church

Only after this fundamental perspective has been established does the poet introduce the ethical and religious absolutes he has carefully refrained from articulating at the beginning.[11] Passus 1 begins with the poem's first piece of overt explanation:

11. The A Prologue is almost entirely free of evaluative, metaphysical religious terminology, as distinct from descriptive sociological terms (such as the names of various types of clergy and of categories of activities and abuses, which, of course, abound). The very few apparent exceptions are dead or semidead metaphor—"Were þe bisshop yblissid & worþ boþe his eris" (A Pro. 75)—or describe observable attitudes—the anchorites "al for loue of oure lorde lyuede wel streite / In hope for to have heuenriche blisse" (A Pro. 26–27). The B poet is a little less careful.

> What þe mounteyne bemeniþ, & ek þe merke dale,
> And ek þe feld ful of folk I shal ȝow faire shewe.
> A louely lady of lire in lynene ycloþid
> Com doun fro þat clyf & callide me faire,
> And seide "sone, slepist þou? sest þou þis peple,
> How besy þei ben aboute þe mase?"
>
> [A 1. 1-6]

The lady's "slepist þou" completes the reversal of the dream convention, as the phrase "com doun fro þat clyf" completes the process of
placing us down on the field with the "tour" of the Prologue looming
over us. Now that we have been maneuvered into viewing this world
of ours with just the mixture of empathy, shrewd scrutiny, and objective evaluation a created poetic world demands, the guide without
whom no self-respecting dream vision can function arrives on cue to
give us an authoritative sketch of the greater world outside and its
relationship with our own. The guide, who introduces herself later as
Lady Holy Church, limits herself ostensibly to explaining the landmarks
in response to such pragmatic questions as what the dreadful looking
donjon is and to whom all the money belongs. But in the course of her
remarks she touches on all the major "landmarks" of Christian belief
except, naturally enough, eschatology; and never have they been so
tersely and snappily surveyed or had more completely the air of being
fired off at random.

Yet the speech in fact falls into three parts, each establishing a general
principle and illustrating it with one or more of the key events in the
history of our world's relation to the larger landscape of which it is an
integral part. Holy Church begins by identifying the first tower and
discussing the nature of the finite world and its proper use, in terms of
the Creation, the rule of Truth (God as creator), and the key concept
of *mesure*. Then she introduces the other two forces active upon man—
the devil (here she explains the second tower and the Fall) and the
Church. Lastly she sketches man's responsibilities in such a scheme of
things. Salvation means, first of all, obedience (positively and negatively
illustrated by the creation of the angels and their fall), because "treuþe"
means not only God himself but also troth in man, the loyalty and

obedience that are a function of one's proper place in the universe. And salvation also means love, both in God and in man; here the Incarnation and Atonement are touched on. These two aspects of salvation are in fact one, since God is both Truth and Love, and Truth is both the ruler in the "tour on the toft" and the treasure man seeks. The lady's terse indication of the order of priority among realities thus lays the basis for all the central concerns of the poem. She sets forth the essential postulates of Revelation, which stands in the same relation to human actuality as the towers do to the fair field. Man faces a struggle to understand and to heal his own experience of life as it comes to him; yet he can only do so in terms of the landmarks which define his situation and hence the true nature of his problems. Holy Church's "map" gives him the basis on which he can try to answer the questions life will raise; yet the questions have neither been begged nor prematurely disposed of. The statement is perfectly definite, and yet it leaves human understanding of the issues open; the human effort to "realize" them, in both senses of the term, is omitted but not prejudiced. What has been affirmed is the particular nature and absolutely objective reality of man's metaphysical surroundings, which ultimately define all aspects of human existence. This explains the admittedly narrow range of examples Holy Church uses to illustrate her remarks. No one can expound principles successfully in the abstract; on the other hand, the poet dares not imperil the delicate balance of his introduction, either by going beyond mere exposition and raising difficult questions which are to be discussed later or by prejudicing the authority of the speaker by letting her appear to oversimplify or judge arbitrarily—hence the necessity for choosing examples that are matter-of-fact but dramatic and clear, whether by familiarity, by authority, or by their uncomplicated ethics.

The air of chaotic and idiosyncratic association of ideas that Lady Holy Church imparts to a speech that is, in fact, quite effectively structured is characteristic of many speeches in *Piers Plowman* and results from the fact that the transitions through which the discourse turns to a new point are not theoretical statements—"topic sentences"—but the examples for the last point. Each illustration serves as the jumping-off point for the next heading on the outline while giving the impression of a digression from a digression ad infinitum. This impression is heightened in the present speech by the fact that the angles by which the lady veers from topic to topic seem to add up to 360 degrees, and she characteristically returns to the point from which she took off by announcing —quite justifiably—that this is what she has been talking about all along: "Forþi I seye as I seide er, be siȝte of þise textis: / Whanne alle tresours arn triȝed treuþe is þe beste" (A 1. 123–24, 180–81). This is a dangerous method of constructing an argument, as is any artistic device that brings high mimesis dangerously near to mere duplication of the phenomenon involved (like the stage bore who unfortunately bores the audience). But at its best this technique not only dramatizes how thought actually works but becomes a truly elegant reflection of the exact relationship between two principles through their juxtaposition with the same example. Thus the paradoxical character of the Incarnation is conveyed, not by overt commentary, but by its pivotal position as the example, successively, of God's love and of man's and as the means by which the first sets free the second; and thus the lady anticipates her concluding point, the reciprocity of love as the condition of grace, the spiritual law of "date & dabitur vobis" (A 1. 175).

The organic quality of the speech also contributes to the characterization of the lady as A's first personification. Her terse and executive tone, her habit of hitting the nail on the head apparently quite at random, and her associations of ideas characterize her without making her too human for her function. While her tone is not comic in the sense of "incongruous because unjustified," her high-handed and brisk disposition of explosive material and her snappy style of exegesis induce high delight in the reader:

> "*Reddite cesari*," quaþ god, "þat *cesari* befalliþ
> *Et que sunt dei deo* oþer ellis ȝe don ille."
>
> [A 1. 50–51]

Her imagery is as perceptive as it is irascible:

> For þeiȝ ȝe be trewe of ȝoure tunge & treweliche wynne
> And ek chast as a child þat in chirche wepiþ,
> But ȝif ȝe loue lelly & lene þe pore,
> Of such good as god sent goodlyche parteþ,

ʒe haue no more meryt in masse ne in houres
Þanne malkyn of hire maidenhed þat no man desireþ.

[A 1. 153-58]

She also shares the tendency of such effective clerics as Chaucer's
Pardoner to cope with popular audiences by digressing rapidly from
the main point onto the more interesting sins. Like the dream guide,
the Church is the opener of the way, not a substitute for a journey.
The limitations of the lady's version of Christianity do not constitute
inaccuracy; yet they are in a very real sense occupational and reflect
the executive responsibilities of an authoritative temporal organization
that exists as the transmitter of realities not its own, so that these may
be available for man to start from: "I underfang þe ferst and þi feiþ þe
tauʒte" (A 1. 74).

As far as the Dreamer himself is concerned, passus 1's main contribution is to take the ambiguous quester of the Prologue, idiosyncratic and
defensive, and to set him in the iconographic posture of the seeker after
salvation. We see the Dreamer pictorially portrayed for the first time
since the dream began:

Þanne I knelide on my knes & criʒide hire of grace;
Preiʒede hire pitously to preiʒe for my sennes,
And ek kenne me kyndely on crist to beleue,
But I miʒte werchen his wil þat wrouʒte me to man:
"Teche me to no tresour but tel me this ilke,
How I may sauen my soule, þat seint art yholden."

[A 1. 77-82]

This intense yet stylized moment complements the earlier image of
search provided by the Prologue with its emphasis on sheer curiosity,
socially oriented ethics, and the ambiguousness of human motivation.
As the Prologue and passus 1 work together to define the "landscape"
in which the poem is to unroll, these two vignettes of the Dreamer establish his role in the poem and set up a rich and complex image of search
itself as the basis for the action. But apart from this basic point, the
Dreamer as a "personality" is diminished throughout the scene to
leave room for the expression of the guide's point of view on the

dreamworld. This scene contributes to our picture of him primarily through Holy Church's curious insistence on regarding him as a professional poet or minstrel and treating this fact as intrinsically connected with his attempt to understand his belief and his society. After her discourse on Truth, she first comments, "Leriþ it þus lewide men, for lettrid it knowiþ" (A 1. 125), but later she is more specific: ". . . preche it in þin harpe / Þer þou art mery at mete, if men bidde þe ȝedde" (A 1. 137–38).

Nevertheless, like everything else in the scene, the characterization of both Dreamer and dream guide is kept strictly subservient to the scene's primary function, which is to complement the Prologue, whose elaborate inversion of convention established the "reality" of actual human experience within an actual social structure as the basis of the poetic world. Passus 1 superimposes on it a second and authoritative "reality" of another kind and indicates its relevance to the first without compromising the peculiar kind of primacy proper to each.[12] This strategy establishes the true basis for the action of *Piers Plowman,* both as literal drama and as intellectual dialectic. That basis is an assertion *Piers Plowman* makes about the relationship between cognitive truth and experiential reality that sets it apart from most art, even art based on personal

12. See Heiko Oberman's discussion of "double truth" in the philosophy and theology of the period dominated by nominalism in all its forms, "Some Notes on the Theology of Nominalism," *Harvard Theological Review* 53 (1960): 47–76, especially pp. 56–60. Particularly useful for an understanding of the tension the poet is dramatizing here is Oberman's emphasis on the central quality of nominalism as its differentiation between God's *potentia absoluta,* his power as being unlimited by anything except the law of noncontradiction, and his *potentia ordinata,* "that which God, by virtue of his moving will, is really going to do or has done" (p. 56). In the sphere of *potentia absoluta* God's relation to existence as we know it can be direct, gratuitous, and even arbitrary in terms of the human frame of reference; in that of *potentia ordinata* God has created a hierarchical and, in a sense, autonomous sphere of finite reality which functions according to natural and ethical laws that may be understood in their own right and in which God acts through the ecclesiastical structure he has set up and the revelation he has provided. Man can have certain knowledge only of revelation. Central to all forms of nominalism is "the idea: *finiti et infiniti nulla proportio.* We cannot reason backwards from God's revelation to His being" (p. 57). See also Arnold Hauser's suggestive comments on multiple truth and Gothic art in *The Social History of Art* (New York, 1951), 1: 232–44.

religious experience. Poetry as such creates a fresh awareness of man's experience and a balance of thematic and structural elements that constitutes one kind of resolution of that experience; and both the awareness and the resolution are betrayed by being translated into cognitive terms. *Piers Plowman* is perhaps unique in that it bases this artistic synthesis on two kinds of knowledge that it refuses either to equate or to regard as mutually exclusive.

This raises a number of questions about the role of intellectual formulations of theological material in works of art.[13] The special kind of resolution provided by art springs from and constitutes a perception of reality. If, as modern man characteristically assumes, the only reality of which we can have so authentic a knowledge is human experience, art ought to hold in abeyance the philosophical and metaphysical constructs by which man attempts to define and order the dimensions of reality that his experience suggests but does not include, and art should do the same with the ethical codes that man invokes as an aid in, if not as a substitute for, judging an act or a personality on direct perception of its nature and implications. Art should admit religious or philosophical "truths" only as part of a variety of human phenomena subjected to scrutiny or modified, enriched, and "realized" in terms of the experience provided by the work itself. The richness of such art where the cognitive is subordinated to the experiential is obvious, as are the disastrous artistic results of entirely subordinating the experiential to the cognitive. But what if both the cognitive and the experiential, while remaining incommensurable, constitute experience authentic and urgent enough to be the province of art?

In *Piers Plowman,* human experience in time is not an absolute, though it remains the touchstone for truth. That experience is malleable, incomplete, transformable, often misleading when viewed in isolation, and always self-contradictory. To extrapolate from what we perceive in the finite world alone does not lead to truth; but neither is the universe to

13. What I am discussing here is not the question of the relationship between religious and artistic experience, the kind of problem studied in a work like Henri Brémont, *Priere et poésie* (Paris, 1926), or the way in which the techniques of meditation may be applied in poetry but the tensions created by introducing blocks of intellectual material that are neither dramatic nor lyric into the artistic experience.

be regarded as one vast contradiction. The "metaphysical" realities are given, immutable, and active; it is from them that we ought logically to start, though we cannot actually do so, to achieve a truer perception even of human actuality. Thus, man lives in the presence of two kinds of realities of which he has quite different sorts of knowledge, one given by experience and the other by revelation mediated by authority, which he sees as ultimately complementary, though in the short run tragically incommensurable. The tension between them points toward a potential state of resolution, in which an effort of the individual equivalent to a sustained act of creation brings to birth a new experiential knowledge or cognitive experience in which the two are synthesized, like man's two eyes in focused vision.[14]

Piers Plowman's contemporary, the mystic Julian of Norwich, expresses her sense of the same tension with special vividness. At times she seems overwhelmed by the apparent contradiction between the finite "truth" her own daily observation brings her, the "truth" of the Church and of scriptural revelation, and the "truth" of her own mystical experiences. For instance, in trying to understand how the concept of guilt and sin so central to her own life and to the teaching of the Church can be so completely absent from her visions, she feels something close to desperation:

> If I take it thus that we be no sinners and not blameworthy, it seemeth as I should err and fail of knowing of this truth; and if it be so that we be sinners and blameworthy,—Good Lord, how may it then be that I cannot see this true thing in Thee, which art my God, my Maker, in whom I desire to see all truths? . . . Ah! Lord Jesus, King of bliss, how shall I be eased? Who shall teach me and tell me that [thing] me needeth to know, if I may not at this time see it in Thee? [15]

14. Note the analysis by Isaiah Berlin of related problems in "A Note on Vico's Concept of Knowledge," *The New York Review of Books* 12 (24 April 1969): 23–26, which focuses on Vico's distinction between *verum* and *certum* ("Si physica demonstrare possemus, faceremus"). This analysis is particularly suggestive for the role of history and of imagination in the later development of *Piers Plowman*.

15. *Revelations of Divine Love,* edited and modernized by Grace Warrack (London, 1901), pp. 106–7.

At other times, she can see the different truths as complementary, although the finite are subsumed in the eternal, which has priority:

> And thus I saw full surely that it is readier to us to come to the knowing of God than to know our own Soul. For our Soul is so deep-grounded in God, and so endlessly treasured, that we may not come to the knowing thereof till we have first knowing of God, which is the Maker, to whom it is oned. But, notwithstanding, I saw that we have, for fulness, to desire wisely and truly to know our own Soul: whereby we are learned to seek it where it is, and that is, in God. And thus by gracious leading of the Holy Ghost, we should know them both in one: whether we be stirred to know God or our Soul, both [these stirrings] are good and true.
>
> God is nearer to us than our own Soul: for He is [the] Ground in whom our Soul standeth, and He is [the] Mean that keepeth the Substance and the Sense-nature together so that they shall never dispart . . . and therefore if we will have knowledge of our Soul . . . it behoveth to seek unto our Lord God in whom it is enclosed.[16]

For her, the knowledge that comes from intellect and tradition and the knowledge that comes from one's own normal experience and consciousness are brought to resolution by a third knowledge, the direct but supernatural knowledge of God in this life through mystical experience; and the three work together cumulatively, so that in the hierarchy of truth each is corrected and fulfilled by the reality which is God. This is precisely what makes her a mystic.

But is *Piers Plowman* a poem of mysticism in this sense? A mystic is a person who has supernatural experiences of a religious nature, who directly experiences God in this life. A mystic is not merely a person whose allegiance to Christian belief and ethics is active and personal or who asserts that love is a more fundamental reality than law or who affirms that man will find untimate fulfillment in the direct apprehension of God after death or who insists on the importance of "devotional" prayer and penance in the life of any Christian or who

16. Ibid., p. 135.

lives an ascetic life or who believes that mysticism can exist.[17] Obviously the poet is working in a religious tradition which accepts the importance of mysticism, and many of the theologians with whom he seems most in sympathy were themselves mystics. Obviously he is concerned with a life in which commitment to Christianity has gone far beyond the average man's largely cultural participation and has become the rationale and meaning of one's whole existence. But that is a very different matter from finding, especially in the A and B texts, the special temperament, the particular modes of experience, and the supernatural states properly termed mystical. In A and B, if not in C, Julian's third kind of knowing remains only a theoretical possibility. The struggle to resolve the first two, a struggle as personal and intense as any mystical experience, remains on the plane of the natural powers of man aided by that grace which is offered to mystic and nonmystic alike.

To describe this resolution, this "experiential knowledge" or "focused vision," so passionately sought for throughout the poem and so fitfully achieved, the poet uses the term "kynde knowing," which he distinguishes carefully both from direct experience and from speculative or theoretical knowledge, even that conveyed by revelation.[18] It is essen-

17. Geoffrey Shepherd's introduction to his edition of *Ancrene Wisse*, pts. 6 and 7 (London and Edinburg, 1959), provides a terse and shrewd survey of the distinction between the ascetic, the devotional, and the mystical. Compare, for instance, his comment that in spite of its emphasis on meditation and love and its celebrated image of Christ as knight and lover, "There is little point in speaking of AW as a mystical work. . . . His teaching on contemplation is pre-scholastic and pre-Dionysian. Throughout Part 7 love is thought of as a humble, creaturely communion with God, the outcome of the fulfillment of duty and obligations" (p. lvii).

18. An excellent recent reassertion of the importance of this term, and an argument for its continued significance in the later B text, is found in Sister Mary Clemente Davlin, O.P., *"Kynde Knowyng* As a Major Theme in Piers Plowman," *Review of English Studies,* n.s. 22 (1971): 1–19. Sister Davlin stresses its importance for the aesthetic character of the poem (p. 19) and provides historical background for the concept and a convenient survey of its role in *Piers Plowman* criticism. Her equation of the term with "divine wisdom, *gnosis,* or *sapientia"* (p. 2), however, seems to me to anticipate in the earlier parts of the poem a meaning which only becomes clearly defined by the end and thus to restrict unduly its earlier function of including all experiential cognition, as distinct from faith and authority; this leads her to treat

tial to the poem's structure that this term, which is to become so central
in the A *Vita,* is first introduced in the present scene with Holy Church
and that both the Dreamer and the lady claim it and use it against
each other. Returning to his earlier plea to the lady to "kenne [him]
kyndely," the Dreamer reacts to her account of Truth neither with assent nor with rejection:

> "3et haue I no kynde knowyng," quaþ I, "3e mote kenne me bet
> Be what craft in me cors it compsiþ, & where."
>
> [A I. 127–28]

Holy Church, appropriately, cannot see the problem:

> "Þou dotide daffe," quaþ heo, "dulle arn þine wittes.
> It is a kunde knowyng þat kenneþ in þin herte
> For to loue þi lord leuere þanne þiselue;
> No dedly synne to do, di3e þei3 þou shuldist."
>
> [A I. 129–32]

A person who already has "kynde knowyng" can see that Holy Church
has pointed out an excellent instance of it, but the Dreamer is talking
about the problem of not having it and being unable to tell quite what
it is one lacks except, as in putting together a picture puzzle, by the
shape of the gap. Implicit in Holy Church's emphasis on the Incarnation, of course, is the key not only to the whole problem but to B's
whole future development, and the B poet was to accentuate this in

---

many of the Dreamer's appeals to "kynde knowyng" over against theologically correct statements made to him as irony on the part of the Dreamer or the poet, particularly in her discussion of *Dowel.* Also, as she notes, "An explanation is still
needed of why Langland chose the term *kynde knowyng* to express this concept"
(p. 1). I am inclined to see his choice in terms, not of the wisdom tradition, but of
an attempt to coin a vernacular equivalent for the theological term "natural knowledge"; compare E. F. Jacob's discussion of the attempt by Bishop Pecock, a generation after the C text, to do the same, particularly in connection with Saint Thomas's
"Sic enim fides praesupponit cogitationem naturalem," and the wide and highly
ambiguous range of meanings these coined terms take on ("Reynold Pecock, Bishop
of Chichester," *Essays in Later Medieval History* [New York, 1968], pp. 1–34,
especially pp. 29–30). In view of the extended meanings of "kynde" even in the
A text, Langland is clearly not limiting this distinctively human awareness to the
rational (or to the sensual); cf. Pecock's "doom of resoun."

revision, particularly by additions stressing history and in a powerful
"metaphysical" passage on love, which was to replace A's "loue is þe
leuest þing þat oure lord askiþ, / And ek þe plante of pes" (A 1. 136–
37).[19]

The purpose of the present scene is not to explore the problem of
the two knowledges in its own right but to set up, in complement to
the prologue, the second of the two poles which define the human
situation and to establish that the locus of the poem's action is to be
the consciousness of man, collective and individual, in the face, not of
one or the other of these realities, but of both. As D. W. Robertson
observes, in warning against assuming that pre-Hegelian ages saw such
polarities as good and evil, flesh and spirit, obscenity and decorum,
paganism and Christianity, as opposites: "even when . . . alternatives
conflict, they are not contraries. As William of Auvergne puts it, 'to
desire something and not to consent to the desire are not contraries,'
or, to put the same idea in another way, to desire something simply
and to desire something else as preferable are not contraries." [20]

Though, in such a consciousness, tension in the modern sense may
not be a positive value, it is still a vivid presence. The convergence
upward of many forces and actualities is a tension of a kind, as we

19. The same deeper interest in the psychology of man and its potential cost that
we saw in the "rat parliament" characterizes the B poet's contributions to Lady
Holy Church's exposition. His, of course, is the addition to the Fall of Lucifer that
reminds us of Milton. But his main addition is the long passage on the nature of
love and its relation to God and to man, which he substitutes for A's simpler
formula. This passage, so badly garbled by the scribes, clearly plays on astrological
and alchemical terms as it relates Truth's teaching on love to history (in the Old
Testament), to theology (in the Incarnation), to psychology, to politics (in likening
love to the mayor who is "a mene . . . bitwene the kyng and the comune"), to
justice, and to "kynde knowyng." Its bold wit provides a psychological and philosophical equivalent to the fascination with complementary spheres of action and
with the time dimension in human experience manifested in the Prologue. But
perhaps nothing witnesses better to the matured awareness implicit in the B poet's
treatment than his eliminating A's "loue is þe leuest *þing* þat oure lord askeþ" on
its second occurrence, as well as the first, and his substituting in the last lines of
passus 1 the simple phrase, "Loue is leche of lyf" (B 1. 202).
20. D. W. Robertson, Jr., *A Preface to Chaucer* (Princeton, N. J., 1962; reprint ed.,
Princeton Paperback, 1969), p. 25.

feel it to be in Gothic architecture. And every reality has within it the potential for being experienced either as autonomous or as pointing beyond itself to actualities of a more fulfilling but, by that very fact, faintly incongruous character. A universe ultimately perceivable as perfect repose in perfect reciprocity is vibrant with energy and process in its very perfection. And in finite experience the reciprocity and repose are precarious at best, and the process by which human consciousness moves toward them is full of what appears in the short-term view to be conflict and sacrifice. Yet the very fullness, intensity, and inclusiveness of the medieval consciousness, seen especially in its completely different attitude to ugliness, obscenity, humor, and the marvelous from that of romanticism and postromanticism, are functions of an underlying sense that the universe is whole and hierarchical. So far, the A poet's two knowledges are a function of basic medieval assumptions. But what is just as distinctive about *Piers Plowman* when considered in the context of the "medieval world view" as in any other (the obvious comparison here is with Dante) is the tenacity with which the poem in all its forms accentuates the problem and pushes it into the foreground, making the struggle to reconcile it the basis of the action, refusing to the Dreamer (and, one must add, to the reader) any interim comfort. The poem insists on making the limitations of the human consciousness and the terrible obstinacy of its yearning the center of the action.

THE TRIAL OF LADY MEED: THE PRINCIPLES
OF THE DREAMWORLD

The episode of Lady Meed and her trial before the king of England provides the third stage in the poem's introductory dream. It is really a transitional episode, because it completes the poet's exposition of the dreamworld with an analysis of the forces which give it what cohesiveness it has, while at the same time initiating the "plot" proper of the main poem. The story of Lady Meed is the story of what happens to the body of people on the fair field, and the decision the king makes in passus 4 brings about the remaining action of the *Visio*. More important still, the poet here raises the question of whether human society is perfectible, and if so, by what means. Society is held together by various forces: economic ties, the profit motive, and the remedial action of

law. Can any of these forces provide the energy and the coercion necessary to bring about a better social order? Are they mutually exclusive?
The episode has a curiously modern air, with its shrewd assessment of
the way individual motivation is influenced by socioeconomic forces
that can be manipulated so as to induce men to alter their behavior,
even if they do not alter their motives; yet the poet decisively parts
company with most modern economists and sociologists by taking the
position that social amelioration so brought about cannot be considered
a significant improvement. His analysis of the role of the profit motive
and, to a lesser extent, of legal compulsion results, not in an endorse-
ment of their effects, but in an approach to social reform based on
the transformation of human motivation itself, a position which can
be called more conservative or more radical depending on one's point
of view.[21]

This explains the poet's decision to base the action, in all its brilliant
detail, on yet another of the well-established literary genres, on which
the A poet plays so ingeniously—a debate between two personifications
before a judge. The A poet gives this virtuoso art form an incongruous
realism by making his debaters Meed (or the profit motive) and Conscience and his judge the very king who is deciding what shall become
of the society on the fair field. He has further transformed the convention by making the intellectual argument conclusive (the aspects
of human experience to which Meed calls attention are respected, but
her interpretation of them is decisively rejected) and then incorporating
its conclusions into the larger completion provided by a realistic setting where they are to be put into practice. Thus the episode achieves
an architectural consistency not at all characteristic of the debate form
itself.

The debate analyzes the two features of life on the fair field that the
Prologue stressed almost to the exclusion of any others, economic

21. Criticism of the Meed story illustrates perfectly the divergence between critics
who take *Piers Plowman* as essentially a literal action, which merely employs a
number of personifications as "shorthand" in dealing with the situations it portrays,
and those critics who see the whole action as allegorical. See especially R. W. Frank,
Jr., *Piers Plowman and the Scheme of Salvation* (New Haven, 1957), and Edward
Vasta, *The Spiritual Basis of "Piers Plowman."*

reciprocity and the multiplicity of social function, two related factors that are the basis of a healthy society and the symptoms of a diseased one. Meed is the spokesman for the existing order of men "so besy . . . aboute þe mase" (A 1. 6). She lumps all forms of economic reciprocity under one heading and claims to represent them all. But Conscience analyzes these economic ties into different groups. Some of the cases which Meed cites as instances of reward are redefined by Reason and Conscience as instances of justice; a general wins battles (if he can) because he is a general, and the king recompenses him because he is a king. This is reciprocal productivity, in which each man participates according to his position and ability. It depends on a correct assessment of needs and on whether a piece of work has the realities of its pretensions; it is not strictly a matter of reward at all. Others of Meed's examples, Conscience goes on to show, are examples of injustice pure and simple. God alone rightly gives meed in the strict sense of the term, for two reasons: here alone the response of the "person" and the office are indistinguishable, and here there can be no "justice" since no man fulfills God's standards perfectly enough for God to "owe" him what recompense he receives. God's grace and Meed's bribery, the reality and the parody, stand outside the order of just reciprocity, the one above it and the other below, and both can be defined as "a reward wholly disproportionate to the merits of the recipient." [22]

Such an analysis exposes the corruption of the existing order, which is indeed that of False, since only a coercion not intrinsic to the reality of the situation, that of "mede" and law, keeps human nature under some control. The analysis also provides a plan for the complete renovation of society, undertaken by the king with the aid of Conscience and Reason and the assistance of Buxomness. In this part of the episode, law is subjected to a scrutiny almost as searching as that applied to meed. Law is clearly not a damaging force, since its function is not to evade reality but to define any event's relationship to certain clearly established standards, and thus law is not part of the realm of False.

22. John Lawlor, *Piers Plowman: An Essay in Criticism* (London, 1962), p. 29 (hereafter cited as *Essay*).

But in the new order law is to be surpassed as definitively as meed is to be abandoned. "Lewte" is above law and love above that: "Ac kynde wyt shal come ʒet, & conscience togidere,/And make of lawe a labourer, such loue shal arise" (A 3. 275–76). This development is organic, not revolutionary, since "lewte" subsumes law rather than denying it. Modern English demands that we translate "lewte" as "justice" rather than by its obvious cognate "loyalty," [23] but it is a concept that has to do with relationship; justice even in its remedial aspect is not an abstract commodity but right respective relationship. All the same, the attempt to establish such an order in human society will be revolutionary. Not to use meed, while it increases the possibility of an ideal society, also deprives the kingdom of much of its defense against the extremes of disorder. The king's decision to base his social order on actual human motivation rather than on its manageable though artificially induced equivalents, fear and greed, increases the danger to the same degree that it increases hope.

The peculiar vitality of this scene comes partly from its sound architecture and partly from specific techniques like the contrast Lawlor admires between well-marshaled crowd scenes and the significant gesture of single figures.[24] The brilliance with which vivid detail can achieve dramatic cogency and symbolic comment simultaneously cannot be better illustrated than by the portrait of Meed herself as both a fourteenth-century heiress and the scarlet woman of *Revelations*. Equally important is the bold mixture of allegorical personifications à la Lady Holy Church with the actual people we have been seeing on the fair field all along. Personifications, even when they provide the whole dramatis personae of a story—as here they do not—create allegory of a completely different kind from that in which the action or situation itself is metaphorical.[25] This section of *Piers Plowman* really is about a king deciding whether to harness the profit motive or to bypass it in

23. See Donaldson, *C-Text*, pp. 65–66.

24. *Essay*, pp. 24–25, 209 ff.

25. For a discussion particularly useful in understanding *Piers Plowman's* use of "allegorical" elements within an action not itself allegorical, see Ian Bishop's analysis of the distinction between the "allegory of the poets" and the "allegory of the theologians" in *Pearl in Its Setting* (Oxford, 1968), esp. chap. 5.

reforming his kingdom. This is no more hypothetical than a novel; the difference lies in the kind and degree of amplification provided, the techniques by which the elements and the significance of the story are made cogent to the reader. Personification, here, is simply rhetorical shorthand for literal reality, forcing the reader to synthesize his previous experiential knowledge with the analytical knowledge presented by the poem.

The peculiar force of the poet's handling here, and much of the delight it provides, comes from the flexibility with which he manipulates the degree of literalness with which he represents the action at any given point, so that the two levels of reality, instead of running along parallel like a well-drilled algebraic equation, as they do in *Everyman,* seem to reflect each other back and forth like a pair of fun-fair mirrors, each with its characteristic distortion. Consider the departure of the wedding party for London. The (personified) Meed must get across the (physical) distance from Malvern to London. For (material) conveyance her (hypothetical) body is placed on a (real) sheriff, who thus makes a (metaphorical) horse and as such is said to be (physically) "shod al newe." In another pleasing passage, Conscience and Reason gallop off down the road, the one on an ordinary horse suitable to a court emissary and the other on that allegorical conveyance "suffre til I se my tyme." This, besides being entertaining, is the dramatic equivalent of the rhythmic variations that are the very life of the blank-verse line. Such flexibility also opens up more serious possibilities closed to the directly representational art forms, such as bold ellipses in the action itself. The poet need not introduce Reason or explain in terms of ordinary motivation the appeal to his authority, since the role of reason in Conscience's speech has already done this. He need not worry about disposing of Meed herself at the end if meed is dealt with or settle for such awkwardly restrictive solutions as leaving a gorgeously bejewelled lady in a darkening hall as the court goes off to church, marrying her off, or having her vanish in a puff of smoke. Here action can exist for its relevance alone, as our dreams do.

With the end of the Meed story, the character and rationale of the poetic world have been placed before us, and we are ready to turn back to the body of people on the fair field. Reason's closing tirade with its catalogue of specific characters and abuses effects the transition. When we first saw these people, they were moving in a pattern of endless repetition worthy of Ecclesiastes between the two towers, and the landscape so framed had something of the quality of a painted still life made up of figures frozen in the gestures of violent motion. Now the folk are to leave their timeless, stylized "worching & wandringe" to begin the consecutive action of the poem.

2

The Repentance of the Folk on the Field

THE FOLK AND THE DREAMER

The king has taken the bold step of entrusting to Reason, Conscience, and Obedience the task of reorienting a whole society, not by channeling existing motivations into more constructive channels (marrying Meed to Conscience), but by changing them. The transition from plan to action is the transition from Reason's "manifesto" at the end of passus 4 to Conscience's sermon at the beginning of passus 5, which mentions many of the same people and abuses and in the same order. The poet has returned us to the full panorama of "þe feld ful of folk þat I before tolde." He must now go beyond his external portrayal of human nature by adding an inward and psychological dimension and he must find a means of enacting what happens when conscience brings self-awareness to creatures who are what they are by virtue of the choices to which their own motivations have led them. Though passus 5 is the direct outgrowth of passus 4, the poet splits them apart by introducing the only waking interlude in the *Visio*, before plunging us into action at a deeper level than the preceding essentially diagnostic survey.

One of the main factors in the establishment of this new level is the greater degree of participation by the narrator in the plot. We almost lost sight of him in the objective reportage of the recent passūs, but here he is again, surrounded as before with the derogatory expressions like "feyntise," [1] which reiterate the importance and ambiguousness of the Dreamer's relationship to the dream. Indeed, the Dreamer reports

---

1. This is confirmed by the nervousness of the A text scribes who substituted "a fayntnes" (E) and "fantasye" (RDKW) for "feyntise" (line 5). Skeat glosses "faintness, an attack of weakness," from Old French "feintise" but recognizes that "feintise" itself means "feigning" or, by extension, "cowardice."

most of Conscience's sermon in indirect discourse and with embellishments directed at his own audience whom he addresses in the second person. Then, instead of introducing the confessions that follow with any procession, crowd scene, or collective portrait of the kind so successfully used in the Meed story, the poet moves from sermon to action with no more than two unobtrusive lines: "Þanne ran repentaunce and reherside his teme / And made wil to wepe watir wiþ his eiʒen" (A 5. 43–44).

This innocent looking remark constitutes one of the major "cruxes" in *Piers Plowman.* One's whole understanding of the poem's dramatic structure is affected by the choice one must make here. Is "wil," as nineteenth-century critics automatically assumed, the William Langland to whom the poems are attributed? Or is "wil" an allegorical figure? If so, has he any connection with the Dreamer? There is nothing here to indicate that this fellow is anything but a low-intensity personification like Repentance. But "wil" is to crop up again within the A *Visio* itself, in a passage which prevents our stopping with this simplest interpretation. This passage occurs in passus 8 after the account of Truth's letter to merchants explaining to what degree they participate in his pardon:

> Þanne were marchauntis merye; many wepe for ioye,
> And ʒaf wille for his writyng wollene cloþis;
> For he copiede þus here clause þei couden hym gret mede.
>
> [A 8. 42–44]

Here "wille" cannot be the allegorical human will; it must be the name of the Dreamer who, as Holy Church first explicitly noted, is the supposed author of this poem. But if the audience is to recognize in the first passage a factor which will not be spelled out for them for another three passūs or, indeed, if they are to understand the second passage when they come to it, it can only be because they have known all along that the Dreamer's name was Will, because it was the name of the real poet; in the same way, the reader of the *Divine Comedy* did not get a surprise when the name "Dante" was finally used at the top of Mount Purgatory; he had to know from the first line of the *Inferno* that the rather undignified fellow Virgil rescues is a known poet, but by no means considered—yet—the peer of Virgil himself, and that he loved a historical Beatrice. The reader of Chaucer's dream visions must appreciate the joke that the reluctant scientist, finally addressed as "Geoffrey," who puts his mentor, the learned Eagle, to such pains to speak "lewdly to a lewed man" is the poet whose power is attested in that poem and also the shrewd civil servant and trusted diplomat. The very point of the difference between narrator and poet depends on the audience recognizing the connection.

Personae of this type differ completely in kind from those like Lemuel Gulliver that become possible in an age of printing, in which the dissemination of the book as a distinct, duplicable physical object, divorced from its creator, gives the work of art a new and objective status. (All the same, the problems raised by the tone of Gulliver's fourth voyage attest to the difficulty a writer has in keeping even that sort of persona completely at arm's length.) The first-person narrator in the late Middle Ages is one of the most sophisticated developments in a conception of poetry shaped by the oral tradition and supported by the continuing presence of oral performance. It is a conception of poetry as intrinsically dramatic, a function of the personal encounter between a poet and his audience in a specific situation, exploiting the close connection between composition and performance, between the poet as creator and the poet as finite individual. It would seem almost inevitable, under these circumstances, that for a sophisticated poet his poem should become in part a dramatization of his own relationship to his subject and an exploitation of the tension between the truth of art and the truth of experience; between vicarious participation in the selective world of the mind and actual vulnerability to human experience; between perfection as a maker and perfection as a creature. Indeed this dramatization may become not merely a means of constructing the poem but its very subject.

When we are reading Chaucer or Dante, we have information about the author exterior to the poem that can help us to strike the right balance between reacting to the narrator as if he really were the creator of the poem and reacting to him as a rhetorical device. But where *Piers Plowman* is concerned, establishing that the audience had some reason that passus 5 itself does not supply for relating poet and Dreamer does not give us any more objective knowledge about the poet than we had before.[2] These lines are placed where they are to mark the point at which the Dreamer becomes a participant in the action of the poem rather than remaining that rhetorically useful entity, an observer-pupil. As a participant he is the human will, and the importance of that faculty to the drama ahead is not slighted, as might at first have appeared, but on the contrary is made crucial to the structure of the whole poem.[3] Furthermore, the connection between what the poet learns as Dreamer within the poem and what he creates and becomes outside it in the "real" world becomes intrinsic to the structure of the poem to an extent unparalleled outside Dante and Chaucer. Indeed, what differentiates the A poet's strategy from theirs is the fact that his dreamworld *is* the real world in a sense very different from theirs. Therefore, in the very world in which "Will" is the dreamer he is the artist.[4] Finally, the confessions which follow are not merely those of individual folk or groups of folk on the field but also those of the Dreamer. They must be seen not merely as brilliant satiric analyses of particular deviations but as stages in an action, forming a cumulative whole, a collective portrait of the diseased human will as it manifests itself both in the society and in the individual, an inexorable development from the anarchical self-determination of Pride to complete de-

2. Nor does it permit us to assume the relationship will remain the same in all three versions. For an assessment of the traditional information about the author of the poem and of the authorship controversy, see Kane, *Piers Plowman: The Evidence for Authorship*. See also Donaldson's analysis of the degree of plausibility to be attributed to the "biography" of the Dreamer that can be pieced together from the three texts and of the degree of consistency between them, in *C-Text*.

3. The name "Will" is thus almost too appropriate to be autobiographical; but consider the role of the name "Will" in Shakespeare's sonnets or of "Elizabeth" in Spenser's *Amoretti*. Note, in this connection, Ian Bishop's argument for an auto-biographical nucleus in *Pearl* from the very sketchiness of the exposition, which would be inadequate as a basis for a fictional situation, a point of special relevance to the skimpiness of A's critical lines (*Pearl in Its Setting*, p. 7).

4. It ought to be unnecessary to point out that I do not mean there is necessarily any literal correspondence between the events of the dream and those of the poet's life (see Fritz Krog, "Autobiographische oder typische Zahlen in *Piers Plowman*," *Anglia* 58 [1934]: 318–32) or that the poet actually had a dream in which these events occurred.

generation of the very capacity to will at all, in Sloth. To preserve this subtle relationship between the personified sins and the actuality they represent, the poem presents no formal masque, deployment, or panorama of sins comparable to the murals of the *Roman de la Rose* or to Spenser's pageants in *The Faerie Queene*.

Indeed, the poet avoids any formal parallelism whatever among the portraits, not only exploiting a complete range of techniques and situations for his figures but choosing figures that are intrinsically heterogeneous and range from the sketchy abstraction Lecher to the specific woman with the Jonsonian name of Pernelle Proudheart already mentioned in Reason's tirade and Conscience's sermon. On the other hand, the portraits do have two characteristics in common. First, the integrity of the individual portrait is continually violated by the intrusion of other sins into the analysis of each, and their distinctiveness from each other is burred by the recurrence of similar details of food, clothing, and physical squalor. Secondly, the portraits are not portraits of the sin as such but acts of confession; and it is indeed a nice question what sort of "confession" a sin, as distinct from a sinner, can produce. Both qualities are essential to the total structure.[5]

---

5. That structure became more difficult to grasp as a result of the authorship controversy, since passus 5 is the *locus classicus* for attempts to show that the B poet, by his treatment of this or that particular detail, reveals his failure to understand A and hence shows he was not the A poet. This gave rise to theories that the A scene as we have it is a corruption of the A poet's text, having suffered a variety of losses or dislocations between the time he finished it and the time the B poet began to revise it, so that even B's close adherence to the surviving text of A could be construed as a proof of the B poet's obtuseness. These hypothetical lacunae and displacements are associated with the points in the A poet's scene where he diverges from the logic or the conventions that scholars expect to find him following, especially where transitions seem abrupt or associations of ideas eccentric. Defenders of B or of single authorship have, in a sense, been even worse offenders, since their strategy has seemed to suggest that the A poet's structure is not odd. Now it is certainly not odd in the particular sense that Manly and others took it to be; if we reestablish ourselves among the assumptions of the fourteenth century, the aspects of A which the controversialists found absurd no longer trouble us. But in the process of demonstrating this, the essential boldness and the technical amateurishness of A became alike obscured, together with the rationale for the B revisions and the role of the scene in the plot of the *Visio*. For a useful summary of the theories which

The Unity of the Confession Scene

The function of the confession sequence is to show what happens when the combined powers of Reason and Conscience are brought to bear on the problem of the human condition. The three qualities on whose witness the king bases his decision and to whom he entrusts the governance of his society, Reason, Conscience, and Obedience, are not supernatural qualities or qualities peculiar to the supremely gifted individual. They imply no resources or capacities that transcend the fair field itself, the normal terms of the human condition. They represent what man himself can bring to bear, out of his own resources, on the corruption of the individual and of society. Like Virgil in the *Divine Comedy,* they can reach the human consciousness at whatever point of degeneration it has attained and make it see what it has become. The series of confessions that follows Conscience's sermon reveals just what it means for the human consciousness to be so reached and shows what that implies for the king's plan to reform his kingdom without enlisting the allurements of Lady Meed. The successive stages in the resulting action are marked by the speeches of the successive sins, and this results in a portrayal of two distinct sequences in counterpoint to each other. On the one hand, each sin's account of what his life is like contributes to a cumulative portrayal of how the human spirit decays, from man's initial refusal to accept the subordination of his identity to God's all the way to the near obliteration of that identity itself; on the other hand, the panorama of attitudes to repentance counteracts the pessimism of the first sequence with a positive movement toward regeneration. Like Dante, the A poet is dramatizing Christianity's underlying concept of sin; sin is not an act but a condition which manifests itself in acts, a condition in which no man can be alone since it imposes itself upon others and is contagious in its nature as well as in its

---

postulate major corruptions in the A text erroneously adopted by the B poet and of the subsequent controversy, see T. P. Dunning, *Piers Plowman: An Interpretation of the A-Text* (London, 1937), pp. 79–80 (hereafter cited as *A-Text*). The two main proposals are those of J. M. Manly ("The Lost Leaf of *Piers Plowman,*" *Modern Philology* 3 [1906]: 359–66) and Henry Bradley ("The Misplaced Leaf of *Piers the Plowman,*" *Athenaeum* [April 21, 1906], p. 481).

effects, for indeed no man is an island. It is as organic as disease, with a pathology just as consistent. One could do worse than read passus 5 as a gloss on Julian of Norwich's "And to me was shewed no harder hell than sin." [6] Combined with the savage objectivity of the satirist and the shrewd observation of the social commentator is something of the sense of human damage which made Julian respond to Christ's assurance that "all shall be well, and all shall be well, and all manner of thing shall be well" with a tenacious "Ah! good Lord, how might all be well, for the great hurt that is come by sin to the creature?" and led her to see God's compassion as anything but a glossing over of that reality: "Though the soul be healed, his wounds are seen before God,—not as wounds but as worships." [7]

The order in which the sins confess is essential to the passus structure and the key to the treatment of each. The sequence begins conventionally enough with Pride, but the low-key spareness of the treatment is as disconcerting as the sordid passivity of Dante's Satan. The confession of Pride is not so much a confession as an illustration of the first stage of repentance, through Pernelle's humility and silent self-knowledge:

> Pernel proud herte plat hire to þe erþe
> And lay longe er heo lokide, & "lord mercy" criede,
> And bihiȝte to hym þat vs alle made
> Heo shulde vnsewe hire serke & sette þere an heire
> For to affaiten hire flessh þat fers was to synne:
> "Shal neuere heiȝ herte me hente, but holde me lowe
> And suffre to be misseid, & so dide I neuere.
> But now wile I meke me & mercy beseke
> Of alle þat I haue had enuye in myn herte."

[A 5. 45–53]

She does not describe her sin, except indirectly through the abject humility of her gesture, her appropriate reference to God as "hym þat vs alle made," and the particular reforms she promises.[8] Yet the apparent

6. *Revelations*, p. 83.
7. *Revelations*, pp. 56, 60, 80.
8. Pernelle's undertaking the penance of allowing herself to be falsely accused, which devotional treatises characteristically describe as the great lesson in humility,

anticlimax is necessary to the theological as well as to the dramatic structure. Sin begins with the creature's all-important, yet almost imperceptible shifting of allegiance from his maker to himself, less a positive act than a withdrawal from the positive act of the whole creation. The drama lies not in the moment but in the results, as Dante himself indicates, not in his splendid gallery of portraits of the proud in the *Inferno,* but in his placement of Pride on the bottom cornice of Mount Purgatory. Similarly, repentance begins, not with spectacular withdrawal from major crimes, but with the unspectacular fundamental acceptance that man is not his own master. Furthermore, Pernelle, by virtue of her name and the fact that she is previously known to us, is as much a character on the field as a personification and completes the transition from the folk, via the Dreamer, to the collective action of the sins.

Lecher's confession is even shorter and wholly unspecific:

> Lecchour seide "allas" & to oure lady criede
> To make mercy for his mysdede betwyn god & hym
> Wiþ þat he shulde þe satirday, seue ȝer þeraftir,
> Drinke but wiþ þe doke & dyne but ones.

[A 5. 54–57]

If lechery did not loom large in other parts of the poem, one might assume that the A poet was uninterested in lechery as a sin; instead lechery seems merely the corollary of pride, the spontaneous taking of what seems good to the individual by his own standards (analogous to the role in the *Inferno* of the Paolo and Francesca episode, in contrast to the other kinds of sexual sin further down). Lecher's penance is entirely alimentary, though he appropriately chooses the day of the week most associated with painting the town red for his abstinence from meat and drink; what he contributes to the discussion of sin and repentance comes from the understated message of his appeal—alone among the sins—"to oure lady," a reminder that sin is essentially a distortion of experiences and faculties that are good and which man

---

and her decision to sew her hair shirt into her "serke" (presumably so she will receive no adulation for wearing one) clearly mark her sin as spiritual pride, the root of all other sins.

was meant to have and that repentance is not intrinsically a negative
thing but man's shift from the negative to the positive expression of
his nature.

With Envy we move from setting the self up as its own standard of
appeal to assuming the ascendancy of the self over other selves as an
absolute principle. For Envy this very awareness is a life's work, a
continual agony of effort, manifested with a wholeheartedness and
energy wholly admirable in every facet of his life; like Farinata's dignity, it is an inverse tribute to what the human spirit can achieve.
The confession of Envy marks the poet's most triumphant use of the
personification proper. Although Envy is consistently lay and male,
his most important consistency lies in the cumulative pressure of complementary details, not in any biographical consistency, even of the most
generalized sort. Some details are pure visual emblem:

> Enuye wiþ heuy herte askide aftir shrift,
> And carfulliche his cope comsiþ he to shewe.
> He was as pale as a pellet, in þe palesie he semide;
> He was cloþid in a caurymaury, I couþe it nouȝt descryue;
> A kertil & a courtepy, a knyf be his side,
> Of a Freris frokke were þe foresleuys.
> As a lek þat hadde leyn longe in þe sonne,
> So lokide he wiþ lene chekis, lourande foule.
>
> [A 5. 58–65]

But these are complemented with brilliant social observation whose
implications are implicitly defined by contrast with emblematic details
of altar and crucifix, unobtrusively included:

> Whanne I come to þe kirke & knele to þe rode,
> To preye for þe peple as þe prest techiþ,
> For pilgrymes, for palmers, for al þe peple aftir,
> Þanne I criȝe on my knes þat crist gyue hym sorewe
> Þat bar awey my bolle & my broken shete.
> Awey fro þe auter myn eiȝe I turne
> & beholde how heyne haþ a newe cote.
>
> [A 5. 85–91]

Envy's very mode of coming to shrift exemplifies the sin itself as much as any repentance of it, and his account of his misdeeds is as much innocent self-revelation as a portrayal of the human will in revulsion at a part of itself. Shrift must work as magic, it seems, for the diseased will can no more cure itself than can an ulcer:

> May no sugre ne swet þing swage it an vnche,
> Ne no dyapendyon dryue it fro myn herte.
> ȝif shrift shulde, it shope a gret wondir.
>
> [A 5. 100–102]

This image of disease leaves us with the impression Envy has a penance; his "ulcer" is its own punishment, and his concluding comment to Repentance is brilliantly ironic:

> "ȝis, redily," quaþ repentaunce & redde hym to goode:
> "Sorewe for synne sauiþ wel manye."
> "I am sory," quaþ enuye, "I am but selde oþere,
> And þat makiþ me so mat for I ne may me venge.
>
> [A 5. 103–6]

Envy in all depraved innocence really is sorry; envy does make its victims live in misery, and he even has a little geniune regret at being the man he is. But the incapacity of Envy even to understand what Repentance means by being sorry for sin eptiomizes the incapacity for perception which is the first symptom that sin is cutting man off from the very reality which he hopes to control.[9]

Avarice's confession is a portrait in much the same style as Envy's, introduced by the same stock disclaimer, "I can him nouȝt descryue," because avarice is the corollary of envy. Here Envy's principle of the ascendency of self over others receives a spectacular program of practical implementation which, like Dante's Malbowge, exploits the very integers of man's relationship with man—material necessities, money, and the very words and measures on which their exchange is based. It is an inverse tribute to the power of human ingenuity and enterprise. But unlike Envy, Avarice has a "biography," a name ("sire heruy"), a

9. This, not the break in the text postulated by Manly, explains the fact that Envy's conclusion does not fit the pattern.

wife ("rose þe regratour") who is an even more inspired deceiver, and a consistent commercial career in the cloth and tavern businesses, all of which place him in a category halfway between Pernelle and Envy. Avarice's distinctive feature is his volunteering a penance which is as ironic as Envy's conception of sorrow for sin; Avarice volunteers to go on a pilgrimage with his wife to Walsingham (after all the poet's comments on pilgrimages and after his selection of Walsingham as the destination of his lecherous hermits in the Prologue) and thus provides a more openly sarcastic reference to the incapacity of sin for any real understanding of repentance.[10] And Avarice's response to Repentance is not merely to agree with him while misunderstanding what he means but to see, even in Repentance's admonition, license for his predatory habits and to enlist the very metaphor of Christian rhetoric in the service of his calling as he plans to "bidde þe rode of bromholm bringe me out of dette" (A 5. 145).

The confession of Glutton breaks the last formal consistency the poet has so far observed by deserting the sins' common pose vis-à-vis Repentance. Glutton's confession is a self-contained dramatic incident, joined to the rest only in that it presumably occurs on the fair field and that Conscience's sermon may have started Glutton off on the well-intentioned errand from which he was so soon distracted. His final confession is addressed not to Repentance but to his wife and wench (if not to the air), and whether his waking words, "where is þe bolle?" (A 5. 204), refer to a "hair of the dog" or merely to a basin, they link his repentance to morning-after misery rather than to contrition. He resolves—understandably enough, under the circumstances—to fast "for hungir or þrist" (A 5. 209), but this heroic plan turns out to mean no more than abstaining from fish on Friday. Such is Glutton's view of abstinence. Glutton's drinking bout in a realistic fourteenth-century

---

10. In A, Sir Harvey is the only married sin except Glutton, and this reference to his wife precludes the possibility that this pilgrimage belongs to Sloth and that Sloth's offer of restitution belongs to Avarice, as has been suggested. See Bradley, "The Misplaced Leaf of *Piers the Plowman*." To object because restitution is not discussed here is to misunderstand the poet's strategy, as we will consider when we come to the confession of Sloth. Nevertheless, it is so natural to wonder about restitution at this point that the A poet undoubtedly creates an awkwardness. (The B poet's handling of this problem will be discussed later.)

alehouse has been admired as long as *Piers Plowman* has had critics, both for its vigor and for the convincing character of its sociological detail. These qualities, combined with its tightness and neatness as a dramatic unit, strike a base note of human authenticity in the chord of the whole passus. From the point of view of allegorical technique, it is an extension of the method used in the Meed debate and the opposite of Envy: the personification of a human quality is placed in the midst of actual people, realistically portrayed in a situation that involves that quality, so that Glutton seems almost an emanation from the group as a whole, who, as he swills and swells, seems at last to engulf and pickle all the rest in a triumph of emblematic squalor. This relative passivity on the part of the personification, by comparison with Envy and Avarice, marks the next stage in the degeneration of the individual and of society. The full impact of human intelligence and energy were displayed in Avarice, celebrated in their very misuse; in Glutton's "repentance," not even the wit of Avarice's parody survives, and it becomes impossible to distinguish the symptoms of the sin itself from the last traces of self-revulsion. For Avarice the human community still remains; it is real enough to be exploited and to make the exploitation process sufficiently difficult that the powers of the human mind are challenged. In Glutton's alehouse, Avarice's financial empire has been replaced by handy-dandy, a game which turns on the comparative worth of expendable bits of clothing, and instead of the warmth of human solidarity we find only the sodden Glutton and the squabbling gamesters. In the appeal to Robin the Roper to umpire the contest, some communal coherence remains, but it lasts only long enough to unleash a new drinking bout as full of "lourying" as of "lauȝing." The increasingly sordid detail culminates in the ultimate parody of community, Glutton being sick in Clement's lap.[11]

With Sloth the sequence reaches its culmination. As in the first of the confessions, there is no pyrotechnic display of detail—indeed, there

11. Kane concludes that this last detail (Skeat's A 5. 202–7) actually belongs to the B tradition and crept into the A MSS UEMH [3] by contamination and thus into Skeat's A text (see Kane's note on his A 5. 198). If so, we have here one of the B poet's most strikingly successful amplifications of an idea essential to the A poet's strategy.

is no direct account of the sin at all. The whole subject is summed up and dismissed in one gesture, Sloth's swoon, which places the last confession in formal parallel with the first and makes it a parody of Pernelle's deliberate gesture of submission:

> Sleuþe for sorewe fil doun a swowe
> Til *Vigilate* þe veil fet water at his eiȝen,
> And flattide it on his face & faste on him criede,
> And seide, "war þe for wanhope wile þe betraye. . . ."
>
> [A 5. 213–16]

The details of Sloth's program of amendment, twice as long as any other sin's, function like Pernelle's to provide a definition of the sin which Dante defined as "love deficient," while stressing the positive results of repentance in a way appropriate to the last of the formal confessions. Sloth offers to combat wanhope and paralysis with positive activity that expresses his reacceptance of relationship with God and man; he undertakes a discipline of religious duties designed to interfere with his comforts by making him rise early and put off his evening ale and a program of restitution for a lifetime of financial parasitism. Sloth's place at the end of the list of sins provides a much more imaginative place for the concept of restitution than under Avarice, since it emphasizes that restitution (*Dobest*'s "redde quod debbes") is the necessary shouldering of responsibility that marks repentance for all sin, or, as Holy Church said of "date & dabitur vobis," it is "þe lok of loue þat letiþ out my grace" (A 1. 176). Though its relevance to Sloth is no less great than to any of the other sins, the true function of the restitution passage is to complete the movement from inward-oriented penance like Pernelle's, which focuses on remedial measures applied to one's own psyche, outward into expressing renewed inner health in the relationships that bind each man to every other and to all the realities of the universe.[12]

12. The appropriateness of restitution to Sloth has been hotly debated, but thanks to R. W. Chambers and others, the authorship controversy finally established that ill-gotten gains were traditionally associated with this sin. See Dunning, *A-Text,* pp. 84–85, for a summary of Chambers's earlier arguments which relates them to such general analyses of sloth as Saint Thomas's. For a convenient summary of the

If sloth were merely laziness, no more than an almost genial failing, the poet would be guilty of anticlimax in closing his sequence with a sin usually passed over quickly somewhere in the middle of the series and treated even more comically than gluttony. Yet the one consistent feature of all *Piers Plowman*'s treatments of the deadly sins, in every version, is that the series invariably closes with gluttony followed by sloth.[13] The poem's emphasis on sloth is in fact even more striking than this would suggest if we remember, as the Dreamer's involvement in the confession scene reminds us to do, the persistence with which the poem's treatment of him in all three texts (culminating in the great C preface to the confession scene itself) associates him with a parasitic existence—"lollerene life," as the C poet calls it—and with paralysis of the will itself. So this emphasis on sloth, surprising at first glance, is organic to the poem's whole view of human corruption and regeneration. Nor is Langland unique in this respect. Julian of Norwich, for example, singles out sloth (which she links with impatience, illustrating the much wider sense of the term in medieval usage) and despair, the ultimate development of sloth, as the very heart of human sin and as the form of sin to which the repentant man seeking regeneration is particularly subject:

> Generally, He showed *sin,* wherein that all is comprehended, but in special He shewed only these two. And these two are they that

---

analytical, rather than cataloguing, function of the concept of the "capital sins" and of Dante's view of sloth, see Dorothy L. Sayers's introduction to her Penguin translation of the *Purgatorio* (Harmondsworth: Penguin Books, 1955), pp. 65–67. 13. All three forms of the Meed "feofment" end with gluttony and sloth, in spite of small variations of wording; B and C strengthen the reference to sloth by explicitly adding wanhope (A 2. 64–71; B 2. 92–106; C 3. 97–108). In the confession scene, A and B have the same order; the C poet's changes do not affect the position of gluttony and sloth (in his order—pride, envy, wrath, lechery, avarice, with "ȝyuan ȝeld-aȝeyn" and Robert the Robber discussing restitution, gluttony, and sloth—only lechery and Robert are affected). While Hawkin's confession (B 13) ends with a long digression on the ethics of minstrelsy, the part of it which covers the deadly sins ends with gluttony and sloth, each of which receives a self-contained discussion that sets these two sins off from the other five, which are comparatively jumbled. (There is no comparable structure in C, since he redistributes this Hawkin material under the appropriate headings in his confession scene.)

most do travail and tempest us, according to that which our Lord shewed me; and of them He would have us be amended. I speak of such men and women as for God's love hate sin and dispose themselves to do God's will; then by our spiritual blindness and bodily heaviness we are most inclining to these . . . And the cause why we are travailed with them is for lack in knowing of love.[14]

She links this basic propensity to wanhope specifically with repentance and confession, in terms peculiarly relevant to the structure of A's confession scene: "For right as by the courtesy of God, He forgiveth our sin after the time that we repent us, right so willeth He that *we* forgive our sin, as anent our unskilful heaviness and our doubtful dreads." [15]

Sloth and wanhope are the image of the insubordinate human will losing even its own intrinsic vitality, that responsive individuality which led God to look at the creation and call it good. To strengthen this image and make it emblematic enough to act as the culmination of his series, the A poet avoids any pyrotechnic account of particular misdeeds in which the slothful indulge[16] and keeps this final portrait spare and absolute. Thus, he can make his progression from revolt to degeneration clear while placing it in counterpoint to his cumulative analysis of repentance, from the silent self-knowledge of Pernelle as she "lay longe er heo lokide & 'lord mercy' criede" through various parodies of restitution to the real thing. In the portrait of Sloth, even more than in any other single confession, is illustrated the balance the scene attains between the moral optimism supported by the regeneration sequence and the poet's tragically cumulative portrayal of the Fall of Man.

The subservience of the individual portraits of sins to these two emerging patterns accounts for the fact that the A poet's scene seems chaotic and unanalytical, even incurious, compared to Dante's lucid demonstration of how the multiplicity of human evils may be traced to

---

14. *Revelations,* pp. 178–79.

15. Ibid., p. 180.

16. Manly expected that sort of account, and its absence led him to postulate another break in the text as we have it.

a limited number of basic deviations in the human will. These portraits are in fact one cumulative portrait of the folk and of the Dreamer,
and hence the individual portraits are continually interwoven through
parallel images and details, like those in Chaucer's prologue portraits,
and through inclusion of a variety of sins in each portrait. At the heart
of Pernelle's pride is envy. Lecher is punished in terms of food. Sloth
is avaricious. Envy's confession is one long outpouring of wrath, greed,
hypocrisy, and sheer malicious destructiveness. This certainly produces
psychological and social realism in the individual portraits, but, more
important still, it makes one common organism of these different allegorical focuses, the body of humanity itself:

> A þousand of men þo þrongen togideris
> Wepynge & weylyng for here wykkide dedis;
> Criede vpward to crist & to his clene modir
> To have grace to seke treuþe; god leue þat hy moten!

> [A 5. 251–54]

The Role of Robert the Robber

But these concluding lines are separated from the last of the formal
portraits by a transitional figure, Robert the Robber:

> Robert þe robbour on *reddite* lokide,
> Ac for þere was nouȝt wherewith he wepte swiþe sore.
> And ȝet synful shrewe seide to himselue:
> "Crist, þat on caluarie vpon þe cros diȝedist,
> Þo dismas my broþer besouȝt þe of grace,
> And þou haddist mercy on þat man for *memento* sake,
> Þi wil worþe vpon me, as I haue wel deseruid
> To haue helle for euere ȝif þat hope nere.
> So rewe on þis robert þat *reddere* ne hauiþ,
> Ne neuere wene to wynne wiþ craft þat I owe,
> But for þi muchel mercy mytygacioun I beseche;
> Dampne me nouȝt at domisday for þat I dede so ille."

> [A 5. 233–44]

What is a figure who is not one of the deadly sins doing here? Does
Robert's response to Sloth's discussion of restitution mean he is to be

associated with Sloth, or does the absence from the A text of a confession by the seventh sin, Wrath, mean we should co-opt Robert for
the job? [17] If we try to classify him by considering references to robbers in *Piers Plowman* generally, as well as the nature of the robber's
life and the major attention accorded it in medieval moral theology,
we can see that there is no one of the deadly sins of which a robber
could not be considered an illustration. While a specific theft seems
less destructive than the more spectacular sins, a robber's way of life
epitomizes man's tendency to live as a destructive parasite on reality,
rather than as a contributing member of the larger structure. A robber
is, on top of everything else, willed sloth.[18] As an inclusive image of
all the sins, Robert is the logical capstone of a structure designed to
make the reader see the interdependence of the sins rather than their
distinctness. But Robert's presence is also dictated by other equally important features of the scene.

To conclude the passus successfully, the poet must bring his portrayal of sin into focus with his larger purpose in the *Visio*. As far as
technique is concerned, he must make a transition from the personifications back to the literal level of the confessing folk; but he must
do so without sacrificing the absolute position of his culminating sin,
as he could afford to do with Pride, and without suggesting, as a
processional departure by the sins in a body would do, that their existence is separate from that of the folk themselves. Robert, as a confessing

17. Discussion of Robert the Robber has become inextricably confused with the
absence of Wrath from the A text. The two issues are, however, perfectly distinct,
and the problem of Wrath in both texts will be discussed later in connection with
the B poet's addition of such a confession, since his decision cannot be understood
without an overview of both confession scenes.

18. The modern reader is most conscious of the medieval view of theft in connection with Dante's treatment of robbery as one of the final stages in the disintegration of both the social fabric and the individual identity (*Inferno*, cantos 24–25).
But the ethical distinction between a needy man who takes the bare necessities of
life without paying for them and a thief, a professional parasite, is an important
issue for Saint Thomas and others; see B's discussion of Need in passus 20 and commentary on it, for instance in Morton Bloomfield, *Piers Plowman As a Fourteenth
Century Apocalypse* (New Brunswick, N. J., 1961), p. 136 and elsewhere (hereafter
cited as *Apocalypse*). Note particularly, "Neglect of restitution is not only the sin
of avarice but the sin of sloth" (*Apocalypse*, pp. 218–19, n. 13).

individual who is collective in representing all the sins, achieves this. Thematically, the problem of sin and repentance must be set in its metaphysical context, as Holy Church began to do, so as to bring the analysis of sin back to the question with which the scene began: is human self-knowledge enough to unleash energies which can reform society? What Robert expresses above all is recognition of his helplessness to meet the standards of justice or to find within himself the resources to make himself other than what he is; yet it is in this very recognition of helplessness, marking as it does a sense of his finitude and of the existence of strength beyond his own, that he enacts hope. Finally, a robber is the scriptural prototype of all repentant and forgiven sinners and epitomizes the incommensurability between the standards by which God saves man and the norms of ordinary human justice. The A Dreamer himself puts it forcefully later in the poem:

> A goode friday, I fynde, a feloun was sauid
> Þat hadde lyued al his lyf wiþ lesinges & þefte,
> And for he kneuʒ on þe crois & to crist shrof hym,
> Sonnere hadde he saluacioun þanne seint Ion þe baptist,
> Or adam, or ysaye, or any of þe prophetis
> Þat hadde leyn with lucifer manye long ʒeris;
> A robbere hadde remission raþere þanne þei alle.
>
> [A 11. 279–85]

The figure of a robber is thus the perfect emblem for the situation of man as sinner on which the whole confession scene is based, and Robert's presence makes the sequence of confessions not linear but concentric with Robert at the hub, embodying the central problem. The optimism of Reason's program for reform is in a sense justified, in that to be human is to have, like Robert, the capacity for self-knowledge. Yet Robert has "nouʒt wherewiþ." Reason's hope of basing the reform of society on man's capacity to change his own motivation by changing his intellectual view of himself seems to lead not to action but to paralysis, as has been implicit all along in the poet's paradoxical portrayal of sins confessing. As the Dreamer's appeal to "kynde knowynge" (in contrast to the knowledge provided by Holy Church) suggested, sin is a state of progressive deterioration which takes more than intellectual knowledge to counteract. The king's bold rejection of Meed made a transformation of man's motivation essential to maintaining, let alone improving, human society; yet once we look at the nature of human sin itself, this seems a precarious basis indeed for a just moral order. Can this wailing and thronging crowd provide the prerequisites for its own renewal? The finale of passus 5 leaves the audience hoping that this is indeed possible: "God leue þat hy moten."

The B Confession Scene

Brilliant as A's structure is, it is obscured by the heterogeneous character of the sins, by the lack of overt transition between them, and by the failure to clarify the crucial role of Robert the Robber. Here, for the first time, no well-known literary archetype provides the scaffolding for the scene, and though it draws on traditional descriptions of sins and murals of sins, such analogues do nothing to make the relationship between the sins and the folk or the rationale behind A's order more readily apparent. When the B poet came to revise passus 5, he addressed himself to precisely this problem and devised ways to make clearer the A poet's strategy and his difficult conception of sin, human consciousness poised at the furthest point to which self-knowledge without an enlightened will can take it. Neither the A poet's order, which his additions leave undisturbed, nor his peculiar strategy for each individual sin could be sacrificed. At the same time, the B poet also dealt with precisely the three features of A's scene that were to absorb the attention of scholars on a new continent five hundred years later almost to the exclusion of anything else: the absence of a confession for the traditional seventh sin, Wrath; the fact that restitution is discussed in connection not with Avarice but with Sloth; and the absence of any specific account of Sloth's misdeeds, which reinforces the common misconception of sloth as mere abstention from any activity, good or bad, and thus, by making Sloth's position at the end of the sequence seem anticlimactic, suggests that A's order is merely a random one. In fact, from his behavior, one would suppose the B poet to have been an avid reader of Manly and Bradley.

Unfortunately for his scholarly reputation, the B poet's solution to the absence of Wrath from A proved even more controversial than the situation it attempted to correct, since his Wrath differs from the other sins in being a tempter rather than a sinner.[19] In this, however, B reflects a marked idiosyncrasy in the treatment of wrath throughout both texts, in which wrath in the usual sense is often omitted,[20] while elsewhere wrath plays a role comparable to that of spiritual pride in most moral theology and is presented as the flaming will to rebellion and jealousy of God from which all sin springs.[21] On the other hand,

19. When this discrepancy between the A and B texts was first noted, there seemed no possible explanation except that the A text had once had a confession of Wrath that was lost from the archetype of all surviving A MSS as well as from the one that the B poet used as the basis for his revision; and that, by adding a confession incompatible with the strategy of the others, he convicted himself beyond appeal of misunderstanding his source. But the idea that the deadly sins are necessarily seven is a modern one and rests on an increasing tendency throughout the Middle Ages to standardize its analyses of all features of the religious life in groups of seven (seven sacraments, seven petitions in the Lord's Prayer, seven virtues, seven vices, and so on). Even in the later Middle Ages, deviations occur: see Dorothy L. Owen, *Piers Plowman: A Comparison with Some Earlier and Contemporary French Allegories* (London, 1912), p. 41; Dunning, *A-Text*, pp. 85–86; and Morton Bloomfield, *The Seven Deadly Sins* (East Lansing, Mich., 1952). As for the "conflicting strategies," the deductions drawn from this were based on an assumption of uniformity in the A scene that is simply not justified.

20. Wrath is missing from Meed's marriage contract in A; and the B poet, in contrast with his treatment of the confession scene, does not add it. Wrath gets one vague line in B's confession of Hawkin which links wrath with envy and with "wikked wille" (B 13. 321) as provokers of violence. The C poet does nothing to redress this imbalance; Wrath's is the only confession not expanded in his redistribution of material from B. For the absence of Wrath from various listings of the "seven" sins in *Piers Plowman*, see Allan H. Bright, "Langland and the Seven Deadly Sins," *Modern Language Review* 25 (1930): 133–39, a very useful survey which, however, accounts for these anomalies by supposing that the poet was himself so little subject to wrath that, since his poem was autobiographical, he had to omit this sin, an argument sufficiently refuted by the violently irascible character of the poem as a whole. See also Dunning, *A-Text*, in the passages cited above, n. 19.

21. The only specific account of Wrath within the A text itself occurs in Piers's account of the pilgrimage to Truth in passus 6, and here we find precisely the anomalous conception of Wrath later used by the B poet: Piers warns the folk that Wrath is a tempter who will "enuye" any pilgrims who have managed to get into

in both A and B, anger is not an unambiguously bad thing and, as its role in the development of both Piers and the Dreamer suggests and the violent irascibility of the poem as a whole confirms, is tied up with the central energies of man for good as well as for evil.[22] So unusual a conception of wrath would be sufficient reason for the A poet to have omitted it from a scene that depends for its force and economy on the reader's familiarity with traditional didactic treatments of the sins. In addition, both texts show a strong sense of identification with this sin on the part of the poet, or at least the Dreamer, and the surprising conclusion to the confession of Wrath in the B text reflects precisely this attitude. After Wrath's lurid account of his activities, Repentance admonishes him: " '*Esto sobrius*,' he seyde, and assoilled me after / And bad me wilne to wepe my wikkednesse to amende" (B 5. 186–87). Wrath is the only one of the sins to receive absolution as well as advice; and here alone in the whole confession scene the narrator uses the first-person pronoun about one of the sins.[23] The effect of this very striking detail is accentuated by the fact that the strange expression, "bad me

the castle because he envies "hym þat in þin herte sitteþ" and will incite them to pride so that they will have to wait a hundred winters at the door. B shows an equally surprising stress on wrath as a tempter when the devil's climactic assault on the tree of charity is by means of wrath and, indeed, involves the very same "agent provocateur" methods used by Wrath in the B confession scene.

22. The A *Visio* contains two major instances of wrath in the usual sense of the term. In the first, Piers responds "in wraþþe" to those who "holpen to ere þe half akir wiþ 'hey trolly lolly!' " (7. 109–12). The second and even more striking one is, of course, Piers's tearing of Truth's pardon in "pure tene," which, whatever else it may be, is not a misplaced leaf from the confession scene. What is interesting about both these cases is that, whatever the poet wished us to think about the rightness of these two actions, it was obviously not the wrath itself, as such, which was disturbing him. For the B poet as well, wrath is not necessarily bad; in passus II it is wrath which arouses the Dreamer from the oblivion in which he has lost all interest in "doing well" and sends him back both to the search for DoWell and to the writing of the poem.

23. Only two B MSS have "him," one in the hand of a corrector, one over an erasure. Compare here Dante's specific association of himself with the sins of pride, wrath, and love excessive by having Dante the pilgrim actually participate in the punishments on those cornices of Mount Purgatory. C, characteristically, omits this detail.

wilne to wepe," echoes the scene's one earlier reference to the Dreamer in which Repentance "made wil to wepe water with his ei3en." The B poet's whole portrait of Wrath, then, is in keeping with an unusual attitude to wrath, which he shares with the A poet and which is closely related to both poets' basic conception of the human will; it also strengthens the role of the Dreamer in the confession scene and, although it remains, in its strategy, a compromise, is by no means so incompatible with the other sins as Manly suggested. After all, wrath is, by definition, no particular sort of activity, nor violence as such, nor violence to any utilitarian purpose. Wrath, more than any other sin except pride, *is* a motive, not an act, and may with peculiar appropriateness be portrayed as a tempter.

Where Sloth and restitution are concerned, the B poet accepts A's reasons for placing restitution at the end of the sequence but forestalls premature objections by raising the issue of restitution himself in an extension of Avarice's ironic dialogue with Repentance. After Sir Harvey offers to go to Walsingham to "bidde the rode of Bromeholme brynge me oute of dette," Repentance asks:

"Repentedestow the euere," quod Repentance, "ne restitucioun madest?"
"3us, ones I was herberwed," quod he "with an hep of chapmen,
I roos whan thei were arest and yrifled here males."

[B 5. 232–34]

He insists that he "wende ryflynge were restitucioun" and similarly defends usury as supporting lords "for loue of her mayntenaunce," adding that he has as much pity for the poor "as pedlere hath of cattes" and that in providing himself with food and drink he is "hende as hounde is in kychyne." As for the danger that the reader may misunderstand the nature of Sloth and with it his role in the scene, the B poet adds a detailed and lively account leading up to Sloth's swoon, which he retains, however, so as the preserve the balance of this final emblematic gesture at the end of the sequence against Pernelle's opening one. The first comic lines may seem to reinforce the stereotype of Sloth as the fellow who cannot keep up any activities at all. But no sooner does his confession begin than out pours a flood of detail, all involving activities. If Pride is the root of all sins, Sloth is their manifestation.

He is as lecherous as Lecher, as ingeniously acquisitive and greedy as
Avarice, as malevolent as Envy, as malicious as Wrath, as squalidly
animal as Glutton. Indeed, at the very heart of Sloth there is a self-
regarding rapacity that cuts him off from human perceptions and makes
B's comparison to a hawk brilliantly apt:

> ȝif any man doth me a benfait or helpeth me at nede,
> I am vnkynde aȝein his curteisye and can nouȝt vnderstonde it;
> For I haue and haue hadde some dele haukes maneres,
> I nam nouȝte lured with loue but there ligge auȝte vnder the
>   thombe.

> [B 5. 436–39]

The wanhope which in A was the whole portrait of Sloth is here the
logical culmination of a life centered solely on self. In reading B's hawk
simile one cannot help thinking of its antithesis, Dante's bold conceit
in which the whole created universe becomes a lure which God, the
great falconer, whirls about his head to call man home to him.

These three additions do more than eliminate potential awkwardness
or misunderstandings. They shift the balance of the scene toward the
longer and more realistically detailed confessions which resemble and
reinforce each other. Thus they must be seen as part of the larger pattern
to be discerned in this revision. The overall strategy is to strengthen the
role of Repentance as master of ceremonies throughout the scene and
thus to counteract the discontinuity of the individual confessions by
providing a clear framework for them, from the first reference to Repentance in the two lines about the Dreamer's tears all the way to the
corporate prayer Repentance offers on behalf of the folk. Except for
the first two sins, Pride and Lechery (which are left as spare and
emblematic as before and for the same reasons), each sin has a dialogue of his own with Repentance and makes either a vow or some
ironic inversion of one. Most importantly, Glutton and his alehouse
are brought into line with the other confessions by the sudden appearance
of Repentance at the bedside of the hung-over reveler. Finally, Repentance's prayer, which is offered in response to Robert the Robber's
plea and made on behalf of the whole throng of the folk, completes

the transition from the abstractions to the reality they convey and complements the metaphysical perspective implied by Robert's reference to the Crucifixion with the kind of full-scale historical dimension so characteristic of the B poet. Within a short thirty lines, Repentance relates sin to God's creation of man in his own image, the Fall, the Incarnation, the Atonement, the Harrowing of Hell, and the Resurrection and ends with a plea to God not as the remote Truth in his tower but as one who has chosen to make himself "owre fader and owre brother."

In this short passage, we have in embryo the whole future development of the B text, even to the cross-referencing between historical events and their liturgical mimesis, most striking when Repentance describes the Crucifixion as Christ's "douȝtiest dedes," which "were don in owre armes," and his death "in oure sute" as "mele tyme of seintes" (B 5. 495–501, 508). The paralysis and incomprehension of man, his incapacity to provide the means of transcending himself, are seen to be the crux of Christian revelation: "Non veni vocare iustos, sed peccatores ad penitenciam." [24] Sin is not simply the disease it has been shown to be but, potentially at least, in the classic paradox which Repentance quotes (B 5. 491), "felix culpa." Truth is not merely a detached and precise observer of the human drama, nor does revelation gloss it over; in Repentance's words, Truth does not ignore the captivity of man but rather "Captiuam duxit captiuitatem." [25] When Hope seizes a horn and blows a triumphant "beati quorum remisse sunt iniquitates,[26] the cry of the wailing throng on the field remains the same cry as in A, but it blends with another sound as "alle seyntes" sing the mercy of God.[27] If the B additions to the confessions themselves seem to weight the scene toward pessimism, the conclusion works in the opposite way to accentuate its constructive elements. The result is to leave the bal-

24. Matt. 9:13, "I did not come to call the righteous but sinners to repentance."
25. Eph. 4:8, "He has led captivity captive."
26. Ps. 31:1, "Blessed are they whose sins are forgiven."
27. This section contains significant echoes of the Confiteor at the beginning of the Mass. This probably accounts for the fact that, in certain cases, biblical quotations which do not follow the Vulgate exactly (see Skeat's note on "vivificabis," B 5. 513) correspond with the Missal.

ance much as the A poet left it but to place that delicately balanced image of struggling man in a vast historical and metaphysical perspective.[28] Thus the B poet reveals himself not merely as the most perceptive reader and critic A's scene ever found but as a more mature and balanced craftsman than the A poet, one who could shape his bold and compact sketch into the foundation for a new and larger drama.

28. In doing so, the B poet anticipates developments which do not occur in A until the pardon scene and are not intellectually assimilated in A at all, as the Dreamer's reference to the repentant thief confirms; see chap. 3 below.

3

From Confession to Pardon

The confession scene in passus 5 ends with no overt absolution nor
any indication of a process completed but with a plea by the repentant
folk for the grace to "seek St. Truth." The confessions, with their emphasis on the inability of the sinner to cure himself, bring the folk no
further than the realization of their need. We now find the poem asking what mankind is to do after this first step. Truth in all the meanings the poem has built up so far is precisely what they lack and now
hope to find, just as the problem of what the "truth" of the finite
world is has been made the central question of the poem by the poet's
inversion of the dream-vision formula and by his placing the fair field
in the shadow of the tower where Truth dwells. But however genuine
the folk's wish may be, as far as it goes, their efforts seem likely to
be wasted:

> Ac þere were fewe men so wys þat þe wey þider couþe,
> But blustrid forþ as bestis ouer baches & hilles
> Til late & longe þat hy a lede mette.
>
> [A 6. 1–3]

Not only are they lost, but when they inquire their way of a palmer
who proves never to have heard of Truth it becomes clear that the
folk have no understanding of the difference between the regeneration
they are attempting and the corrupt parody exemplified by this palmer,
any more than Envy and Avarice understood Repentance's exhortations.
The satire on the palmer himself is obvious and quite in keeping with
the poet's previous attitude to professional pilgrims. But a second

irony, more scathing and more compassionate, is directed against the folk themselves.

In short, the folk's attempt seems to have reached a dead end before it has really begun. But now the poet acknowledges that the dilemma he portrays is artificial in that it leaves out one further factor in the human situation, which man himself can discern by bringing his own conscience and reason to bear on the panorama of human behavior. This factor the poet included in his initial portrait of the fair field by beginning his survey of the professions with the honest plowmen, but he has systematically excluded it from the part of his drama that responds to the Dreamer's plea, "kenne me by sum craft to knowe þe false" (A 2. 4). Not all are false. If a corrupt man cannot supply what is needed to reverse the trend of his own corruption, what about mankind's remaining resource, its healthy integers? There are others besides palmers who could respond to a query about Truth:

> "Petir," quaþ a plouȝman and putte forþ his hed,
> I knowe hym as kyndely as clerk doþ his bokis.
> Clene conscience & wyt kende me to his place,
> And dede me sure hym siþþe to serue hym for euere . . ."
>
> [A 6. 25–28]

Piers Plowman's confident and practical account of his life gives a sympathetic and hopeful picture of man embodying precisely the standards of obedience and "mesure" which Holy Church expounded in passus 1. Piers knows truth and troth in precisely the way in which Envy knew envy. His life is characterized over and over by the word "kyndely"; it is natural, as evil is always essentially unnatural. Its virtues are those which result from filling one's appointed place and responsibility in the universe, according to faithful common sense, in just the terms of "fel, face & fiue wyttes" which Truth set up as the human condition. Surely this must be the answer to mankind's problems. Piers himself feels nothing but optimism: "Þere is no labourer in his lordsshipe þat he louiþ better / For, þeiȝ I sey it myself, I serue hym to pay" (A 6. 30–36). He feels no doubt that his service is adequate and that he fully understands the terms he and Truth are on. His commendation of Truth as a master is the practical evaluation of one who knows just where they stand with each other, and Piers's very existence seems to confirm Holy Church's brisk assumption that the good life is at bottom a very simple matter.

Piers's world is an idyll in the sense that it contains no factors that confront him with any problems but practical ones that can be solved by the exercise of honesty, skill, and tenacity. Even his profession itself is peculiarly in accord with Truth—as a farmer he is directly in touch with the elements that Truth created to serve man and created man to use—and illustrates two of the poet's central themes, the productive and natural dependence of the finite on the infinite and the interdependence of individual perfection and social function. In his literal character as the farmer of another's land, Piers becomes the archetype of all those whose vocation in the world is their mode of serving God and man and their school of Truth.[1] In an even larger sense, Piers as a farmer suggests archetypal man in the terms used of his creation in Genesis: "Tulit ergo Dominus Deus hominem, et posuit eum in paradiso voluptatis ut operaretur et custodiret eum." The farmer is also the emblem of man bearing and responding to the effects of the Fall: "Maledicta terra in opere tuo; in laboribus comedes eam cunctis diebus vitae tuae. . . . In sudore vultus tui vesceris pane, donec revertaris in terram de qua sumptus es." [2] Thus, Piers raises the two most basic questions about man: what was he meant to be, and what has he become in the world in which he must now define himself?

After a speech describing the way to Truth, the practical and psycho-

1. This is clarified by the subsidiary clauses of the pardon in passus 8, which establish the degree to which each profession constitutes "helping Piers Plowman."
2. Gen. 2:15, "And the Lord God took the man and placed him in the Garden of Eden to till and keep it." Gen. 3:17, 19, "Cursed is the ground because of you; in toil shall you eat of it all the days of your life. . . . In the sweat of your face shall you eat bread till you return to the ground for out of it you were taken." Since it seems impossible to establish what variant of the Vulgate text the poet used, all citations follow *Biblia Sacra Iuxta Vulgatam Versionem,* ed. Bonifatio Fischer, OSB, et al., 2 vols. (Stuttgart, 1969); punctuation mine. The eclectic translations attempt to provide a "trot" while preserving the effect, so central to *Piers Plowman,* of the contrast between a poem in one's "birthtongue" and quotations in an authoritative, incantatory, universal, and to that extent elevated style.

logical corollary to the principles Holy Church enunciated in passus 1,[3] Piers places his experience at the folk's disposal, and it would seem that they are now in the fairest way for a not-too-distant happy ending, with the whole human race as healthy, virtuous, and frugally prosperous as Piers. But this hoped-for development depends on providing for the material necessities of life. The arrangements Piers makes for plowing his half acre are the practical corollary of the Meed trial and exemplify the hierarchical division of labor that is the economic and social reflection of a hierarchical universe. At first, Piers's moral ascendancy seems enough to make the experiment work, but soon the lazy abandon the course, and Piers's attempts to deal with the situation merely turn this laziness into deceit and then drive Waster into open revolt. Piers then appeals to the second sanction, the protection of the knight or the force of law and order, but this merely makes Waster obstinate and a stalemate is reached. Finally, Piers, in a rage, falls back on the only remaining temporal sanction, Hunger, the inevitable consequence of human irresponsibility. At first Hunger galvanizes even hermits into frenzied activity, but as the approaching harvest reduces him to torpor the last semblance of order on the half acre disappears; the corrupt stop working, and even the industrious become greedy and dissatisfied. The passus ends with a tirade by the Dreamer on the coming famine, which is the only possible result of an irresponsible and self-centered society.

In other words, the kind of force represented by Piers, however admirable it may be, is as helpless to remedy human corruption as the corrupt themselves, as helpless as Virgil before the gates of Dis.[4] Al-

3. It is significant that Piers does not describe either the good life or the pilgrimage with which he images it realistically. The poet's subject at this point is not brooks, crofts, and castles, in the same sense as plowmen, corrupt taverners, and repentance. Nor is the poet describing the nature of obedience, honesty, mercy, or humility. He is only conveying the relation in which they stand to each other by equating each with an element in a simple and familiar pattern which is applicable only in being roughly analogous. In short, this image is didactic rather than dramatic, its artificiality calls attention to its teaching function, and that function is dramatically justified by the role of Piers's speech in the literal story.

4. Many critics of the poem have not agreed that the half-acre scene is to be taken literally or that Piers can be seen as other than the perfect illuminated man of the

though there is nothing wrong with Piers's values, he cannot get at the central problem of the social and moral order, the motivation of the folk. If that cannot be changed, then the rejection of Meed as a force of social cohesion must inevitably lead to the even cruder compulsion of Hunger, either as a deliberately invoked sanction for correct social behavior or as an inevitable result of its absence. The moral perfectioning of society presupposes material support; and the meeting of material needs presupposes moral qualifications in those who sustain the social fabric: the result is a vicious circle. By the end of passus 7 the fair field full of folk has regressed to where it was in the Prologue; still worse, it has jettisoned the makeshift structures that were protecting it from the worst excesses.[5] It has brought itself to despair, since all the resources man can bring to bear "kyndely" on the problem of his own condition have been exhausted. The implications of taking human society as a self-contained "dreamworld" have been worked out to their ultimate conclusions.

FARMER AND DREAMER

Before we can go on to look at the pardon in the light of the events that lead up to it, we must look more closely at the figure of Piers, who is so sympathetically portrayed, yet whose obvious excellence does not seem sanctioned by the outcome of his efforts. As far as the plot about the folk is concerned, he is here in a double capacity: on the one hand, he is a foil for the folk, since he has exactly those virtues that the folk lack and that are the strict complement to the kind of corruption revealed in the Meed debate and the confession scene; on the other

---

later B text. See, for instance, D. W. Robertson, Jr., and Bernard Huppé, *Piers Plowman and Scriptural Tradition* (Princeton, 1951), pp. 83–85; and Vasta, *The Spiritual Basis of "Piers Plowman,"* pp. 107–36 and elsewhere. But compare Lawlor, *Essay,* p. 255, and *"Piers Plowman:* The Pardon Reconsidered," *Modern Language Review* 45 (1950): 452.

5. Since the social order of the half acre is clearly one of which the poet approves, critics have assumed that the plowing is a success, with the exception of Lawlor who suggests that at the end of the scene "We are back in the individualistic world of the Prologue" (*Essay,* p. 70), though he retains his earlier interpretation of the pardon which depends on the opposite view ("The world of the *Visio* has been set to rights," *Essay,* p. 82).

hand, he is here to test whether virtue of his kind is the basic solution to the problems of human nature and human society. Piers's virtue provides a norm of stability within a society almost paralyzed in its corruption; he seems to sum up in his own person the alternative to the psychology propounded by Lady Meed, the diseased state of the deadly sins, and the helpless craving of Robert the Robber. Yet all his efforts have failed to reverse the pattern of man's attempts to improve himself; like the proverbial frog in the well, society has now made three efforts and for each leap forward has fallen back two. In the poem so far, Piers is the best, but is the best the Good?

Piers's virtue is instinctive and simplistic. It is derivative from an established pattern of life in which he has always existed; that is why the pastoral image of a plowman as an ethical norm is so useful to the poet. This is not a reflection on Piers, but he is as unable to provide the prerequisites for that way as Envy or Sloth or Robert the Robber; and the whole force of the poem's analysis has been directed not to human behavior as such but to its basis, not to corruption and virtue as such but to the problem of turning the one into the other. Piers's virtue is *pietas* rather than *caritas*.[6] What the action of the half acre brings home to the reader more than anything else is the growing anger and puzzlement, even resentment, of Piers as the whole gamut of means available to the well-intentioned for the amelioration of society are inexorably revealed, one by one, to be useless for anything but temporary palliation. What Piers represents is simply not the answer to the tragic character of the human situation.

The satiric function of the figure of Piers as a foil for the folk is obvious enough; what is less immediately obvious, though no less important, is that Piers is still more fundamentally the complement to the Dreamer, to whom he is related in a way which the modern reader cannot help associating with Yeats's self and antiself and which the poem's use of personifications would have made natural in its own time. The two seem like complementary poles in a cumulative portrayal of Everyman. Piers is all purity, practicality, authority, confidence. He is

6. I am indebted here to an unpublished essay by Prof. David McCarthy, delivered in a seminar at Brown University, 1969.

disciplined, extroverted, productive. He sees life in terms of its manageable elements; he is totally unprepared for a world which does not respond to recognized treatment. He has a contractual conception of the relationship between God and man, an "Old Testament" conception, quite innocent of the consciousness Paul saw as its corollary, in which the very awareness of law brings a self-knowledge which is a kind of death: "I had not known sin but by the law. . . . The commandment which was ordained to life I found to be unto death." [7] Piers's account of the way to Truth does not confine itself to the Ten Commandments. Its emphasis on "loue & louȝnesse," the role of grace and mercy, and references to the pope, the sacrament of penance, and so on, make it clear that no identification between Piers and a pre-Christian ethic in the historical sense is intended. But his emphasis is on the fulfillment, point by point, of an established code, and above all on the confidence that a man who fulfills this code can count on an equally established and predictable response from God: Truth is "þe presteste payere þat pore men knowen," and Piers can say, "þeiȝ I sey it myself, I serue hym to paye" (A 6. 36). In Piers's view, in contrast to Conscience's in the Meed debate, God gives not "reward" but justice. In short, although the content of Piers's religion is not "Old Testament," the contractual psychology of it is.[8]

But in our recognition of what Piers exemplifies in the religious sense, we must not forget that he is also one kind of emblem of man as artist, *homo faber*, mind and will shaping the elements of his world as form shapes matter; he is, as the fourteenth century called the poet, a "maker," not with words but with the elements of his environment. For the medieval audience (unlike the modern one, since we are used to thinking of art as a special and privileged human activity produced by a unique faculty, the imagination), the parallel would be perfectly

7. Rom. 7:7, 10, ". . . peccatum non cognovi, nisi per legem . . . inventum est mihi mandatum quod erat ad vitam, hoc esse ad mortem."
8. While it is true that the decalogue is considered by typological exegetes a prefiguring of the law of charity, to consider it so here is to obscure the distinction, even more important to the poem as a whole and especially to these passūs, between law and charity, between a legal covenant-ethic and a love-ethic.

natural. Furthermore, until he starts to use other human beings as his
"matter," he is a successful one, much more successful, it would appear,
than the Dreamer. Piers would have no patience with the Dreamer's
megrims; he would have responded to him, as Holy Church did to his
fuzzy ideas about "kynde knowing": "þou doted daffe!" He would
surely have lumped the Dreamer with the other unproductive characters on the half acre and cut off his rations along with Waster's.

Now the one character who clearly displays just this opinion of the
Dreamer is the Dreamer himself. His calling himself an unholy hermit
and a minstrel, his hypersensitivity on the subject of the wandering
professions, and his role in the confession scene all indicate this. If Piers
is man as agent, the Dreamer is man in search of a basis for action, the
"kynde knowyng" which can resolve the tragedy of his incapacity to
will and do.[9] But for all his apparent weakness, ethical and practical,
the Dreamer's tenacity is in its own way as great as Piers's. He is not
exactly a walking definition of Keats's "negative capability," since he
cannot manage to remain in "uncertainties, Mysteries and doubts"
without "irritable reaching after fact & reason,"[10] but he does insist on
remaining there *with* them. And surely no poem ever had a narrator
who followed Keats's advice so thoroughly (and his practice so little)
when it comes to having "the confidence to put down his half-seeing"
and not censoring out the inconsistent responses of the "chameleon
poet." The dreamer's determination to accept no premature palliations
or securities in his attempt to understand the human situation, to go
on refusing one explanation after another in the name of "kynde
knowyng," to remain vulnerable and open to each aspect of the problem as it arises—these make him the polar opposite of Piers. Indeed,
Piers and the Dreamer correspond closely with the two alternatives
which Moneta presents to the dreaming poet in *The Fall of Hyperion*:
those who "labor for mortal good" and those who, on the other hand,
at the cost of being "a dreaming thing, A fever of thyself," one who
"venoms all his days, Bearing more woe than all his sins deserve,"
become visionaries because they are "those to whom the miseries of the

9. McCarthy, unpub. essay.
10. To George and Thomas Keats, 21, 27 [?] December 1817 (Rollins, *Letters*,
1:193).

world Are misery, and will not let them rest." [11] These qualities make
the Dreamer seem perfectly useless; they also make Piers's brisk view
of man, to say nothing of Lady Holy Church's definition of man as
"fel, face & fiue wittes," seem childlike, if not tragically limited. One is
sharply reminded of the contrast Keats saw between his own nature and
that of his theologically minded friend Bailey:

> Yes on my Soul my dear Bailey you are too simple for the World
> —and that Idea makes me sick of it—How is it that by extreme
> opposites we have as it were got disconted [*sic;* discontented?]
> nerves . . . although you have been so deceived you make a simple
> appeal—the world has something else to do, and I am glad of it—
> were it in my choice I would reject a petrarchal coronation—on
> account of my dying day, and because women have Cancers. I
> should not by rights speak in this tone to you—for it is an incendiary
> spirit that would do so. Yet I am not old enough or magnanimous
> enough to anihilate self—and it would perhaps be paying you an
> ill compliment.[12]

The price of the Dreamer's attitude to human sin and need is that it
makes him to some degree its accomplice and divorces his perceptions
from natural expression in action or in lucid exposition: "Until we are
sick, we understand not." [13]

The two figures of the Dreamer and Piers are to remain the poles
of the poem's structure through all three versions of *Piers Plowman*.
Both figures will evolve, while keeping their complementarity, into
more and more emblematic images of man's nature. B's transfigured
Piers will be "plowing" all of disintegrating Christendom as his
Dreamer approaches the annihilation of death. By the end, these two
roles will become so fully symbolic and complementary that Conscience,
as he takes over the Dreamer's role of quester, will voice his final hope

11. Canto I. Compare also Keats's comment on the difference between "imaginary"
evils and "real" ones: "The imaginary nail a man down for a sufferer, as on a
cross; the real spur him up into an agent" (to Charles Brown, 23 September 1819
[Rollins, *Letters,* 2:181]).
12. To Benjamin Bailey, 10 June 1818 (ibid., 1:292).
13. To Reynolds, 3 May 1818 (ibid., p. 279).

not in terms of finding but of *having* Piers Plowman: "sende me happe
and hele til I haue Piers the Plowman" (B 20. 383).

Passus 7 ended with the Dreamer's vision of the disasters that will
inevitably follow the failure of the experiment on the half acre. Passus 8
begins abruptly from that point in the plot:

> Treuþe herde telle hereof, & to peris sente
> To take his tem & tilien þe erþe,
> And purchacide hym a pardoun *a pena & a culpa*
> For hym & for hise heires eueremore aftir,
> And bad hym holde hym at hom & erien his laiȝes.
> And alle þat holpen to erien or to sowen,
> Or any maner mester þat miȝte peris helpen,
> Part in þat pardoun þe pope haþ hem grauntid.

[A 8. 1–8]

The next sixty-nine lines deal with what these "mesters" are and to
what degree they count as "helping Piers." Then suddenly two further
characters, one new and one old, are drawn into the scene:

> "Piers," quaþ a prest þo, "þi pardon muste I rede,
> For I shal construe iche clause & kenne it þe on englissh."
> And peris at his preyour þe pardoun vnfoldiþ,
> And I behynde hem boþe beheld al þe bulle.
> In two lynes it lay & nouȝt o lettre more,
> And was writen riȝt þus in witnesse of treuþe:
> *Et qui bona egerunt ibunt in vitam eternam;*
> *Qui vero mala in ignem eternum.*
> "Petir," quaþ þe prest þo, "I can no pardoun fynde
> But do wel & haue wel, & god shal haue þi soule,
> And do euele & haue euele, & hope þou non oþer
> Þat after þi deþ day to helle shalt þou wende."
> And piers for pure tene pulde it assondir
> & seide *"Si ambulauero in medio umbre mortis*
> *Non timebo mala quoniam tu mecum es.*

[A 8. 89–103]

Piers then announces he intends to live a new kind of life that is not so concerned with material necessities, the priest picks a quarrel with him by referring sarcastically to Piers's sudden erudition about the Latin Bible, and the shouting wakes the Dreamer who seems completely baffled by the whole affair:

> Al þis makiþ me on metelis to þinke
> Manye tymes at mydniȝt whan men shulde slepe,
> On peris þe plouȝman, whiche a pardoun he hauiþ,
> And how þe prest inpugnid it al be pure resoun.
>
> [A 8. 149–52]

However, he soon escapes from this dilemma into some unimpeachable conclusions about how much better it is to do well than to dely on pardons and indulgences:

> Forþi I counseil alle cristene to criȝe god mercy,
> And marie his modir to be mene betwene,
> Þat god ȝiue vs grace er we go hennis
> Suche werkis to werche, whiles we ben here,
> Þat, aftir oure deþ day, dowel reherse
> Þat at þe day of dome we dede as he hiȝte.
>
> [A 8. 179–84]

And with that the *Visio* ends.

Any reader of this scene recognizes the symptoms of intellectual indigestion described by the Dreamer. An extraordinary number of problems arise in these few lines. Truth invades the closed world of the poem like a *deus ex machina;* what he sends is a pardon; he "purchased" it. And it is to Piers he sends it, not to Robert and his like. Furthermore, the "pardon" turns out to look exceedingly unlike a pardon; it is nothing but two lines from the Athanasian Creed, and their impact is well described by Lawlor: "'All in two lines it lay,' utterly uncompromising; so far from making any concessions to human frailty, its effect is to bring that frailty out of the realm of ambiguity into the steady light of Divine Justice. . . . Its impact is as sharp and terrible as a sword stroke," [14] Worst of all, Piers tears the pardon up.[15] In case we should not be sufficiently shocked and might think he had merely decided it had nothing to do with him or that its existence in writing was superfluous, we are told he tears it "for pure tene." In case we should only be shocked and view this as a purely vicious action, however psychologically convincing, we see Piers instantly transformed into a new kind of person altogether, whose motto is no longer "þeiȝ I se it myself, I serue hym to pay" but "though I walk through the valley of the shadow of death, I shall fear no evil, for thou art with me." [16] Then he appears to disobey Truth's injunction to "holde hym at hom & erien hise laiȝes":[17] in fact, his conduct and the explanations he gives for it become quite unintelligible by ordinary logic.

In short, the pardon is nothing less than an *aenigma,* that device under which medieval rhetoric classed both irony and allegory. The text itself presents us with a statement which, as it stands, has a plain, natural, and familiar meaning but whose context is incompatible with that meaning. Statement and context together force the reader to extrapolate to find a further meaning that will reconcile them and give point to the original contradiction. The pardon is marked as an aenigma because its words clearly state the law of reward and punishment, whose existence has been the crux of the plot and which was presented by Conscience as the antithesis to the order of Lady Meed and endorsed by Piers in his "pilgrimage to Truth"; it should please and comfort the man who once said "þeiȝ I sey it myself, I serue hym to pay." Yet this once familiar landmark looks anything but comforting after the recent events which have clearly demonstrated the naïveté of seeing ethical

14. *"Piers Plowman:* The Pardon Reconsidered," p. 455.

15. It is this action, above all, that needs explanation. Much of the best recent discussion of the pardon has fallen back on the assumption that this act of Piers's cannot be what it appears and that there is no adequate meaning for it, so that the best the critic can do is understand why Langland's ideas were too much for his craftsmanship. See, for instance, John Burrow, "The Action of Langland's Second Vision," *Essays in Criticism* 15 (1965): 247–68, with its important emphasis on seeing the pardon in the context of the preceding events.

16. See below, chap. 5, for the liturgical associations of Piers's three Latin quotations and their relevance to this scene and to B's passus 11.

17. Donaldson, *C-Text,* pp. 166–67.

goodness as sanctioned by results or as an adequate solution to the human predicament. Instead of comforting Piers, it fills him with rage. And above all, this statement, like the Renaissance emblem, bears a title which labels it authoritatively as the one thing which it seems impossible for it to be: a pardon. All of this forces us to take the document sent to Piers, and with it the very existence of law in the human psyche and in society, as a riddle, the central riddle of human history. Man can live neither with law nor without it. What, then, is it?

That this paradoxical, shocking, and enigmatic character of the scene must on no account be explained away is indicated by the stylistic and dramatic ingenuity with which the A poet has accentuated it. For instance, the poet's manipulation of the reader's reaction to the pardon is as brilliant as anything in the poem to date. As Piers unfolds his pardon, we instinctively accept his view of the situation: he got out of his depth on the half acre, but his intentions were of the best, and Truth is responding like the kind, just employer Piers described earlier; he sends Piers back to his natural job and takes care of both the results and the responsibility by dispatching a document that goes so far beyond the claims of the most extravagant pardoner as to eliminate not only the *pena* but the *culpa*. In short, Piers is being decorated on the field by a grateful commander. Thus the words of the pardon come as a complete shock; we recoil with the thought, "That's not a pardon!" No sooner has this thought formed itself than the priest takes the words right out of our mouths: "Petir . . . I can no pardoun fynde." Suddenly we are no longer looking at the action from Piers's point of view but from that of his opponents, and Piers begins to recede from us. This effect is intensified as the scene proceeds by the difficulty of understanding what he seems suddenly to find so clear, an effect which prepares us for his subsequent disappearance from the action of the poem. On the other hand, we are made uncomfortable by this separation and by having so disagreeable a man as the priest be our spokesman. We begin to doubt our own instinctive reaction and to wonder if perhaps the pardon really could be a pardon after all. This sudden self-doubt heightens our appreciation of Piers and contributes to our sense that he is being transformed before our eyes into more than himself. The poet's craftsmanship also intensifies the shock value of the scene through pacing. The long disquisition on what vocations constitute "helping Piers Plowman" reinforces up to the last minute our instinctive expectation that by fulfilling a code of prescribed good actions a man acquires a claim on God; the universe is manageable if you know the rules. Again, the sheer lyricism of Piers's speech after tearing the pardon, particularly the lines about God's care for the birds in winter, is set between the violence of tearing the pardon and the violence of the quarrel, accentuating the effect of all three with extraordinary economy.

In short, the point of the scene cannot be to "explain" anything but rather to show a completely new rationale, incommensurable with everything that has gone before, overriding the dramatic, ethical, and psychological assumptions in terms of which the poem has worked. From the moment that Truth, hitherto left in convenient isolation in his tower on the borders of man's domain, intervenes within that domain, the status of the fair field as a self-contained world is destroyed. Hitherto the poem has traced with tragic realism the efforts of that world to perfect itself by its own resources. When Truth supersedes man's responsibility, does this interference destroy the drama of the *Visio*? What becomes of our understanding of man in this new context? What stature has man when faced with the stature of God? This is an artistic as well as a philosophical problem, and its challenge to the unity and integrity of the *Visio* can hardly be overstressed.

Piers's response reinforces this effect. When the rules of the game are changed on him, he first reacts with perfectly understandable outrage. He has made what seem like "superhuman" efforts; yet he receives no special commendation of his own way of life, merely a statement addressed to all men, no special tribute to his efforts but an epitome of the difference between God's standards and his own which can only deepen his sense of failure. This is all the more exasperating since it purports to be not a statement of wrath, which a man can stand up to, but a statement of patience. If this is a pardon, and Truth says it is, then its terms are an enactment. That must mean that the salvation of good men to which it refers is not a wage earned, that it would not occur except by a gratuitous gift of God to which he is not compelled by justice as human logic understands it. If this is a pardon, accepting it means accepting God's acceptance of man's finitude; if this be freedom afterward, it is gall before. To man's self-respect, the pardon is more unbearable as an act of patronage than as an act of punishment. If this is the only way out of our constantly disintegrating efforts to take care of our own problems, then indeed we cannot call our souls— or our world—our own. This superseding of man's autonomy, with all it implies, has been implicit in the poem all along, in the framing of the fair field by the two towers, in Holy Church's metaphysics, in Conscience's shocking assertion that God's meed is more nearly analogous to Lady Meed's than to justice. But no "kynde knowyng" of it is possible to man until every other alternative has been inexorably snatched away from him by experience, and he will evade this realization as long as any avenue remains untried.

Consequently, the dramatic impact of the scene on the reader is absolutely essential to the whole strategy of the poem. But the scene itself can only be defended if the action which produces the effect does, in fact, make sense in its own terms, although not in those of the Dreamer, the folk, and—at the actual moment of experience—the reader. Is the poet merely shocking us toward new awareness by insulting our emotions and intelligence as the Zen master does his disciple (which is insufficient justification for a work of art with any pretensions beyond the dadaist lyric), or is there something behind the paradox of pardons that aren't pardons and outraged destruction that turns into radiant docility? This is precisely where commentary on the pardon scene embroils itself.

There are two fundamental problems that come up once one attempts an intellectual analysis, and both must be admitted to result naturally from certain choices the poet has made. The first is a result of the calculated risk he takes in using as his central image the ambiguous idea of a pardon, ambiguous even in the fourteenth century and a major stumbling block to a modern reader.[18] Yet, here, what the poet gains by his choice justifies the increased difficulty of the scene. On the one hand, pardons are those legal or ecclesiastical clearances that, regardless of the theoretical position of the Church (or of the state for that matter), continued to be construed by the average man as a finan-

18. Bishop (*Pearl in Its Setting*, pp. 64–65) uses this scene to explain the close connection between "allegory" and "irony" insisted on by medieval rhetoricians.

cial transaction by which he bought himself off or by which someone richer or more important on whom he had a claim did it for him. In that sense, a "pardon" is the epitome of injustice and of human capacity to obscure the issue of good and evil. On the other hand, "pardon" as God's response to human sin is the very cornerstone of Christian doctrine; Christ's act of atonement is the point on which history turns like a hinge. In short, a "pardon" is the very image of the two kinds of "mede" in terms of which Conscience classified human motivation, the one evading, the other surpassing and fulfilling human justice.

The efficacy of this paradox is a function of the true meaning of "pardon." The term "pardon," like the term "lewte," which the poet uses where modern English uses "justice," defines not a commodity but a relationship. It implies a situation where a relationship which exists between two persons is vitiated by the act of one, so that the relationship continues to exist, but as a negative factor rather than a positive one. A pardon means that the situation has been resolved, not by the action of the party "in the wrong" vis-à-vis the relationship, but by the sheer creativity of the "injured" party, who has acted in such a way that the original relationship is in fact restored and the fruits of a positive relationship again grow from it. Real pardon is not a violation of justice, such as is implied by merely forgetting the facts. The point of a pardon is that it is an agent, an enactment which produces as a result what it could not demand as a prerequisite, a certain quality of relationship and action between two people. It sets free what it could not presuppose. Thus a "Pardoner's pardon" is a parody in the strictest sense of the word; it is an empty but devastatingly close imitation of the real thing. When what Piers thought was a pardon in the socialized sense turns out to be pardon indeed, his action provides exactly the image the poet needs. Only at the cost of his "self-respect" can man achieve that for which he cannot provide the prerequisites or endure the real cost. The "scandal" of the Christian God substituting his own cost in the person of Christ for making Robert the Robber meet the conditions of the law —that is more closely analogous to the Pardoner's parody than to Piers's painstaking faithfulness.

The second problem has to do with the number of possible states

being played against each other in this scene. To see them as two—
the states of Piers before and after tearing the pardon—is not wrong,
since the scene does indeed have major affinities, as has been suggested
more than once, with the story in Matthew 19:16–22 of the young man
who asked Christ what he should do to inherit eternal life and was first
told he should obey the law; when he insisted he had always done so,
Christ replied, "If thou wouldst be perfect, sell all thou hast, and give
to the poor and then thou shalt have treasure in heaven, and come,
follow me." Nevertheless, if we stand back from the scene, we see its
drama in the context of the whole *Visio* as concerned with a threefold
comparison between the man who falls below the law (like the whole
cast of the poem until the appearance of Piers), the man motivated by
the law, and the man who has gone beyond the law. The point of the
scene is the basic difference of psychology between these three states
and their incommensurability, and if we view it this way it ceases to
be a puzzle, though it remains, as it was meant to, a shock.[19]

We naturally turn to the Bible for analogues which may help us
understand the strange demands of Truth and the still stranger rebellion
and acquiescence of Piers. Apart from the story of the young man in
Matthew, one of the more significant suggestions has been Mary
Carruthers's argument that there is a parallel between Piers tearing the
pardon and Moses breaking the tablets of the law.[20] A still more illuminating analogy can be seen between Piers and Job, the good man
whose experience deprives him remorselessly of his confidence in a
relationship to God governed by covenant, in which God exists as the
prescriber and the guarantor for ethics. The righteous Job, faced with a
universe that no longer seems to sanction his goodness, rejects the ex-
plantations of his friends (who insist that he must be a sinner since
he is suffering) and demands a reason from God; and he is answered
not with reason but with an annihilating vision of how far God's
nature exceeds man's: "Canst thou draw out Leviathan with a hook?" [21]

19. The danger here is a premature correlation between these states and the "three
lives," the analyses of DoWell, DoBet, and DoBest with which the *Vita* is concerned; see below, chaps. 6 and 7.
20. See her "The Mind of Will" (diss., Yale University, 1964).
21. Job 41:1, "An extrahere poteris leviathan hamo?" (Vulg. 40:20).

The Voice's arguments from nature culminate in complete rebuke whose terms are peculiarly relevant to Piers's situation:

> Deck thyself now with majesty and excellency; and array thyself with glory and beauty.
>
> Cast abroad the rage of thy wrath: and behold everyone that is proud and abase him.
>
> Look on everyone that is proud, and bring him low; and tread down the wicked in their place.
>
> Hide them in the dust together; and bind their faces in secret.
>
> Then will I confess unto thee that thy own right hand can save thee.[22]

This Job accepts:

> . . . I have uttered that I understand not; things too wonderful for me, which I knew not. . . .
>
> I have heard of thee by the hearing of the ear; but now mine eye seeth thee:
>
> Wherefore I abhor myself, and repent in dust and ashes.[23]

Significantly, God's response to this combination of rebellion and self-abnegation is to justify Job to his friends: "Ye have not spoken of me what is right as my servant Job hath." [24]

But the greatest commentary on the pardon scene is Paul's Epistle to the Romans. What it provides is not an analogue or a "source" but a commentary on the central assertion of Christianity about the relation between ethics and salvation, between human effort and the action of God. But it is a commentary which presents striking analogies to the thought of the A poet in the way the issues are set up, in the anguished ambivalence of the writer's attitude to ethical goodness, in the rigor

22. Job 40:10–14, "Circumda tibi decorem, et in sublime erigere, et esto gloriosus, et speciosis induere vestibus. Disperge superbes in furore tuo, et respiciens omnem arrogantem humilia. Respice cunctos superbos, et confunde eos, et contere impios in loco suo. Absconde eos in pulvere simul, et facies eorum demerge in foueam. Et ego confitebor quod salvare te possit dextera tua" (Vulg. 40:5–9).

23. Job 42:3, 5–6, "Ideo insipienter locutus sum, et quae ultra modum excederent scientiam meam. . . . Auditu auris audivi te, nunc autem oculos meus vidit te. Idcirco ipse me reprehendo, et ago penitentiam in favilla et cinere."

24. Job 42:5, "Quoniam non estis locuti coram me rectum, sicut servus meus Job."

with which the intellectual analysis brings out in all its drastic implications the primacy of God's act over man's best achievements.[25]
    What makes Romans so moving is its recognition of the tragic in-
commensurability between the order of law and the order of Christ,
projected through the anguish with which Paul asserts his identity
with the tradition of Judaic law simultaneously with his conviction that
it has been superseded: "Quia major serviet minori." [26] Many of the
passages in which he expresses this are intensely moving: "Optabam
enim ipse ego anathama esse a Christo pro fratribus meis, qui sunt
cognati mei secundum carnem. Qui sunt Israhelitae, quorum adoptio est
filiorum, et gloria, et testamenta, et legislatio, et obsequium, et prom-
issa." [27] As he goes on to explain, "Israhel vero sectans legem iusticiae,
in legem iusticiae non pervenit. Quare? Quia non ex fide sed quasi ex
operibus. . . . Testimonium enim perhibeo illis quod aemulationem Dei
habent, sed non secundem scientiam. Ignorantes enim Dei iustitiam, et
suam quaerentes statuere, iustitiae Dei non sunt subiecti. Finis enim
legis Christus." [28] Yet he sees this failure, analogous to the despair that

25. Hence, of course, its crucial role in the great upheavals of Christian history, of
which the Reformation is only one. A good corrective to an anachronistically post-
Reformation view of Romans is its role in the thought of Saint Bernard (see Etienne
Gilson, *The Mystical Theology of St. Bernard,* trans. A. C. Downes [London and
New York, 1940], and note also Gilson's discussion of Abelard's *Espositio in Epist.
Pauli ad Romanos* in app. 2). For an extremely useful survey of the way in which
both Reformation and counter-Reformation attitudes to Romans represent polariza-
tions and fragmentations of medieval thought on Paul, see Stanislas Lyonet, S.J.,
"Gratuité de la justification et gratuité du salut: le problème de la foi et des
oeuvres," *Studiorum Paulinorum Congressus Internationalis Catholicus* 1961 (*Analecta
Biblica* 17–18), Rome, 1963, pp. 95–110.
26. Rom. 9:12, "The elder shall serve the younger."
27. Rom. 9:3–4, "For I could wish that myself were accursed and cut off from
Christ for my brethren, my kinsmen according to the flesh; Who are Israelites: to
whom appertaineth the adoption, and the glory, and the covenants, and the giving
of the law, and the service of God, and the promises."
28. Rom. 9:31–32, 10:2–4, "Israel, which followed after the law of righteousness,
hath not attained to the law of righteousness. Wherefore? Because they sought it
not by faith but as it were by the works of the law. . . . For I bear them record
that they have a zeal of God, but not according to knowledge. For they, being
ignorant of God's righteousness, and going about to establish their own righteousness,
have not submitted themselves unto the righteousness of God. For Christ is the end
of the law."

he described earlier as the psychological corollary of living by the law, as the key to the whole process of redemption for Israel as well as for the Gentiles: "Dico ergo: Numquid sic offenderent ut caderent? Absit. Sed illorum delicto, salus Gentibus ut illos aemulentur. . . . Si enim amissio eorum, reconciliatio est mundi: quae adsumption, nisi vita ex mortuis?" [29]

Paul, though he sees himself as a Jew and a Roman citizen, and as such has been trained twice over in the primacy of law, is in a difficult position in writing to the Roman Church. He is the apostle to the Gentiles, and the Romans represent the bloc within the new Christian Church that thought in terms of continuity between the old law and the new, between being a Jew and being a Christian. Also, Paul must deal with the fact that the Romans clearly associate his ministry with the destruction of ethical standards in the name of salvation by faith: "Et non (sicut blasphemamur, et sicut aiunt quidam dicere) faciamus mala ut veniant bona: quorum damnatio iusta est." [30] He continually stops short in his argument to make sure he is not misunderstood about this: "Legem ergo destruimus per fidem? Absit: sed legem statuimus." "Quid ergo dicemus? lex peccatum est? Absit." "Quid ergo? peccavimus, quoniam non sumus sub lege, sed sub gratia? Absit." [31]

Thus the crux of his argument is the absolutely fundamental difference of psychology or motivation between the order of the law and the order of grace, not the suggestion that one *code* of behavior should be substituted for another. This he presents in terms of a threefold distinction between the state of man without law, man's state under law, and the state in which law is superseded and fulfilled. All three states

29. Rom. 11:11, 15, "I say then, Have they stumbled, that they should fall? God forbid: but rather through their fall salvation is come to the Gentiles. . . . For if the casting away of them be the reconciling of the world, what shall the receiving of them be, but life from the dead?"

30. Rom. 3:8, "And let us not (as we would be blaspheming if we said, and as some slanderously affirm that we do say) do evil that good may come; the damnation of such is just."

31. Rom. 3:31, "Do we then overthrow the law by this faith? By no means!"; Rom. 7:7, "What shall we say then? Is the law sin? God forbid!"; Rom. 6:15, "What then? shall we sin because we are not under the law, but under grace? God forbid!"

he sees about him in his own time; they are also the consecutive stages of history, and they may be psychological stages in the individual as well. Man without law is given over to his own depraved reason, and the outward characteristics of this state as he describes them (Rom. 1:28–34) resemble A's portrayal of the folk on the field. Nevertheless there is a kind of innocence about this state: "Usque ad legem enim peccatum erat in mundo: peccatum autem non imputabatur, cum lex non esset." Or, more personally, "Ego autem vivebam sine lege aliquando. Sed cum venisset mandatum, peccatum revixit. Ego autem mortuus sum." [32]

In contrast to this, there is the revelation of the law: "Si autem tu Iudaeus cognominaris, et requiescis in lege, et gloriaris in Deo; Et nosti voluntatem, et probas utiliora, instructus per legem, Confidis te ipsum ducem esse caecorum, lumen eorum, qui in tenebris sunt, Eruditorem insipientium, magistrum infantium, habentem formam scientiae et veritatis in lege." [33] The splendor of this picture, so excellent a description of the Piers of passus 6, is nevertheless not a sufficient answer to the human dilemma, either for the law-abiding man or for the overt sinner. Apart from the problem of managing to keep the law perfectly (and Paul insists on the impossibility of doing so), the law changes the human consciousness itself drastically: "Per legem enim cognitio peccati." The ultimate result of this is despair: "Infelix ego homo, quis me liberabit de corpore mortis hujus?" Apart from any specific acts of wrongdoing, all "egent gloria Dei." [34] At this stage God intervenes: "Nihil ergo nunc damnationis est his, qui sunt in Christo Jesu. . . .

32. Rom. 5:13, "Until the law, sin was in the world, but sin is not imputed when there is no law"; Rom. 7:9–10, "For I was alive without the law once, but when the commandment came, sin revived and I died" (AV 7:9).
33. Rom. 2:17–20, "Behold, thou art called a Jew, and restest in the law, and makest thy boast of God, And knowest his will, and approvest the things that are more excellent, being instructed out of the law; And art confident that thou thyself art a guide of the blind, a light of them that are in darkness, An instructor of the foolish, a teacher of babes, which has the form of knowledge and of the truth in the law."
34. Rom. 3:20, "Through the law comes knowledge of sin"; Rom. 7:24, "Miserable man that I am, who shall deliver me from the body of this death?"; Rom. 3:23, "All have . . . come short of the glory of God."

Nam quod inpossibile erat legis. . . . Deus filium suum mittens. . . .
Ut iustificatio legis impleretur in nobis." [35] Thus the law is not denied
but fulfilled "in libertatem gloriae filiorum Dei." [36] What has happened
is not that the standards of perfection have been changed but that the
basis for man's relationship to them has been altered: "Non enim
accepistis spiritum servitutis iterum in timore, sed accepistis Spiritum
adoptionis filiorum, in quo clamamus: Abba (Pater). Ipse Spiritus
testimonium reddit spiritui nostro quod sumus fili Dei." [37] Paul keeps
returning to the question "Quid ergo amplius Judaeo est?" and answers
both "Multum per omnem modum" and "Nequaquam." [38] If, then,
even the system of the law itself depends on God's action, what happens to the stature and dignity of man? "Ubi est ergo gloritatio tua?
Exclusa est. Per quam legem? Factorum? Non: sed per legem fidei." [39]

Now the pardon scene may be viewed as an actualization in dramatic
terms of several features of this argument. Piers is being shown to us
contrasted, on the one hand, with the state of the folk and the dreamer
and, on the other, with a mysterious new state on which he enters
after passing through the crisis which recognition of the full implications
of law creates. For Paul, the terms "pagan," "Jew," and "Christian"
refer in the first place to historical sociological groups. But the thrust of
Paul's argument is to divorce the terms from this meeting and to make
them metaphors for three differently motivated attitudes to the same
basic factors of the human condition. His states are perfectly applicable
to different orientations within the basic teachings of Christianity itself,
once these have become codified. The point was made earlier that Piers
is not to be identified with any historical pre-Christian state, but he

35. Rom. 8:1, 3–4, "There is now no condemnation for those who are in Jesus
Christ. . . . For God has done what the law could not do, . . . in order that the just
requirement of the law might be fulfilled in us."

36. Rom. 8:21, "in the glorious liberty of the children of God."

37. Rom. 8:15–16, "For ye have not received the spirit of bondage again to fear;
but ye have received the spirit of adoption, whereby we cry 'Abba Father.' The Spirit
itself beareth witness with our spirit, that we are the children of God."

38. Rom. 3:1–2, "What advantage then has the Jew? Much in every way"; (Rom.
3:9), "None at all."

39. Rom. 3:27, "Then what becomes of our boasting? It is excluded. On what principle? The principle of works? No, but on the principle of faith."

represents the kind of allegiance within Christian teaching which is the psychological equivalent to covenant religion; he is an epitome of what, at its best, it can and cannot achieve. The spectrum provided by the group of folk, Piers, and the new state on which Piers now enters provides a metaphor for Paul's three states in terms of the poet's own intellectual and social milieu.

But useful as this perspective on the scene may be, it tells us nothing about what is, after all, the real problem—the "plot," what actually takes place and how. It is here that Paul leads us to the explanation of the *aenigma's* most enigmatic feature: Why couch this pardon in words which are a formulation of the law? The answer lies in Paul's most epigramatic formulation of the process by which man crosses the gulf between state and state: "Ego enim per legem legi mortuus sum" (Gal. 2:19)—"By the law I died to the law." It is easy enough to see how perception of the law brings the corrupt to an awareness of the ethical. What is crucial to the structure of the *Visio* is that it is also awareness of the law that brings a man across the second and deeper gulf from law to faith. And the paradox that what seems to be wages is actually "pardon" or gift—in Conscience's earlier words, "mede" not justice—is a paradox that comes from Romans itself: "Ei autem, qui operatur, merces non imputatur secundum gratiam, sed secundum debitum. Ei vero, qui non operatur, credenti autem in eum, qui justificat impium, reputatur fides eius ad justitiam." [40] Or as Paul puts it even more epigramatically, "*Stipendia* enim peccati, mors. *Gratia* autem Dei, vita aeterna." [41]

The difficulties of the scene are consequently not a matter of theme or structure but only of accessibility. What is missing from the A poet's metaphorical enactment of this hierarchy of states is, on the one hand, any intellectual analysis of just how Piers's new state will actually differ from his old and, on the other, any discursive explanation of the catalytic process by which this transformation from the order of law to the order of faith is achieved. The first of these lacks is not characteristic of

40. Rom. 4:4–5, "Now to a man who works, his wages are not reckoned as a gift but as his due. To him, indeed, who does not work, but believes in Him who justifies the sinner, his faith is reckoned as righteousness."
41. Rom. 6:23, "For the *wages* of sin are death, but the *gift* of God is eternal life."

Romans but is understandable in writing which is dramatic rather than discursive. If the poet were to teach us one thing by describing Piers's new state in concrete terms, he would fail to teach us another through making us feel the shock of being left behind by Piers as he moves into a state beyond the reader's comprehension. Secondly, he would inevitably appear to be substituting one outward code for another, which would destroy his central point. Therefore he can only characterize Piers's new state by its "tone," its psychological orientation. But the second lack in the pardon scene, the absence of explanation for the transition process, *is* characteristic of Romans. Paul continually reminds the Romans that what brings transformation about is a psychological event within each man which corresponds to and depends on the crucifixion of Christ, in which the resentment of the righteous man at Christ's claims, superseding his whole view of human responsibility, destroys him; and this "death," the Atonement, is what releases man from bondage—just as in history God acted, man destroyed what he sent, and that destructive act transformed man. But Paul makes no attempt to explain this doctrine; he assumes it, and the A poet does not explain it either. Instead, he has Piers enact an analogous psychological sequence whereby man vents his resentment at God's transcendent superiority on God's immanent manifestation of himself (the pardon) by destroying the manifestation, thereby releasing its energies. The poet can go no further without spoiling the relationship between the reader and the action that his entire strategy is designed to bring about, substituting for this scene the kind of historical reconstruction and analysis of the Incarnation, Crucifixion, Harrowing of Hell, and Resurrection, with its accompanying intellectual analysis, which the B poet was to make the climax of his differently oriented drama. The culminating stroke in the A poet's strategy is not to elucidate the affair but to show that it is unintelligible first to the priest and then to the Dreamer, who falls back on remarks about DoWell, which display precisely the covenant psychology which Piers has left behind, underlining the total incompatibility between the order of law and the order of spirit.

Here the poet has seized for us the image of man in the act of being transformed neither "kyndely" nor yet without "kynde," just as he pictured man earlier, in the confession scene, balanced between the self-knowledge that is death and the self-knowledge that is life. This image of transforming confrontation between God and man cannot be understood in the terms associated with a sentimental "loving God" or even in terms of the kind of mutual cherishing embodied in Michelangelo's *Creation of Adam*; for this poet, the point of intersection between the divine and the human is no meeting of fingertips but an explosive confrontation, will against will, as if the very nature of each were to be defined in terms of the energy of will itself. If we are to choose an analogy for Piers from Michelangelo, it should be, not his Adam or Moses, but his unfinished captives, pulling themselves out of their blocks of stone. The energy of Piers's wrath provides the impetus by which trust, based on a real if limited knowledge of Truth, can break through its limitations into a new and radical dependence on God. (It is here that the analogy with Job is most helpful.)

The subtlety and complexity, both psychological and theological, of this view of man's transformation through his confrontation with God, emerges with particular vividness if we contrast the pardon scene with the comparable, yet radically different scene in *Pilgrim's Progress,* in which Christian's burden falls from his shoulders:

Now I saw in my Dream, that the high way up which *Christian* was to go, was fenced on either side with a Wall, and that Wall is called *Salvation*. Up this way therefore did burdened *Christian* run, but not without great difficulty, because of the load on his back.

He ran thus till he came at a place somewhat ascending; and upon that place stood a *Cross,* and a little below in the bottom, a Sepulcher. So I saw in my Dream, that just as *Christian* came up with the *Cross,* his burden loosed from off his Shoulders, and fell from off his back; and began to tumble; and so continued to do, till it came to the mouth of the Sepulcher, where it fell in, and I saw it no more.

Then was *Christian* glad and lightsom, and said with a merry heart, *He hath given me rest, by his sorrow; and life, by his death.* Then he stood still a while, to look and wonder; for it was very surprizing to him, that the sight of the Cross should thus ease

him of his burden. He looked therefore, and looked again, even
till the springs that were in his head sent the waters down his
cheeks.[42]

Both scenes dramatize, not the Passion, but the moment when the fact
of God's action in the Crucifixion transformingly impinges on an already committed, yet still imprisoned consciousness. The A poet explicitly prevents our taking the pardon-tearing as the Crucifixion itself,
since he tells us that the pardon was "purchased" already before it was
sent to Piers. The essential order is the same in both scenes: strain and
hope; then perception of the symbol of God's act; then release, which
brings both joy and tears, and a change from viewing the symbol as a
thing to seeing God as a person. By comparison with Bunyan, the
tension and complexity of the A poet's drama is thrown into relief.
His concern is not limited to stressing the paradox of revelation and
the incompatibility, intellectual and psychological, between the state of
sin and the new state on which Piers enters. His very conception of sin,
grace, and human nature and his insistence that God's mercy reaffirms
the demands of justice while surpassing them make the scene more demanding both aesthetically and theologically. The A poet's drama depends on his distinguishing, by means of the contrast between Piers
and the folk, between two kinds of sin. The first, the folk's, is the "sin"
that consists of evil and damaging motives and actions; the other,
Piers's, is the "state of sin," the culpable finitude which is man's as
long as he regards himself as self-justifying, complete and psychologically independent, even though he may, as a result of this very attitude,
be free of sin in the first sense. Above all, the A poet's scene marks, as
does no comparable one, the ambivalence in man's attitude to salvation,
which he resists as much as he desires it. This element is focused in

42. *Grace Abounding to the Chief of Sinners* and *The Pilgrim's Progress from This World to That Which Is to Come*, ed. Roger Sharrock (London, 1966), p. 169. I do not mean to suggest that Bunyan's conception of sin is intrinsically simplistic or that his conception of allegory excludes great subtlety, complexity, and power in his whole structure, of which the passage I quote forms a small and early incident. For a recent and provocative discussion of Bunyan's aesthetic and its relation to Protestant tradition, see Milo Kaufmann, *The Pilgrim's Progress and Traditions in Puritan Meditation* (New Haven, 1966).

the one aspect of his sequence that has no parallel in Bunyan and that even the C poet backed away from: the tearing of the pardon. Only when the energy of the will in its very desire to maintain its autonomy becomes a part of the confrontation between man and God does an inner transformation, as distinct from an exterior commitment, take place.[43]

It is precisely these aspects of salvation and "justification" that were in the forefront of theological debate in the fourteenth century, particularly in England.[44] In fact, the pardon scene can be read as an attempt to present in dramatic terms a resolution to the conflict raging in the poet's own day between a characteristically nominalist view of salvation and one which, by adopting a more strictly "Augustinian"

43. For background for the poet's making Truth's violation of the autonomy of the fair field (and of human ethics) the logical culmination of the *Visio* argument, see Oberman's discussion of the way in which nominalism's stress on the distinction between God's *potentia absoluta* and *potentia ordinata* paradoxically fostered both "a recovery of the sense of divine immediacy" and "an autonomous antropology" in which "the supernatural world . . . has receded and has become a hemisphere, a dome. This dome shuts out the world of God's non-realized possibilities and provides room on the inside for man's own realm, in which he, as the image of God, thinks and acts. This thinking, though never able to reach unshakeable truth outside this domain, can, nevertheless transcend the dome; this acting, however good, can never go beyond this boundary line. Here this acting *ex puris naturalibus* has to be promoted from moral goodness to meritorious goodness" ("The Theology of Nominalism," pp. 61, 63).

44. Heiko Oberman has made an excellent example of this conflict available in translation in *Forerunners of the Reformation: The Shape of Late Medieval Thought* (New York, 1966), which gives selections from Robert Holcot, *Lectures on the Wisdom of Solomon,* and Thomas Bradwardine, *The Cause of God against the Pelagians,* along with selections from Gabriel Biel and Johann von Staupitz. Oberman's introduction, particularly the section, "From Middle Ages to Reformation: Continuity or Discontinuity" (pp. 32–43), and his introduction to the selections on justification (pp. 123–141) provide a readily intelligible analysis of the problem. Oberman's major study is *The Harvest of Medieval Theology: Gabriel Biel and Late Medieval Nominalism* (Cambridge, Mass., 1963). Its glossary (pp. 459–476) is a particularly useful introduction to the key concepts. See also Paul Vignaux, *Justification et prédestination au XIVe siècle: Duns Scotus, Pierre d'Auriole, Guillaume d'Occam, Gregoire de Rimini* (Paris, 1934). For a recent discussion of the problem which illuminates its implications for the question of how man may attempt to improve himself, see William J. Courtenay, "Covenant and Causality in Pierre d'Ailly," *Speculum* 46 (January 1971): 94–119.

position, came very close to the total rejection of works as a means to salvation that we consider characteristic of the Reformation. Both positions reject the Pelagian idea that man, by performing the requisite moral acts, can compel God to save him. For all of them, "all our righteousness is as filthy rags," and the best man can do remains so far short of good that salvation is always more than man deserves. But the nominalist theologians attempted to reconcile the Biblical demand for faith and the equally Biblical demand for works by asserting that, though man can exercise no compulsion on God, God can compel himself and has freely bound himself to accept good works as a token of man's acceptance of divine ascendancy.[45] In the classic formula, "God will not withhold his grace from those who do their very best [*quod in se est*]."[46] To more strictly Augustinian theologians, even this formula seemed an infringement on the autonomy of God and on the gratuitousness of grace; for them, the very best works done by a man whose will is not wholly reoriented into radical dependence on God and on nothing else are so fundamentally vitiated that they remain totally irrelevant to salvation. The pardon scene presents a "model" of the process of justification in which the requirements of both positions are met simultaneously and in which the apparent conflict between them, a conflict which goes back to the New Testament itself, is resolved.

Such a resolution, asserting that ethics both do and do not play a role in salvation, can only be conveyed to the audience by shocking, offending, and baffling them into active participation in the action. The resolution must come through an image, not through a formula. Paradox must be central dramatically as well as thematically. Thus the scene's strategy seems almost a dramatization of Paul's words to the Corinthians:

45. See the glossary in Oberman, *Harvest*, s.v. "gratia gratis data," "gratia gratum faciens."

46. See the Oberman, *Harvest*, glossary for the distinction between "meritum de condigno," an act worthy of divine acceptation, and "meritum de congruo," an act of the kind accepted by God on no other grounds than his generosity. See also "facere quod in se est."

Verbum enim crucis pereuntibus quidem stultitia est: his autem,
qui salvi fiunt, id est nobis, virtus Dei est. Scriptum est enim?
  Perdam sapientiam sapientium:
  et prudentiam prudentium reprobabo.
Ubi sapiens? ubi scriba? ubi conquisitor huius saeculi? Nonne
stultam fecit Deus sapientiam huius mundi? Nam quia in Dei
sapientia non cognovit mundus per sapientiam Deum, placuit Deo
per stultitiam praedicationis salvos facere credentes. Quoniam et
Iudaei signa petunt et Graeci sapientiam quaerunt: nos autem
praedicamus Christum crucifixum, Iudaeis quidem scandalum, gentibus autem stultitiam: ipsis autem vocatis Iudaeis atque Graecis
Christum Dei virtutem et Dei sapientiam.[47]

The result is a scene which not only fails to make clear what Piers
will do next—or how his tearing of the pardon can have these miraculous
effects—but also raises a series of secondary questions. Some have to
do with the poet's refusal to do what our commentary has just done;
that is, to relate the events explicitly to the historical-theological context of the Atonement. Clearly what is being portrayed here is what
happens to Piers, not the nature of God's action itself. But that leaves
us with the question of how and where Truth "purchased" the pardon,
how it is effective, and precisely what is wrong with the righteous, such
as Piers. Does the change in Piers's relationship to God mean a change
in his relationship to society? Is a change of psychology necessarily a
change of vocation? What is the nature of man's humanity, and what
becomes of it in the new order? What in particular becomes of free

47. 1 Cor. 1:18–24, "For the word of the cross is folly to those who are perishing,
but to us who are being saved it is the power of God. For it is written, 'I will destroy
the wisdom of the wise, and the prudence of the prudent I will reject.' Where is
the wise man? Where is the scribe? Where is the investigator of this age? For since
in the wisdom of God, the world did not know God through wisdom, it pleased
God through the folly of our preaching to save those who believe. Has God not made
foolish the wisdom of this world? For the Jews demand signs and the Greeks seek
wisdom, but we preach Christ crucified: to the Jews a stumbling block and to the
Gentiles folly, but to those who are called, both Jews and Greeks, Christ the power
and the wisdom of God."

will if man is so literally at the mercy of God? How can man comprehend or accept God's judgments if his standards in evaluating men are so incommensurable with the highest insights of human ethics? And the subsequent quarrel with the priest raises the further question of the value of human learning.

It is a highly significant feature of the A text that this list of questions is precisely the list that turns up in the tirade with which the Dreamer ends the A text, a point to which we will return later. For the present, what we need to note is that these questions, the obvious corollaries of the scene, are not raised here and that the waking Dreamer is portrayed as not having grasped what was happening well enough to ask them, let alone answer them. He falls back on the concept of doing well, which was what Piers, by contrast with Dreamer and folk, originally stood for. As the Dreamer muses on the difficulty and importance of doing well, there emerges into the world of the poem a new character, DoWell, who is to be a witness in man's defense at the Day of Judgment. It is from this point, and not from the point reached by Piers, that the rest of the A text develops.

4

The A *Vita*

THE ACTION OF *Dowel*

The *Vita de Dowel* is the most intellectually difficult and artistically demanding section of *Piers Plowman* in all its versions. Not only does it present riddle after riddle as taxing as those in the densest modern poetry, but it is dry and recalcitrant; it seems, especially in its earlier passūs, to repel empathy and frustrate curiosity. If, as Wit says of human development, there is "a rose, þat red is and sweet" at the end of the process, it certainly grows from "a raggit rote and a rouȝ brere." We encounter one after another the issues that have most troubled Christian and non-Christian alike in the history of Western thought and are denied even the respite of interim clarity or a vivid story line. Yet here the links which hold this strange poem together are forged, and here there emerges a portrayal of thought as action in its own right, which can claim a place among the achievements of poetry. As Lawlor comments, "The author of the *Vita de Dowel* may with justice be regarded as one of our greatest poets of the *activity* of thought, in all its arbitrary and non-consecutive movement. Langland . . . admits us to thought in its very context, not its ordered expression." [1] Or, as he put it elsewhere, "Langland's poem thus succeeds in communicating not a cumulative effect of discursive thinking, but the very pressure of experience itself." [2] Both the difficulty and the vitality of *Dowel* come from its urgency toward a truth inclusive enough to be relevant to the growth of a whole human being. Rigid as the argument itself is, this urgency reminds us of Julian of Norwich's desperation when she feels a conflict

1. *"Piers Plowman:* The Pardon Reconsidered," p. 450.
2. "The Imaginative Unity of *Piers Plowman," Review of English Studies,* n.s. (1957): 113–126.

between what she sees around her, what she finds in the teaching of the Church, and what she sees in her revelations: "I cried inwardly, with all my might seeking unto God for help, saying thus: Ah! Lord Jesus, King of bliss, how shall I be eased? Who shall teach me and tell me that [thing] me needeth to know, if I may not at this time see it in thee?" [3] That such a drama is integral to the larger action of the B text admits of no doubt, and it involves the poet in an intellectual and dramatic strategy that places almost intolerable demands on the reader but that is, nevertheless, intrinsic to his subject. His object here is not to write a clear, vivid, and aesthetically attractive exposition of the matter a Christian should know but to engage in the drama of knowing, the drama of resistance and desire through which the individual arrives at that special synthesis of knowledge, commitment, and empathy he terms "kynde knowyng."

It is not so clear whether the A *Vita* can be defended on the same grounds or whether anyone uninfluenced by knowledge of B would think of doing so. In addition to the difficulties of the B *Vita,* the A *Vita* is a fragment whose length, intellectual coherence, and relation to the *Visio* are a matter of disagreement. Here we have more to face than the problems raised by any poem whose action is a series of colloquies with abstractions; we must consider whether its argument has anything to do with the *Visio,* whether it is complete or an abortive attempt at a longer work, and, even, how long it is. [4] Do its theme and structure really develop out of the *Visio,* or is the *Vita* in fact a separate poem, whatever its poet may have meant it to be? The very fact that these

3. *Revelations,* p. 107.
4. Some A MSS have eight passūs, some eleven, and three a fragmentary twelfth, of which at least the last lines are openly identified as a "continuation" by one John Butt. Kane's study of the manuscripts in which the A text appears (the quire arrangement, manuscript condition, length of other poems included) and his evidence for what genetic relationships we can be sure of, in the complex editorial situation, indicate that the three A MSS which terminate within the *Visio* originally had at least eleven passūs. No further certainty, however, can be arrived at from the manuscripts themselves. For instance, the names the manuscripts give to the different sections of the poem and their systems of numbering do not support any given interpretation of the *Vita*; what they appear to suggest in one place they invariably contradict somewhere else.

problems exist seems bound up with the nature of the poem and must
be treated as we treat the variants in each line that point the editor
toward the *durior lectio.* There must be a "harder definition" of the
A *Vita* which will account for all these phenomena.

THE *Vita* PROLOGUE

The *Vita's* relation to the *Visio* and the nature of its action are precisely the factors defined in the opening lines of passus 9. Here a new
dream begins, whose frame parallels the earlier waking intervals, and
establishes the complete dependence of the *Vita* on the foregoing action.
But the emphasis on searching for DoWell, which is what ties the *Vita*
inextricably to the *Visio,* is precisely what makes the relationship between the two poems contradictory and is the principal cause of the
Vita's peculiarities. The idea of DoWell as a person to be searched for
derives from the pardon scene and makes the *Vita* meaningless without
the immediate context of the *Visio* conclusion; and yet the Dreamer's
idea of DoWell represents an attempt to carry on within the very patterns of thought that the pardon scene has superseded. To follow the
Dreamer through the vicissitudes of the *Vita* is to be constantly reminded of the *Visio* while being forced to set aside one's own principal
reaction to it.[5] Thus the distinction between the action proper and the
Dreamer-narrator through whom we view it, so basic to the *Visio,* is
carried a step further, and the Dreamer and his consciousness are brought
into new prominence as the basis for the ensuing action. This change of
strategy places a new kind of emphasis on the very nature of search and
understanding, especially on the "kynde knowyng," which the Dreamer
has all along insisted was a completely different matter from intellectual
cognition.

Hence the crucial importance of the one element in the *Vita* opening
which has no parallel in the *Visio,* the meeting with the friars. This is
the only occasion on which the A poet shows us the waking Dreamer

---

5. As Vasta, defending the C poet's omission of Piers's "ne solliciti sitis" speech in
revising the pardon scene, rather than exploring the A-B strategy, so shrewdly observes, "The *ne sollicitis sitis* speech makes a poor transition to *Dowel* because it
looks forward to the end of *Dowel* rather than to its beginning" (*The Spiritual Basis
of "Piers Plowman,"* p. 137, n.8).

contrasted with other specific, "real world" people; he does it here in order to contrast the Dreamer's attitude with theirs, so as to preface the poem's search with an analysis of search itself. That two fourteenth-century friars should claim that they are—"and euere shal hereaftir" be—DoWell is egregious; and the complicated, anticlimactic logic and stumbling syntax to which the Dreamer resorts in rejecting this solution are comedy indeed. And the exemplum by which the friar proves to the confounding of all critics and the alleviation of all anxieties that one can be DoWell otherwise than by doing well illustrates precisely the damaging role the friars were so commonly accused of playing at the time and which the B poet was later to portray when he showed them drugging the garrison of Unity and bringing its resistance to Antichrist to an end, the very role played in *Pilgrim's Progress* by Mr. Worldly Wiseman at the outset of Christian's journey. Like the comedy of the Dreamer's "feintise," creed, and rosary in passus 5, this humor introduces in an oblique and ironic form one of the key issues of the ensuing action, the fallibility of the just and well-intentioned man that so concerned Paul: "Non enim quod volo bonum, hoc facio; sed quod nolo malum, hoc ago." [6] But for the friar, "the evil I would not" is simply nothing to worry about.[7]

The purpose of the scene is to contrast this kind of invincible ignorance with the ignorance of the Dreamer, who can defend himself against the friar only by the genuineness of his desire to know and by the shrewdness and tenacity with which he can tell whether an explanation has explained anything or not. His courtesy is so exquisite that we almost overlook the flatness with which he rejects the friar's definition of DoWell as the friars:

6. Rom. 7:19, "For the good I would I do not, but the evil I would not, that I do."
7. The analogy itself won't stand up on inspection; for instance, if the boat is the body, "falling out" ought to be death, not sins of the will as opposed to sins of frailty. And while charity is surely the motivation within man and the help from without that is the decisive factor in the transformation of the human soul, no meaning yet attributed to the term DoWell will support equating it with charity, and the whole remaining argument of the *Vita,* even in A, contradicts it. So far DoWell is unambiguously a matter of right actions in an ethical sense, and charity as a motivation is a later development.

"I haue no kynde knowyng," quaþ I, "to conseyue þi wordis,
Ac ȝif I may lyuen & loken I shal go lerne betere.
I bekenne ȝow crist þat on þe crois deiȝede."

[A 9. 48–50]

It is only from an attitude like the Dreamer's (comic as it looks here,
confusing and inefficient as it certainly is, and implying complicity with
the very evils against which he struggles) that the unity of intellect
and life called "kynde knowyng" can arise, a state where, as Lawlor
says of the B Dreamer, man can "apprehend as vision what eluded him
as discourse." [8] The search may or may not correspond to a process of
intellectual argumentation (in *Dowel* it does; in B's *Dobet* and *Dobest*
it does not), and even as argument it will be completely different in
character from Euclidian or scholastic constructs. It will necessarily be
tentative, accretive, and cyclical and present a series of positions which
are neither obviously complementary nor obviously dismissed in favor
of alternative interpretations. It will necessarily shift from one frame
of reference to another as various aspects of human personality view
DoWell from their particular perspectives, especially since these factors
are, in one sense, subjective—Wit is a man's own wit—and, in another,
objective witnesses to the common experience and cumulative insight
of man in general—wit is intellect as such. The dialogues of the *Vita*
objectify not merely a struggle for self-awareness and self-knowledge
but also what Bloomfield has called "a dialectical relationship . . . between the world and the questing hero." [9] The very process of trying
to understand is one kind of "experience" which, as Roger Bacon insisted, "certifies" knowledge "ut quiescat animus in intuitu veritatis";
and we must not let Bacon's role in the history of science obscure the
fact that for him "experience" includes everything experiential from
scientific experimentation to immediate divine illumination.[10] The coherence of the *Vita* inheres, not in the intellectual arguments in their
own right, but in the human drama which Lawlor has called "the

8. "The Imaginative Unity of *Piers Plowman*," p. 119.

9. Bloomfield, *Apocalypse*, p. 16.

10. Paul Vignaux, *Philosophy in the Middle Ages: An Introduction,* trans. E. C.
Hall (New York: Meridan Paperback, 1959), p. 101.

activity of thought," and it will require a fresh analysis of man's nature and psychology and a new understanding of how the elements of his personality relate to each other and to his world. Lady Holy Church's cavalier definition of man as "fel, face and fiue wittes" is no longer enough to work from. Yet this is all directed toward the achievement of an integration of mind and heart in which the argument itself will be superseded, just as law and justice, according to Reason's plans in passus 4, were to be superseded by love.

As soon as the dream itself begins, we see that the action is to be just such an inward journey, rather than a predominantly exterior drama like that of the *Visio*. There is no landscape. Thought does not come *from* anywhere, as Lady Holy Church did. He is defined by the fact that his answer sums up the Dreamer's own thoughts as he emerges from the *Visio* and, like the Dreamer's conclusion to passus 8, both evokes and evades its argument. Thought assumes that human behavior is graduated; DoWell is the behavior of a good citizen, the minimum decency that forms a sound basis for society, but he has two companions, DoBet the altruist and DoBest the spiritual leader.[11] The Dreamer's reaction to Thought is polite, grateful, unsurprised, but firm:

> I þankide þouȝt þo þat he me so tauȝte.
> "Ac ȝet sauouriþ me nouȝt þi segging, so me god helpe;
> More kynde knowyng I coueyte to lere,
> How dowel, dobet & dobest don on þis erþe."
>
> [A 9. 101–4]

---

11. Thought's speech involves the kind of analysis by social function that underlay the Meed story (and that we have seen in B's coronation procession). DoBet is not a contemplative; his outward activities include DoWell's but go beyond his self-sustaining honesty to altruism by sharing money or learning, whichever he has. DoBest is the religious authority responsible for the welfare of DoWell and DoBet but not a civil authority, since a king must be crowned to bear the responsibility for the social order. Thought is speaking sociologically, sorting observable behavior into categories, without confronting any of the difficulties of this kind of approach which the *Visio* has been raising since the Meed episode. Both as the Dreamer's thought and in keeping with his place in scholastic psychology, he merely presents to the intellect a conceptualization of observation and experience without going beyond them.

Although he makes no attempt to refute Thought, he is undeterred, repeating his desire for "kynde knowyng." This Thought cannot provide, but he offers to take him to Wit.

WIT: THE MAP OF THE HUMAN PERSONALITY

Wit's speech is to the *Vita* what Holy Church's is to the *Visio,* an authoritative, if somewhat spare and limited, outline of the factors in terms of which the problems under consideration must be understood. Unlike Thought, the mere observer, Wit is an analyst. He surveys the inner constituents of human behavior and sees the three Do's as distinct but complementary and coexistent aspects of man, hierarchical in order of achievement and in the dependence of each state on the one before but not mutually exclusive. Wit's theoretical analysis is framed by two analogies, each of which sets up a picture drawn from real life and designed to render comprehensible the structure of the human personality and the basic states which give rise to the multiplicity of human conduct.

Wit begins with an "algebraic" analogy: A lady lives in a castle built for her by her absent lover, protected against the attacks of a rival suitor, a "proud prikere of Fraunce," by the "duk of þise marchis," to whom the lover has delegated the defense of the whole territory, and by the "cunstable" of the castle and his five sons, who are in charge of defending the castle itself. The lady is waited on by her "damysele," the duke's own daughter. Thanks to all these people, she will be kept safe and beautiful until the time comes when her lover will either come for her or send for her and take care of her himself. Wit then translates his image: the lady is Anima or Life, and the castle is Caro, the flesh. The lover is "Kynde," which means Nature but is clearly identified with God the Creator:

> Kynde . . . is creatour of alle kenis bestis
> Fadir & fourmour, þe ferste of alle þing.
> And þat is þe grete god þat gynnyng had neuere,
> Þe lord of lif & of liȝt, of lisse & of peyne.
>
> [A 10. 27–30]

The rival lover is *Princeps huius mundi,* the devil. The duke is DoWell, and his daughter, the lady-in-waiting, is DoBet; DoWell, then, is applicable to the whole territory, whereas the lady's DoBet, though derived from DoWell, is individually her own. The constable is Inwit: conscience and consciousness. His five sons are

> Sire se wel & sey wel, & here wel þe hende,
> Sire werche wel wiþ þin hond, a wiȝt man of strengþe,
> And sire godefrey go wel, grete lordis alle.

[A 10. 19–21]

In other words, the five sons of Inwit, who correspond to what Thought believed to be DoWell, are here distinguished from him. Presumably the time when "kynde come oþer sende and kepe hire himselue" will be DoBest.[12]

All this is, of course, strongly reminiscent of Piers's "pilgrimage to Truth": the image of the castle; the view of ethical law as a means toward a state which will surpass it; and the style, in which the image is used not because it is an instance of the subject but because the interconnections within the image are applicable to the subject, a style which may give rise to an incongruity between "tenor" and "vehicle" as great as in a metaphysical conceit, although the incongruity is not even an aim in itself. The process is as mechanical as slipping one drawing behind another and holding the paper up to the light to establish certain correspondences of outline. But Wit's speech, in the form in which it occurs in A, achieves outstanding excellence in the rather specialized and presently underrated genre of "expository poetry," the poetry of intellectual perception. This is first of all a function of its lucidity, then of the fact that its conscious formality and spareness are in character and illustrate the nature of the speculative intellect as distinct from other faculties and experience. Behind this lies the fact that the romance connotations of the story suggest the human realities of love, protection, defense, and future liberation, contributing directly to our understanding of soul and body, creation and temptation, God and man. Such an image emphasizes the active roles of God: God the Father, the creator,

12. But DoBest is also mentioned earlier along with the other two Do's as already "maistris of þis maner" (line 14), without other explanation.

involving himself more intimately in making man than in all the rest
of his creation; God the Son, the lover and champion; and God the
Holy Spirit, the future liberator and immediate presence.[13]

Wit then turns from his analogy to an explicit definition of the
three Do's:

> Þanne is dowel a duc þat destroyeþ vices,
> And sauiþ þe soule þat synne haþ no miȝt
> To routen ne to resten ne roten in þin herte;
> And þat is dred of god, dowel it makiþ.
> It is begynnyng of goodnesse god for to douten.
>
> [A 10. 76–80]

Sin is intrinsically as destructive as disease, but God has not left man
in a vicious circle where only the positive goodness he does not yet
have can keep him safe from destruction long enough for him to develop positive goodness. God provides fear:

> For doute men doþ þe bet; dred is such a maister
> Þat he makiþ men meke & mylde of here speche,
> And alle kynde scoleris in scole to lerne.
>
> [A 10. 83–85]

Fear, however limited as an ethical motivation, can at least rescue man
from the state portrayed in the confession of the seven deadly sins,
where man can know his corruption, yet be unable to provide the force
to break out of it. (Wit appropriately personifies DoWell as a general
outside the castle itself, whose authority is accepted by those within.)

Dread does not merely enforce exterior norms; it eventually produces a
second state, an inner attitude of acceptance and positive obedience,
which is still a result of exterior discipline but a more positive one:

> Þanne is dobet to ben ywar for betyng of þe ȝarde,
> And þerof seiþ þe sauter, þe salme þou miȝt rede:
> *Virga tua & baculus tuus ipsa me consolata sunt.*
>
> [A 10. 85–87]

13. Compare Julian of Norwich's fondness for thinking of the Trinity in terms of
the Maker, the Keeper, and the Lover.

The acceptance of the surgery of dread is freedom within the rules that dread dictates, as the artist is free in and through his obedience to his form and material or the athlete within the rules of the game. And thus the fullness of life which sin inhibits may develop.[14]

As in the castle image, Wit is at his vaguest (though also at his most eloquent) in explaining DoBest. DoBest seems to be related to DoBet as DoBet to DoWell; it is a changed state of soul in which what was once achieved by discipline is now the free expression of one's nature:

> And þus of dred & his dede dobest arisiþ,
> Which is þe flour & þe fruyt fostrid of boþe.
> Riȝt as a rose, þat red is and swet,
> Out of a raggit rote and a rouȝ brere
> Springeþ & sprediþ, þat spiceris desiriþ,
> Or as whete out of weed waxiþ, out of þe erþe,
> So dobest out of dobet & dowel gynneþ springe
> Among men of þis molde þat mek ben & kynde.

> [A 10. 121–28]

This state is the coming of Kynde himself into the life of a man, in an altogether new sense:

> For loue of here louȝnesse oure lord ȝiueþ hem grace
> Such werkis to werche þat he is wiþ paied.

> [A 10. 129–30]

There, for the first time, man fully meets the standards of ethics, in the very stage in which ethics as such, and the man's own efforts, have been superseded by grace. Having clarified the microcosm of man, Wit turns outward to the macrocosm and finds the same factors written large in the structure of society, and here his emphasis is on DoWell, which he illustrates by the relationship of marriage to the whole body politic.

Wit concludes with a summary of his definitions:

14. Compare Julian of Norwich's analysis of the constructive and destructive forms of dread (*Revelations*, pp. 180–82) and the threats that make up Conscience's sermon in passus 5.

Þanne is dowel to dreden, & dobet to suffre,
And so comiþ dobest aboute, and bringeþ doun mody,
And þat is wykkide wil þat many werk shendiþ.

[A 10. 216–18]

For the first time we see the exact nature of the change provided by
DoBest. The state described earlier as the flowering of a plant or as
the direct care of Kynde himself is the state when the "wykkide wil,"
which is the underlying reason for man's responsiveness to forces of
evil without, is eliminated, so that man, at last, does as the free and
natural expression of his own identity what he achieved before, im-
perfectly, as obedience to the law, first upon compulsion and then
through complete inner docility toward the ascendancy of God and
his standards for human life. The transformation is not merely a "magic"
applied from without; nor is it wholly man's own work, for man cannot free himself. It is only here, at last, that man "pleases" God in the
full sense:[15] "For loue of here louȝnesse oure lord ȝiueþ hem grace /
Such werkis to werche þat he is wiþ paied" (A 10. 129–30).

It is obvious that Wit's argument holds the clew to the difference
between God's meed and man's, to the paralysis of the "repentant" sins,
and to the pardon scene. Yet Wit does not deal directly with any of
the elements that make the *Visio*'s analysis of man hard for man to

15. "Meritum de condigno" in theological terms (see Oberman, *Harvest*, glossary).
DoWell, DoBet, and DoBest, as Wit describes them, are strongly suggestive of Saint
Bernard's three stages of the inner life, not the three stages of mystical experience,
humility, charity, and unity but his more generally applicable analysis of how human
motivation evolves so that the soul's lost likeness to God is restored and the three
freedoms of the will are recovered. Although the discipline of the Cistercian life, the
scola caritatis, is directed toward the accomplishment of this process, the stages do not
apply to the monk alone. Etienne Gilson summarizes them in words which render
the likeness between Wit's triad and Saint Bernard's very clear: "God is charity; by
the gift of charity He dwells in us and we in Him; . . . but to attain to this
beatifying union we must set out from the state of fear, divest ourselves, by way of
humility, of all self will, until at last, charity now taking the place of fear, we
shall henceforth accomplish the will of God by love" (*Mystical Theology,* p. 31).
Not only is the sequence—fear, humility, and love—the same, but in both schemes
the first two stages are ordered in different ways by fear; with DoBest freedom and
love replace fear, and kinship between God and man becomes possible because man's
true nature is restored.

accept or that make the pardon scene so intellectually inconclusive. And it does not give the Dreamer, as he complained to Thought, "More kynde knowyng . . . How dowel, dobet & dobest don on þis erþe." Throughout the whole speech, Wit does not mention love (though both his analogies are based on it) or any of the revealed "facts" which Holy Church said were not only central to an understanding of man's situation but capable of awakening responses in kind from man and lifting him out of his paralysis. Wit's whole account is theoretical and stoic in tone, as his very appearance suggested from the beginning:

> He was long & lene, lyk to non oþer,
> Was no pride on his apparail ne no pouert noþer,
> Sad of his semblaunt & of a softe speche.

[A 10. 110–12]

STUDY: KNOWLEDGE AND PROCESS

It is with considerable relief, then, that we find Wit's exposition rudely interrupted by the raciest, most vibrant, and most convincing of A's personifications: Wit's spouse, Dame Study, whose Wife-of-Bath rhetoric instantly reduces austere, elegant, awesome Wit to sheepish and undignified submission and even to covert complicity with the Dreamer. To represent the relationship of the discipline study to the faculty intellect through the medieval tradition of the shrewish wife is an engaging conceit, and her outrage at her husband and the Dreamer, together with her thumbnail accounts of the various skills, tools, and disciplines she has invented, are comic, realistically appropriate to her character, thematically the perfect complement to Wit's theorizing, and above all endearing. The shopworn critic of *Piers Plowman* can only feel gratitude for her account of theology:

> Ac theologie haþ tenid me ten score tymes,
> For þe more I muse þeron þe mistlokere it semiþ,
> And þe deppere I deuynide þe derkere me þou3te;
> It is no science forsoþe for to sotile þereinne.
> Ne were þe loue þat liþ þerein a wel lewid þing it were.
> Ac for it lat best be loue I loue it þe bettere,
> For þere þat loue is lord lakkiþ neuere grace.

[A 11. 137–43]

As far as the *Vita*'s argument is concerned, Study's main contribution is her attack on the Dreamer for exploiting Wit under false pretenses. She is particularly concerned about the misuse of logic and language and treats herself to an extensive analysis of false logicians and entertainers who complicate man's attempt to understand his world, like the entertainer who tells "harloterie" or the cynical logician who asks unanswerable questions like "Why did God create the snake?" Intellect is not a self-sufficient, self-governing function. It is a faculty by which we place ourselves at the disposal of Truth, and it is intrinsically related to action. Her motto is *non plus sapere quam oportet sapere:* "Al was as he wolde; lord, yworsshipid be þou / And al worþ as þou wilt, whatso we telle" (A 11. 85–86). Inquiry must always be subordinated to the facts, including those facts outside the realm of man's competence.

Her immediate ire is directed to Wit for "casting pearls before swine" by sharing his ideas with someone who has not shown he has the prerequisites for responsible use of the intellect. As for the Dreamer, Study, like Holy Church, takes him without any hesitation for a minstrel, and for the worst and most irresponsible sort at that. Even intellectual understanding of DoWell presupposes an underlying commitment to it, she insists:

> And now comiþ a conyon & wolde cacche of my wittes
> What is dowel fro dobet; now def mote he worþe
> Siþen he wilneþ to wyte which þei ben alle.
> But he lyue in þe leste degre þat longiþ to dowel
> I dar be his bolde boruȝ do bet wile he neuere,
> Þeiȝ dobest drawe on hym day aftir oþer.

>   [A 11. 87–92]

Coached by Wit's hints, glances, and gestures, the Dreamer replies:

> . . . "mercy madame, ȝour man shal I worþe
> For to werche ȝour wil while my lif duriþ,
> To kenne me kyndely to knowe what is dowel."

>   [A 11. 101–3]

This causes a complete about-face on her part; apparently these few words have sufficed to class the Dreamer as in "the least degree that longeth to DoWell" and therefore constitute an implicit definition. Her only explicit amplification of them comes after her comment on theology and love: "Leue lelly þeron if þou þenke do wel, / For dobet & dobest ben drawen of louis scole" (A 11. 144–45).[16] The Dreamer, "fayn as foul of fair morewen, / Gladdere þanne þe gleman þat gold haþ to ȝifte," supplied with a clear ethical road map, sets off to visit Study's ex-pupils, her cousin Clergy and his new wife, Scripture, for whom Study "wrot" the Bible and glossed the Psalter, and the scene ends on a high note of optimism.

The Disintegration of the A *Vita*

For the Dreamer to arrive at the home of Clergy and Scripture would seem to be the culmination not only of the *Vita*'s argument but of the *Visio*'s as well. He has gone from false security (the friars) to search, and the search has followed a sequence which, though it is in a sense that of subjective, personal growth, is in another an objective development through the modes of knowing available to the human mind: thought, wit, study, clergy, and scripture. The first three are natural human faculties and correspond to the *Visio*'s portrayal of man's successive attempts to deal with his own situation through his own resources; the last two are more than human, the authority which can complement the natural insight of man with that of Revelation and

16. These two brief comments, however, carry Wit's analysis of the three Do's a step further by stressing their complementarity and interdependence. She does not discuss the role of dread, but she excludes DoWell from "loues school." This distinction between DoWell and the other two is as Bernardine as Wit's earlier analysis, "Fear comes first: it is only a preparation for wisdom. With the former you receive a preparation, with the latter a beginning" (Saint Bernard, *Sup. Cant.* 23:14, quoted in Jean LeClerq, *The Love of Learning and the Desire for God,* trans. Catherine Misrahi [New York, 1961], p. 267. For both Wit and Study, DoBest is a state apart from the other two: for Wit it was a transformation wrought by the grace of God which, for the first time, eliminates the "wicked will" in man and makes his acts at last pleasing to God; Study sees it as a *telos* that draws a potential for right action into DoWell and DoWell into DoBet. In neither case does man provide it out of his own resources.

relate the evolution of man to the Atonement. Instead of finding anything of the kind, however, the Dreamer's high hopes are dashed as
remorselessly as the high hopes of the folk at the end of the confession
scene, and we should not really be surprised. The *Vita,* in spite of the
eloquence of a few of Wit's passages and the vivacity of Study, has been
ominously lacking in the dramatic intensity and richness of the *Visio.*
The scope and momentum of the poem have steadily diminished since
the pardon scene, and as soon as we get to Clergy himself, the argument, instead of reaching its resolution, is blocked. Clergy propounds a
perfectly straightforward and narrow definition of the three Do's by
social function, definitions which closely resemble Thought's but lack
even the minimal ethical criteria Thought included (A 9. 71–75).[17]
The Dreamer underlines this resemblance by picking up Thought's discussion of kingship and asking if temporal administrators ("kinghed,
& kniȝthed, and caisers with Erlis") are the three Do's. Scripture then
enters the discussion to rebut this suggestion, on the grounds that these
activities "helpiþ nouȝt to heuenward," the simplest definition yet (and
reminiscent of the Dreamer's conclusions from the pardon scene), adding
that not the rich but "pore men in pacience & penaunce togidere" will
go to heaven. The Dreamer reverts to his manner with the friars and
refutes her with still another definition:

> "Contra," quaþ I, "be crist! þat can I þe wiþsigge,
> And prouen it be þe pistil þat petir is nempnid:
> *"Qui crediderit et baptizatus fuerit saluus erit."*
>
> [A 11. 232–34]

While Scripture agrees that this is valid for a dying pagan, she defines
the Christian (abandoning any hierarchy of Do's) as one who loves

---

17. Clergy's DoWell is the "active life" in the narrowest sense of the term, the life
of those who earn an honest living. Clergy is not even using the term in the
extended sense current in more sophisticated theological and mystical thought to
mean the first stage in the inner life, as has been suggested: see T. P. Dunning, "the
good works of the active life are works of religion and devotion" ("The Structure
of the B-text of *Piers Plowman,*" *Review of English Studies,* n.s. 7 [1956]: 225–37),
and Lawlor's reference to "the confusion of 'active life' with mere activity, action as
opposed to contemplation, in which a good deal of comment upon Piers Plowman
has been entangled" ("The Imaginative Unity of *Piers Plowman,*" p. 8).

God and his neighbor, the latter including even the heathen. Finally, she reverts to the view, presented in Conscience's sermon, that God will revenge himself for all misdeeds.

This series of heterogeneous definitions—there have been eight in eighty lines, of which eighteen lines were taken up with Clergy's attack on the modern religious—is not simply a series of non sequiturs, though the argument induces vertigo. These definitions have regressed steadily down the path by which the *Vita* argument has brought us this far—back to Thought, the friars, and the Dreamer's conclusions from the pardon scene, back to the pre-pardon *Visio*'s simplest conceptions of the good life in terms of heavenly wages for simple obedience to essentially social ethics—without even attempting to deal with the limitations of those ideas that the whole drama of the poem to date has been exploring. In addition, a series of new themes, new to the A text but only too painfully familiar to the student of B, have been introduced at random only to be dropped again: the salvation of the heathen; the dangers of wealth and power as such; the sovereign effects of poverty, patience and penance; the nature of baptism; the relative value of faith and works; and the respective mandates of the Church hierarchy and the king. The fact that Scripture drops any attempt to justify the honest workingman as such (her praise of the poor is praise of accepted suffering, a very different matter) is particularly suggestive of B.

The argument of the *Vita* has fallen apart, but it is of the greatest significance for the whole *Piers Plowman* problem that this is no random disintegration. We are seeing the poem unraveling or coming unglued along the very lines and in the very order in which it was constructed. Even more significantly, the breakdown of A's argument is clearly associated not only with the *Vita*'s past but with its future, since it coincides with the introduction of a particular group of quite specific theological and ethical problems, whose emergence does not seem explicable by any inherent logic but which are unquestionably those to which B's development of A's argument will lead.

At this crucial point a tirade begins literally out of nowhere; it lacks even the eerie, landscapeless introduction with which Thought initiated the *Vita* dream. There is no setting, no attribution (although the contents reveal that the speaker is the Dreamer); it seems to have no dramatic context at all. It is not addressed to Clergy and Scripture, nor is it a direct response to what they have said or to any part of it. It begins on a note of hopelessness:

> ȝet am I neuere þe ner for nouȝt I haue walkid
> To wyte what is dowel witterly in herte.
>
> [A 11. 258–59]

But the reasons given for this hopelessness have nothing directly to do with the specific path we have seen the Dreamer walking. What makes him hopeless, as he explains with mounting excitement and with an eloquence unlike most of the *Vita,* is the very nature of the God whose being overrides man's will. God's omniscience and omnipotence imply predestination for his creatures, which seems to render human action meaningless:

> For howso I werche in þis world, wrong oþer ellis,
> I was markid wiþoute mercy, & myn name entrid
> In þe legende of lif longe er I were,
> Or ellis vnwriten. . . .
>
> [A 11. 260–63]

Furthermore, the standards by which God approves or disapproves of human actions are not merely unintelligible, they are an affront to human standards of goodness and justice. Who was more just than Solomon? Who was wiser and more essential to Everyman's salvation than Aristotle? "And al holy chirche holden hem in helle." God selects for his favorites people marked with corruption and violence:

> Þanne marie þe maudeleyn who miȝte do wers?
> Or who dede wers þanne dauid þat vrie destroyede,
> Or poule þe apostil þat no pite hadde
> Christene kynde to kille to deþe?
>
> [A 11. 287–90]

The archetypal instance of salvation is the archetype of injustice:

> A goode friday, I fynde, a feloun was sauid
> Þat hadde lyued al his lyf wiþ lesinges & þefte,

And for he kneuȝ on þe crois & to crist shrof hym,
Sonnere hadde he saluacioun þanne seint Ion þe baptist,
Or adam, or ysaye, or any of þe prophetis
Þat hadde leyn with lucifer manye longe ȝeris;
A robbere hadde remission raþere þanne þei alle.

[A 11. 279–85]

The very attempt to understand this brings the Dreamer to despair, not only over the problems but over the method he has been using to solve them, the commitment to intellectual inquiry itself:

Arn none raþere yrauisshid fro þe riȝte beleue
Þanne arn þise kete clerkis þat conne many bokis,
Ne none sonnere ysauid, ne saddere of consience,
Þanne pore peple, as plouȝmen, and pastours of bestis,
Souteris & seweris; suche lewide iottes
Percen wiþ a *paternoster* þe paleis of heuene
Wiþoute penaunce at here partyng, into þe heiȝe bliss.

[A 11. 307–13]

And here the A text breaks off without any awakening.

The fact that the Dreamer can still use a term like "right belief" at such a juncture shows an ambivalence—even a resistance—toward his own despairing conclusions. This explains his retreat from the issues he raises into nostalgia for the time before these problems arose and for the kind of life in which, since it lacks consciousness in the sense that he himself has it, they cannot arise. This sort of anti-intellectualism (as distinct from an insistence that "kynde knowyng" is the purpose of intellectual inquiry) is certainly not characteristic of the A text as a whole and does not constitute a "conclusion" of its argument in any serious sense of the term. There is a sense, however, in which the tirade is the natural result of A's argument. As Paul de Man has observed of comparable nostalgia for the primitive in modern literature and art,

> As a consciousness develops and progresses, it is bound to encounter an increasing resistance to its own growth. The more it understands its own progression, the more difficult or even painful this progression becomes. Naturally enough, this increased resistance leads to

a nostalgic regret for earlier, less advanced stages of self-awareness that may seem surrounded by an aura of innocent simplicity. Hence the tendency, in periods of acute self-consciousness, to regress towards more primitive levels of experience and to idealize them into something very different from what they actually are. All modern writers and thinkers have moments during which they give in to such regressive tendencies, especially when they feel tempted to undertake vast, general syntheses.[18]

The tirade is also the conclusion of the whole poem, *Visio* and *Vita,* in the rather special sense that its contents arise from that argument and bring it to a halt. Although the issues it raises are new to the *Vita* analysis, they are crucial to the *Visio*. They are the very issues which underlie the pardon scene, upon which an understanding of it depends, and which it was the central strategy of that strange piece of drama not to explain. They are the very issues which the Dreamer so strikingly evaded in his colorless conclusions about DoWell and in his pursuit of DoWell in the *Vita*. What becomes of the fair field full of folk if it is at the mercy of a *deus ex machina?* How can we comprehend the goodness of man, his dignity, his struggle to be accountable for his own evil and, at the same time, face the total ascendancy of God? The Dreamer presents the problem in heightened coloring and phrases it in such a way as to obscure the issue from the theologian's point of view; as he phrases the problems, they sound like the unanswerable questions Study was so severe about earlier. This does not conceal, however, the fact that Christianity raises exactly these questions and that nothing in the poem has done justice to its answers, either in intellectual terms or in dramatic empathy. The *Vita* argument covered up these fundamental questions, but they remained like buried land mines, ready to explode as soon as the argument approached the critical issues—God's ascendancy over man's knowledge and the dependence of man's growth at each stage on God's initiative and authority. The very appearance of Clergy and Scripture inevitably detonated them; their speeches and

18. In a review article, "What is Modern?," on *The Modern Tradition: Backgrounds of Modern Literature,* ed. Richard Ellman and Charles Feidelson, in *The New York Review of Books* 5 (26 August 1965): 10–13.

the ensuing dialogue constitute a rapid and increasingly hectic retreat from everything to which the action of the poem has been building. Even this new evasion cannot prevent the explosion and the resulting abandonment of the poem itself.

A's thoroughly eccentric, difficult, and yet profoundly moving sequence from the pardon to the Dreamer's already superseded conception of DoWell, through a series of precarious theoretical analyses to evasion, anger, despair, nostalgia, and silence, is based on taking the limitations and difficulties of a highly idiosyncratic Dreamer, rather than the objective demands of the subject matter, as the basis of the poem. One might say that A's Dreamer swamped the poem—or rather, to speak less pejoratively, A's Dreamer undergoes a drastic change of function as the poem progresses. From the beginning he is portrayed with extraordinary vividness as an idiosyncratic, complex, and troubling personality. The frequency, immediacy, and vividness of his intrusions into the poem are striking, but, nevertheless, he is, at first, essentially a rhetorical device, an example of the first-person narrator, who speaks as the author of the poem simply as a means of transmitting and commenting upon the drama it presents. Such a persona may even be an important character in the poem in his own right; the involvement of the *Pearl* narrator, Dante the Pilgrim, or the narrator of Chaucer's *Troilus* in the poems they narrate is even greater than the A Dreamer's seems at first to be. But as the poem develops, the pose of being an author taking part in the action of his own poem seems, like Pygmalion's statue, to come alive, and the narrator's relation to the subject matter becomes the subject matter. The conflict between the autonomy of man and the ascendancy of God, objectively dramatized in the *Visio,* becomes gradually interiorized and the drama redefined until the subject of the *Vita* becomes the conflict between the implications of the *Visio* and the narrator's resistance to them. The strategy of the pardon scene required that the action outstrip the narrator; it did not require an erroneous and regressive summation like the Dreamer's musings on DoWell, let alone a long subsequent argument which appears to build on the *Visio* while evading its central implications. As it stands, the A *Vita* is intrinsically inconcludable.

THE REVISION OF THE A *Vita*

To someone thinking in terms of the A text alone and managing to be influenced by knowledge of what the B and C poets were to make of it, the greatest riddle of the B text is why its poet did not scrap the A *Vita*. To anyone lacking the hindsight of history, the A *Vita* as it stands should have looked like a dead end; its argument starts in the wrong place and from the wrong assumptions and can be made to lead back to the basic questions the *Visio* asked only by an outrageously complicated detour. As far as the basic, abstractable, intellectual skeleton of the B text is concerned, the B poet could have gone straight from the pardon scene to the banquet with surprisingly little adjustment. (Certainly the C poet did not flinch from equally drastic if more scattered revisions of B).

If the B poet took over A's eccentric and often tedious and arbitrary-looking construction, it can only have been because what seemed irrelevant, even deleterious, to the main structure from a syllogist's point of view seemed to him essential. He must have felt that, whether the A *Vita* starts in the "right" place or the "wrong" place by the standards of the craftsman or the logician, it was the only place to start. The very nature and order of the A Dreamer's development must have seemed privileged subject matter to the B poet, the clew to further intellectual growth, material he could only work through, not around, just as the tenacity with which A's Dreamer had held onto these "wrong" questions because they were the ones that made sense to him had ultimately led him to asking, if not answering, the "right" ones. And the B poet's results, difficult though they are, bear him out. In his hands, a latent coherence and objectivity about the order and even the non sequiturs of the later A *Vita* emerge into articulateness. What was recalcitrant fact in A receives the fully defined and developed truth of art.

For the B poet to achieve this, he had to do more than merely append to A new action that would clarify the pardon scene and carry its perspective on human affairs forward. Before he could do so, he had to construct a series of scenes to resolve the specific problems that were blocking the Dreamer's progress and to explain the process by which the writing of the poem was abandoned and resumed. In preparation for this, he had to revise the friars-Thought-Wit-Study sequence so as to accentuate whatever relevance it had to the general problem of human development and to differentiate the actual nature of the faculties portrayed from the condition of the Dreamer himself. Unfortunately, any serious study of how this part of the revision was carried out must await a more accurate text; according to Professor Donaldson, these passūs, particularly the critical scene with Wit in passus 10, are so corrupt that any conclusions drawn from Skeat's edition must be merely tentative.[19] Finally, the B poet had to recast the scene with Clergy and Scripture so that, instead of pointing backward, it would prepare the ground for events to come and provoke the tirade directly; and the tirade itself had to be made into a serious psychological and intellectual portrayal of the Dreamer's position.

Drastic revision, then, begins with Clergy. B's Clergy has a completely new speech so that, as in A the learning process as such triggered the tirade, in B Learning's remarks do so by bringing to the fore precisely the elements in the relationship of man to a transcendent God, witnessed to by an authoritative, temporal Church, that are at the heart of the Dreamer's resistance. Clergy's speech is still a definition of the three Do's but no longer a regressive, sociological one; Clergy's Do's are now consecutive psychological stages like Wit's but oriented toward Clergy's special concern for the clerical function in society. Clergy's first stage, belief, corresponds to Wit's "dred," but Clergy, like the intellectual he is, centers on the submission of the mind to the

19. Skeat's passus 10, for instance, would suggest that in revising Wit's crucial speech the B poet preserved the castle analogy while omitting most of the conclusions which A's Wit drew from it in the form of explicit definitions, thus sharply differentiating the material to which the Dreamer is exposed from any understanding of it achieved by him; the B poet would appear to be deliberately "spoiling" the A poet's scene precisely because it was too good for the function it must now serve. In many speeches, B appears to be introducing a large body of detail which limits the characters more strictly to the function their names define while building up a complex of images, biblical quotations with their traditional commentary, parables, and liturgical echoes which focus upon and define the key doctrines the Dreamer is portrayed as struggling unsuccessfully to understand. (Biblical and patristic elements in this complex are explored in Thomas Ryan, "The Poetry of Reform" [diss., Brown University, 1971].)

authority of certain revealed "facts," the integers of the faith, and particularly to the intransigent ascendancy of God's being:

"It is a comune lyf," quod Clergye, "on holycherche to bileue,
With alle the artikles of the feithe that falleth to be knowe.
And that is to bileue lelly, bothe lered and lewed,
On the grete god that gynnyng had neuere,
And the sothfaste sone that saued mankynde
Fro the dedly deth and the deueles power,
Thorwgh the helpe of the holy goste the whiche goste is of bothe;
Three propre persones ac nouȝt in plurel noumbre,
For al is but on god and eche is god hym-selue.

[B 10. 230–38] [20]

This emphasis on the nature of God, and especially on the Trinity, raises one of the main issues of the pardon scene and of the tirade and also provides the first move in B's design to make the Trinity a dominant triad in the rest of the poem. For the second stage, that of DoBet, Clergy actually borrows the term A's Wit used, "suffre," to describe the inner acceptance and assimilation of what the first stage of submission demands:

Thanne is Dobet to suffre for thi soules helth
Al that the boke bit by holycherche techyng;
And that is—"man, bi thi miȝte for mercies sake,
Loke thow worche it in werke that thi worde sheweth;
Suche as thow semest in siȝte be in assay y-founde;
   Appare quod es, vel esto quod appares.

[B 10. 249–53]

DoBest is to exercise outwardly the authority conferred by this inner transformation:

[So] is Dobest to be bolde to blame the gylty,
Sithenes thow seest thiself as in soule clene;
Ac blame thow neuere body and thow be blame-worthy.

[B 10. 256–58]

20. "Comune": "communal, in common (i.e., not one of singularity)," *not* modern "frequent, ordinary."

He then goes on to contrast the corruptions of the clergy with the
religious and humanist ideal they betray:

> For if heuene be on this erthe and ese to any soule,
> It is in cloistere or in scole be many skilles I fynde;
> For in cloistre cometh no man to [carpe] ne to fiȝte,
> But alle is buxumnesse there and bokes to rede and to lerne.
> In scole there is scorne but if a clerke wil lerne,
> And grete loue and lykynge for eche [loweþ hym to] other.
>
> [B 10. 300–306]

B certainly does not idealize "clergye." Except for the one hint of
nostalgia for the academic community, the speech is dry and cerebral;
a little patronizing and uncomfortably absolute; stoic rather than generous (these Do's were surely never "drawen of loues scole"); tending
to see man's response to God in terms of a mental response to a body
of ideas and its ultimate expression the prevention of vice in others;
prone to shoptalk about its own profession, to finding all its colleagues
villains, and to relating all human problems to the exercise of its own
vocation. Nevertheless, this discourse sets up in advance a sharp corrective to the Dreamer's wild accusations against learning and prepares
us to see them better for what they are: epiphenomena.

The material between Clergy and the Dreamer's outburst seems
altered only enough to make what were non sequiturs in A organic
to their context and to make additions to Scripture prepare for the
crucial role of learning, patient poverty, and baptism in the next
passus.[21]

---

21. In B, Clergy ends with a fine flourish with his celebrated prophecy of the
"Abbot of Abyndoun" who will "Haue a knokke of a kinge and incurable the
wounde." This instance of a king being "bolde to blame the gylty" like DoBest
provokes the Dreamer's response, "Thanne is Dowel and Dobet . . . *dominus* and
kniȝthod" (10. 331; cf. A 11. 219–24); while still a non sequitur that shows exactly
how much of the preceding definitions sank in, it is an understandable error, and
an error in context, which no longer reminds us of Thought. As before, it brings
Scripture into the argument. B adds enough to Scripture's praise of patient poverty
(A 11. 229–31; B 10. 336–44) to make it a genuine foreshadowing of the later B
argument and adds extensive discussion of the Christian life in terms of love and
caring for others. This acts as a corrective to Clergy's remarks on belief; brings the

In the context the B poet has set up, the Dreamer can address Scripture and Clergy directly, and his objections to Christianity become legitimate objections to the course of the argument as it has unrolled. The tirade, which was so heterogeneous in A, thus coheres around the issue of mind and its relation to other values. The A Dreamer shot off his disparate complaints like so many firecrackers. B refocuses each attack to make it a serious formulation of a real problem: the apparent implications of predestination, itself implied by the omnipotence of God; the tragedy of the righteous heathen, inseparable from Christianity's "scandal of particularity," its integral relationship to a particular historical milieu; the observable fact that the more man increases his potential for good by becoming more self-conscious and highly trained, the more he also increases his potential for evil. In one sense the Dreamer's objections make less electrifying emotional statements than in A. B's complaint about predestination is in a lower key, but it is also a fairer and therefore more remorseless statement of the difficulty. An even more striking instance is the qualifications B introduces into A's conclusion, admitting that A's "lewed iottes" lived "imparfitly" and defining the failings of the clergy. The A poet's celebrated "note of finality" disappears, but so does the crudeness of his escapism. The same is true of the Dreamer's ambivalence about his own conclusions (which A showed in such paradoxes as the continued use of the term "right belief"): the B poet integrates this element into his overt statement and shows the Dreamer circling about among qualifications, admissions, and reassertions.[22] The resulting speech is a

problem of the righteous pagan to the fore, since Scripture's prime example of caring for others is the Jewish community, not Christian society; and prepares for the coming discussion of baptism and the Crucifixion so crucial to the resumption of the poem. Her emphasis on love "in dede" and on the Crucifixion as the key to the relationship between God's love and man's not only complements Clergy's summary of Christian doctrine but harks back to Holy Church and the elements in her speech that Clergy left out. Nevertheless, Scripture's argument is no less intransigent than Clergy's about God's absolute demand for allegiance and the stringent requirements of the social gospel and contains not even a reference to the three Do's.

22. The most striking instance comes in the new passage B adds to A's discussion of the righteous heathen. It begins with the famous quotation from Ecclesiastes, "Sunt iusti atque sapientes; et opera eorum in manu dei sunt," with its elegiac resig-

much more intellectual argument, and much more sharply and sustainedly defined as the attitude of a specific character responding to particular ideas and pressures rather than making an absolute statement. As a dramatic monologue it has become less the hortatory Elizabethan soliloquy and more the analytical Browning portrait.

That the argument is still escapist all the same is clear. Scripture replies "multi multa sciunt et seipsos nesciunt," [23] and with that, as with a fairy tale's stroke of midnight, the scene dissolves, and the Dreamer, weeping "for wo and wratth," is plunged into a deeper dream. There the man who has just eulogized one kind of oblivion turns instead to the kind which is really possible for him—Fortune, Concupiscentia-carnis, Coueytise-of-eyes, Pryde-of-parfyte-lyuynge, Recchelesnes, Fauntlete, and the easy absolution of the friars, all of which he follows so successfully "That of Dowel ne Dobet no deyntee me ne thouȝte; / I had no lykynge, leue me, [the leste of hem to knowe]" (B 11. 47–48).

---

nation, then modulates into the bitterness of the proverbial "qant OPORTET vyant en place yl ny a que PATI" and on to the cynicism of "For sothest words that euere god seyde was tho he seyde *nemo bonus*" (10. 430–41). Note the great relevance of the rest of Eccles. 9 to the tirade and the next passus.

23. "Many know much and do not know themselves" (see Skeat's note).

5

The B Poet's *Vita de Dowel*

In the process of reorienting the A *Vita de Dowel* in such a way as to
bring the poem back to the point reached by the pardon scene while
making A's long detour relevant to it, the B poet circles three times
across the issues and questions that the argument of A raised. He
recasts the actual text of A and then adds two distinct but closely related blocks of new action, which cover basically the same ground: the
Oblivion-Justice-Scripture-Trajan sequence and a more concise one in
which the Dreamer meets Nature, Reason, and Imagination. Each of
these blocks of new action begins with a vision of Middle Earth and
goes on through a defeat or rejection; an acknowledgment of the need
to continue the "dream," which conjures out of nowhere the figure
that is to carry the argument a step further; justification for writing the
poem itself; and then an answer to specific problems raised by A. The
second block is not only more conclusive than the first; it is more
cosmic and completes the B poet's modulation from A's story of
private defeat to his own universal drama.

The process of reorienting the Dreamer begins in the very scene
which dramatizes his rejection of the search the poem embodies. In
the deeper dream which succeeds the tirade, Fortune, echoing the Prologue's first description of the Dreamer as going "Wyde in þis worlde
wondres to here," makes him look into "the myroure that hiȝt Mydlerd"
in "the londe of Longynge," telling him he will "se wondres, And
knowe what thow coueytest." At last he comes face to face with the
truth about himself. Thanks to the blandishments of Fortune and her
daughters and the easy absolution of the friars, "of Dowel ne Dobet no
deyntee me ne thouȝte; / I had no lykynge, leue me, [the leste of hem

to knowe]" (B 11. 47–48). The first truth the mirror has shown him is that he does not really want the "simple life" or DoWell but release, surcease for the pain of consciousness and knowledge and the tension of effort, and he finds it in an oblivion that lasts a symbolic "fourty wynter and a fifte" until age, poverty, and the fear of death remorselessly take his drugs from him. Only then does the man who has been living on the friars' "cheap grace" find he wants to be buried, not with them, but in his own parish. With this moment of awareness he finds himself in the midst of a serious quarrel with the friars about an objective issue, the role of the Church, and especially—most important for the ensuing action—about baptism. This conjures a new character, Justice, into the poem:

> And lewte [louʒ] on me [for] I loured [on þe frere]
> "Wherfore lourestow?" quod Lewte and loked on me harde,
> "ʒif I durste," quod I, "amonges men this meteles auowe!"
>
> [B 11. 84–86]

The ensuing argument between two such different observers of society, the satirist and the judge, about the legitimacy of "admitting the dream" marks the resumption of composition.

Here we come to the first overt discussion in *Piers Plowman* of the issue which has haunted the narrator throughout both texts, his need to justify his vocation as dreamer, parasite, minstrel, fool, amateur theologian, social critic, and as the writer of the poem. This first discussion limits the justification of the poem to its simplest role as satire; yet, even so, it is crucial. For the first time what distinguishes the Dreamer from legitimate clerics (what makes his "habite as an hermite" that of an "vnholy" one and his "shroudes" only an imitation of a "shepe") receives authorization, giving him a legitimate function distinct from theirs. Justice puts it legalistically:

> It is *licitum* for lewed men to [l]egge the sothe,
> If hem lyketh and leste, eche a lawe it graunteth,
> Excepte persones and prestes and prelates of holy cherche,
> It falleth nouʒte for that folke no tales to telle,
> Though the tale were trewe and it touched synne.

Thinge that al the worlde wote wherfor shuldestow spare
To reden it in retoryke to arate dedly synne?

[B 11. 92–98] [1]

Justice's attempt to distinguish between legitimate satire and mere tale-
bearing, malicious gloating, or passing judgment on one's fellowman
to one's own peril ("Judge not, that ye be not judged") is purely ethical,
not aesthetic:

Ac be neuere more the fyrste the defaute to blame;
Thouȝe thow se yuel, sey it nouȝt fyrste, be sorye it nere amended.
[Þ]inge that is pryue publice thow it neuere,
Neyther for loue [looue] it nouȝt ne lakke it for enuye.

[B 11. 99–102]

What matters is that it dignifies the very "minstrelsy" about which the
Dreamer feels such loneliness and ambivalence with a kind of "rule of
the confessional."

With this acceptance of his own nature and of the drama in which
he is portraying himself, the Dreamer instantly finds himself back in
the abandoned scene with Scripture, who no sooner accepts his justification than she reaffirms the very element in the gospel that has most
repelled him:

"He seith sothe," quod Scripture tho and skipte an heigh, and
    preched,
Ac the matere that she meued if lewed men it knewe,
The lasse, as I leue, louyen [thei wolde
The bileue of oure lord þat lettred men techeþ.]
This was her teme and her tyxte, I toke ful gode hede;
"*Multi* to a maungerye and to the mete were sompned,
And whan the peple was plenere comen, the porter vnpynned the
    ȝate,

1. Note that the difficulties Skeat raised about this passage in his notes—since the
poet is not a "lewed man"—are unnecessary if we remember that the exception in
line 94 is not for the literate as opposed to the ignorant but for priests, beneficed
clergy who have a public office. This the poet clearly portrays himself as not being.

And plukked in *pauci* priueliche and let the remenaunt go rowme!"
Al for tene of her tyxte trembled myn herte,
And in a were gan I waxe. . . .

[B 11. 103-11]

This moment is the turning point of the whole argument, since what the Dreamer is experiencing here—the apparent acceptance of a man in his vocation, the "tyxte" from God which turns out to be only a reiteration of his uncompromising standards (and a piece of the common heritage at that), and "tene"—is precisely what happened to Piers when Truth sent him a pardon. The passage from Ecclesiastes which B added to the Dreamer's tirade goes on: ". . . nescit homo utrum amore, an odio dignus sit: Sed omnia in futuro servantur incerta, eo quod universa aeque eveniant iusto et impio, bono et malo, mundo et inmundo, immolanti victimas et sacrificia contemnenti. Sicut bonus, sic et peccator." [2] The moment that came to the good man at the end of his resources comes now to his antiself, and he feels what Piers must have felt when the pardon was translated: "And in a were gan I waxe and with my-self to dispute, / Whether I were chosen or nouȝt chosen" (B 11. 112-13).

But this time the stages which lead a man from the desire to be justified in his own right ("thouȝe I seye it my-self I serue hym to paye") to the relationship between his will and the realities within and without, in which he says "si ambulavero in medio umbre mortis, non timebo mala; quoniam tu mecum es," [3] will be clearly dramatized. The Dreamer who sees himself already "in medio umbre mortis" now takes his first steps into the realm which so long ago swallowed up Piers:

. . . on Holicherche I thouȝte,
That vnderfonge me atte fonte for one of goddis chosen;

2. Eccles. 9:1-2, "A man does not know whether he is worthy of love or of hate; but all things in becoming are subject to uncertainty, because all things are brought to the same conclusion for the just and the impious, the good and the evil, the clean and the unclean, the man who makes sacrifices and the man who scorns them. As is the good man, so is the sinner."
3. B 5. 556, 7. 117-29 ("If I should walk in the midst of the shadow of death, I shall fear no evil, for thou art with me").

For Cryste cleped vs alle come if we wolde,
Saracenes and scismatikes and so he dyd the Iewes,
   O vos omnes scicientes, venite, &c.
And badde hem souke for synne sauf[te] at his breste,
And drynke bote for bale, brouke it who so myȝte.
   "Thanne may alle Crystene come," quod I, "and cleyme there
     entre
By the blode that he bouȝte vs with and þorough baptesme after,
   Qui crediderit & baptizatus fuerit, &c.

                          [B 11. 112–19] [4]

The Dreamer goes on to think of his own distant baptism as an event
which admitted him to "the household of the faith" only in the sense
in which a "churl" goes on belonging to his lord, whether he chooses
to accept that relationship and experience it as benevolence or to reject
it and experience the same relationship as judgment. Once you are
within the household, to "reneye" your presence there is impossible; you
can only choose between being there in the house and being there in
the dungeon. Contrition is the only possible beginning for the man who
has realized this; and that will bring mercy:

"That is soth," seyde Scripture, "may no synne lette
Mercy alle to amende and mekenesse hir folwe,
For they beth as owre bokes telleth aboue goddes werkes,
   Misericordia eius super omnis opera eius."

                          [B 11. 132–34]

4. Isa. 55:1, "O you who thirst, come [to the waters, and those who have no money,
make haste, buy, and eat; come, buy wine and milk without money and without
price]." That the reading "scicientes" in Skeat's B represents "sitientes" is confirmed by the subsequent verbs "souke" and 'drynke" as well as by C's quotation,
"O uos omnes sitientes, venite ad acquas!" (Confusion of "c" and "t" is very common
in Latin passages in the Laud MS as in MSS generally, as they are indistinguishable
in some hands.) Mark 16:16 (glossed by Skeat as Matthew), "He who shall believe
and be baptized [shall be saved]." Note that C quotes as far as "saved" before
adding "etc." which suggests that the next words, "and he who does not believe
shall be condemned. And signs shall accompany those who believe. . . ." may be
relevant as well.

It is expressly *for sinners* that baptism and redemption exist. In a moment the whole idea of predestination as understood—more or less perversely—by the earlier Dreamer has been reversed and subsumed in a total vision of the Creator and his creation converging with relentless compassion on each of his creatures. Freedom is the freedom of response in the human will; there is no other.

In this passage themes and images that have run all through the poem converge. The Dreamer's concern with baptism goes back to his quarrel with the friars, which, in turn, goes back to Scripture's emphasis on baptism and the Atonement, much of which is new in B. It moves toward resolution of the "righteous heathen" difficulty by placing the Dreamer, the Christian, the Jew, and the "saracene" all on the same footing. It subsumes a series of suggested definitions of DoWell—dread (Wit), belief (Clergy), poverty with patience (Scripture), baptism, and later, contrition (the Dreamer), to say nothing of Study's elusive "least degree that longeth to DoWell"—in a new one: thirst. Scripture's summation in terms of mercy recalls the role of Mercy in Piers's pilgrimage to Truth, as the image of the churl imprisoned in the dungeon of his lord's castle suggests Piers's castle of Truth and the two towers of the Prologue. Most obvious of all is the echo of the words with which Holy Church introduced herself:

> "Holicherche I am," quod she, "thow ou3test me to knowe,
> I vnderfonge the firste and [þi]feyth [þee] tau3te,
> Þou brou3test me borwes my biddyng to werche."

> [B 11. 75–77]

We remember that one of the B poet's first major changes was to add several passages on love and the Atonement to Holy Church's speech, including one describing the Incarnation in highly metaphysical terms, and to make her summation "loue is leche of lyf." Thus, not simply in content but in style, the passages are akin, since the resolution of themes embodied here is achieved through a highly "metaphysical" complex of images, which turns on the basic metaphor of thirst. The Crucifixion in which Christ sheds the "blode that he bou3te vs with" is seen as the spring of water for the thirsty; the healing of those who would "drynke bote for bale"; the return to the mother's arms for those who "souke for synne sauf[te] at his brest"; the "wine and milk" of the Isaiah verse; the "mele tyme of seintes" in which, as B's Repentance tells the folk, God feeds "with thi fresche blode owre forfaders in derknesse"; the "maungerye" of Scripture's sermon; and the ultimate answer to the physical hunger of the *Visio*. Finally, the speech relates the Crucifixion, explicitly and through the image of water, with baptism. This complex of images makes the Atonement the crux of all the problems involved both in the Dreamer's revolt and in the pardon scene: the nature of God's ascendancy over man and of men's responsibility; the nature of the attitude from which human growth truly begins; the relationship between belief and virtue, mercy and judgment, law and love.

This coalescing of images around the Passion and the association between what is happening to the Dreamer and what happened earlier to Piers are reinforced by the fact that the two quotations involved— "O vos omnes sitientes" and "qui crediderit"—are associated with the Atonement by their role in the Easter liturgy and come specifically from contexts in which we find two out of the three quotations in Piers's corresponding "ne solliciti sitis" speech.[5] Whether or not the

5. The Isaiah passage occurs twice in the Easter season. It appears in one of the twelve prophecies read in the Holy Saturday liturgy which involves the lighting of the paschal candle and the blessing of the baptismal font, whose tractus includes Piers's "Fuerunt mihi lacrymae meae" passage (Ps. 42). It occurs again, this time in conjunction with Piers's "Si ambulavero": "O vos omnes" is the introit for the Saturday before Passion Sunday when the first two verses of the 23d Psalm are the Communion, and "Si ambulavero" itself is the introit the Saturday before that, as well as, understandably, the gradual in votive masses for pilgrims and travelers and for the grace of dying well. Furthermore, "O vos omnes" would almost certainly suggest the other verse which haunts the Passion liturgy and which had such an influence on the medieval religious lyric: "O vos omnes qui transitis per viam, attendite et videte si est dolor similis dolor mea," an association supported by the fact that B and C both quote Isa. 55 as beginning "O vos omnes," whereas the Vulgate reads "Omnes sitientes" and the missal "Sitientes, venite. . . ." "Qui crediderit" comes from the account of the Resurrection in Mark 16 and is the lesson for mass on Ascension Day. B's association of texts with liturgical rather than biblical contexts is illustrated by his citation of Ps. 71:20, Hope's horn in passus 5, not in its Vulgate form but in the form in which it occurs in the missal in the exchange that follows the Confiteor. For the stages by which the proper of the

poet expected the reader to notice this, it indicates clearly that the A poet associated the pardon scene with Easter (and his omission of overt reference to it was, as suggested earlier, deliberate) and that the B poet associates the Dreamer's new credo with the pardon.

The Dreamer's capitulation speech, then, achieves thematic and imagistic resolution of great complexity with even greater simplicity. At this point there reemerges a singing, affirmative note that has been missing from the poem since Piers's own capitulation, with its momentary lyricism between the tearing of the pardon and the quarrel with the priest. The sudden contrast with everything since the end of the *Visio* provided by this incantatory emotional intensity, following upon intellectual complexity and foreshadowing its resolution, is the more striking since the B poet seems to have omitted Wit's rose image in which the same note was briefly heard, and he toned down the cathartic emotionalism of A's tirade. Unlike the tirade, the emotion of the capitulation speech is not narrowly personal. Here is seen clearly for the first time B's sublimation of one man's development into a pageant of mankind's common experience, revealed in history and reenacted by each individual mind, just as the human embryo reenacts the evolution of the body. In that sense, this song is not strictly lyric but choral, and the liturgical aura imparted by the sound of the Latin (if by nothing else) is essential.

If this release comes for the Dreamer through awareness of his baptism, then the problem of the "righteous heathen" becomes more urgent than ever, both for its own sake and for the sake of a proper understanding of baptism. In the Dreamer's speech itself, baptism was already presented as derivative from a central act of Christ's, addressed to "vs alle," "Saracenes and scismatikes and . . . Iewes." Scripture's concluding words on the supreme mercy of God provoke vociferous approval from a new voice. Just as A capped the sequence of abstractions in passus 5 with the witness of a "real person," Robert the Robber,

---

mass evolved, see J. A. Jungmann, S.J., *The Mass of the Roman Rite,* trans. F. S. Brunner (New York, vol. 1, 1951; vol. 2, 1955); for variations in English usage, see chap. 6 below; for the Holy Saturday observances in England, see the Sarum Customary in W. H. Frere, *The Use of Sarum* (Cambridge, 1898), 1: 149–53.

so B's sequence from Thought through Wit, Study, and Clergy to Scripture brings us to the Emperor Trajan:

> "Ʒee! baw for bokes!" quod one was broken oute of helle,
> ["I,] *Troianus,* a trewe knyʒte, t[a]ke witnesse at a pope,
> How [I] was ded and dampned to dwellen in pyne,
> For an vncristene creature; clerkis wyten the sothe,
> That all the clergye vnder Cryste ne miʒte me cracche from helle,
> But onliche loue and leaute and my lawful domes.
>
> [B 11. 135–40] [6]

Pope Gregory, he says, "By loue and by lernynge of my lyuyng in treuthe / Brouʒte me fro bitter peyne." Unlike most forms of the legend, B's does not say that Trajan was revived and baptized: he was saved "Nouʒt thorw preyere of a pope but for his pure treuthe." In fact, the picture of Trajan is the complement to the Dreamer's new understanding of baptism, which will receive its explicit formulation from Imagination. The justice and humility of Trajan—he is one of Dante's two instances of humility on the cornice of pride[7]—and the irresistibility of his need mark the response of God to man, not on the basis of what, in his limitation, he cannot be, but on what he does know and do. Trajan also complements the "pardoning" of the Dreamer with an instance, closer to the "pardoning" of Piers, of God's rescuing the virtuous from their inherent limitations. The rescue of Trajan is not something he "earned," though without his "pure trothe" he would not have been rescued. Similarly, the Dreamer's baptism, the awareness of which rescues him from the vicious circle of argument in which he has entangled himself, does not put him in a position of superiority to Trajan or dispense him from the realities of ethics. Like the pardon itself, which did not dispense anyone from anything, it is merely the beginning of the beginning.

The discourse on "lele loue," poverty, and patience that follows is the

---

6. Note that the form of the name—Troianus—suggests, like that of Chaucer's Troilus, his central quality of truth and troth and prepares for Imagination's argument that the salvation of Trajan is not an exception but a principle.

7. *Purgatorio* 10. 73–93; the Virgin Mary is the other.

discursive complement to the trust in God manifested by the Dreamer and by Trajan (as well as by the postpardon Piers), and its text could well be Piers's *ne solliciti sitis* itself.[8] The speaker seems to be Scripture,[9] and the key text, "Qui non diligit, manet in morte," significantly translated as "Who so loueth nouȝt, leue me, he lyueth in deth-deyinge" (B 11. 173), sums up the poem's changed perspective on salvation; salvation is the quality in human life that can make it life rather than life-in-death. It is in this speech that the poet introduces for the first time the crucial passage from Matthew that has been seen by critics as the corollary of the pardon:

> *Si vis perfectus esse, vade & vende, &c.,*
> And is to mene to men that on this molde lyuen,

8. Even the extensive discussion of clerical ethics turns on the necessity for priests to be provided for outside of their own efforts and the inappropriateness of charging a fee for their services.

9. There is no attribution in the text as we have it, but much of the contents seems inappropriate to Trajan, and the line at the end, "moche more in metynge thus with me gan one dispute," along with references to Trajan in the third person, suggests that Trajan is not the speaker. Because of the basic theme of patient poverty that Scripture introduced, other themes (like the need to care for the needy) that Scripture stressed, the marked emphasis on scriptural quotations and the *Legenda Sanctorum,* and the role of Scripture as the character who provides the continuity between the two halves of the scene on either side of the tirade, the speech seems to be hers. After all, for such an important element in religious growth, she has had very little to say. Skeat attributes the discourse to Lewte, which does not seem to fit the contents (although, since he is Justice, one can make a better case for him as Trajan's spokesman than Skeat did). Donaldson has persuasively argued that the speaker is the Dreamer, but this seems to me inconsistent with his present stage of development. In any case, in view of the close connection between the Dreamer and all the *Vita* abstractions, Donaldson's argument for the role of Recklessness in C would not be affected; see *C-Text,* pp. 173–74. In view of B's coy conclusion ("with me gan one dispute"), it seems probable that at least some dreamlike and suggestive anonymity is deliberate, as an attempt to make the speech a sort of concluding emanation from the whole argument. It should be noted, however, that in the Kane and Donaldson B text, some of the most awkward third-person pronouns are eliminated (cf. lines 135–40, quoted above), and, if one could assume that a saved Trajan would have clerical ethics on his mind, the whole speech could be his, and "with me gan one dispute" could be an echo of the opening "quod one was broken out of helle" (11. 135).

> Who so wil be pure parfyt mote possessioun forsake,
> Or selle it, as seith the boke, and the syluer dele
> To beggeres that begge and bidden for goddes loue.
> For failled neuere man mete that myȝtful god serued.
>
> [B 11. 265a–68]

The problem of whether to define the good life in terms of its motives or of its manifestations, in terms of faith or of works, is now resolved: as Scripture puts it very simply, "Whoso leneth nouȝte, he loueth nouȝt, [lord] wot the sothe" (B 11. 174). The active love of man is our link with the love of God:

> For owre Ioye and owre [Iuel], Iesu Cryst of heuene,
> In a pore mannes apparaille pursueth vs euere,
> And loketh on vs in her liknesse. . . .
>
> [B 11. 179–81]

Since the Redemption, we are no longer "sons of man" but "sons of God" and brothers, who "carry one another's burdens." "Thanne is byleue a lele helpe, aboue logyke or lawe" (B 11. 213). The discipline it demands is not arbitrary but intrinsic, and not ultimately unnatural:

> As on a walnot with-oute is a bitter barke,
> And after that bitter barke, (be the shelle aweye),
> Is a kirnelle of conforte, kynde to restore.
>
> [B 11. 251–53]

B's second and even more conclusive synthesis of the problems created by the A poet begins when the Dreamer, once again, banishes himself from an experience which is bringing him to the verge of understanding the central demands of an omnipotent if benevolent God. Scripture's discourse melts into the coming of Kynde who, in a clear parallel with the earlier action of Fortune, shows the Dreamer "the wondres of this worlde" from "a mountaigne that Mydelerd hiȝte." [10]

10. Note that the C poet accentuated the parallel between the two visions by making both take place in the same mirror, at the cost of eliminating B's suggestive contrast between mirror and mountain, the latter suggesting panorama rather than introspection and perhaps echoing Christ's temptation to suggest that this vision is the kind of test that confirms or denies a vocation.

But this time, in one of the most splendid lyric passages in the poem, he sees there something more than himself and his own desires: "I was fette forth by [forbisnes] to knowe, / Thorugh eche a creature and Kynde my creatoure to louye" (B 11. 316–17). First he sees the splendor of the material world itself:

> I seigh the sonne and the see and the sonde after,
> And where that bryddes and bestes by here makes thei ȝeden,
> Wylde wormes in wodes and wonderful foules,
> With flekked fetheres and of fele coloures.
>
> [B 11. 318–22]

Finally he sees human society in terms that sum up the fair field of the *Visio* Prologue:

> Man and his make I myȝte [se] bothe
> Pouerte and plente, bothe pees and werre,
> Blisse and bale bothe I seigh at ones,
> And how men token mede and mercy refused.
>
> [B 11. 322–25]

As he sees the elaboration, intricacy, splendor, and measure of the entire creation, human society stands out as a cosmic exception. He watches the variety with which birds adapt their lives to all sorts of circumstances; then the scope of the vision widens:

> And sythen I loked vpon the see and so forth vpon the sterres,
> Many selcouthes I seygh ben nought to seye nouthe.
> I seigh floures in the fritthe and her faire coloures,
> And how amonge the grene grasse grewe so many hewes,
> And somme soure and some swete selcouthe me thouȝte;
> Of her kinde and her coloure to carpe it were to longe.
> Ac that moste moeued me and my mode chaunged
> That Resoun rewarded and reuled alle bestes,
> Saue man and his make. . . .
>
> [B 11. 354–62]

The Dreamer's reaction is only to lash out at Reason for permitting this, in an abdication of responsibility for himself which is also a fundamental misunderstanding of what, for better or worse, distinguishes man, *animal rationale,* from the beasts.[11] As Reason rebukes him harshly, the dream dissolves and the Dreamer finds himself experiencing "kyndely" what he told Scripture with such assurance not long ago: contrition is the only liberation for man when he has seen reality:

> Tho cauȝte I coloure anon and comsed to ben aschamed
> And awaked ther-with; wo was me thanne
> That I in meteles ne myȝte more haue yknowen.
> [Þ]anne seyde I to my-self ["slepynge I hadde grace
> To wite what dowel is, ac wakyng neuer."]
>
> [B 11. 395–99]

With this moment of recognition, the Dreamer finds that a figure has materialized and, like Lewte earlier, is eyeing him:

> And as I caste vp myn eyghen one looked on me.
> ["What is dowel?" quod þat wiȝt. "Ywisse sire," I seide,]
> "To se moche and suffre more, certes," quod I, "is Dowel."
>
> [B 11. 400–402]

To perceive and accept what is, is not merely the only possible starting point for living but the beginning of humility through admission of one's creaturely status. The mysterious observer accepts this definition tacitly since he makes it the basis for explaining Reason's disappearance; a man is unteachable until, like the drunk in the ditch, he has not only felt but admitted shame and need. The Dreamer demonstrates an untypical ability to put two and two together and see himself:

> "Why ȝe wisse me thus," quod I, "was for I rebuked Resoun."
> "Certes," quod he, "that is soth," and shope hym for to walken;
> And I aros vp riȝt with that and [reuerenced hym faire
> And if his wille were he wolde his name telle].
>
> [B 11. 428–31]

With this image of the Dreamer tagging along in the wake of his teacher, a new passus begins.

The mysterious stranger introduces himself as Ymagynatyf, who

11. I owe this point to Professor Donaldson.

exercises the function alloted to him in scholastic psychology as *ars commemorativa:* he reconciles the Dreamer with Reason by unsnarling the remaining problems raised by the A text, and his relation to memory is clearly established in the first elegiac lines of the passus. In medieval psychology, "imagination" has nothing to do with artistic creation,[12] and that Imagination discourses on DoWell, learning, the righteous heathen, and the repentant thief would seem incongruous to a contemporary reader only because imagination is so comparatively unimportant a faculty.[13] Having accepted the Dreamer's unanalytic definition of DoWell, Imagination complements it with a new triad, Paul's faith, hope, and charity. He then provides the final resolution to the Dreamer's special problems by explaining the role of learning, the heavenly status of the repentant thief, and the salvation of the righteous heathen; in connection with the latter, he at last formulates the new conception of baptism which has been developing since passus 10:

> . . . there is fullyng of fonte and fullyng in blode-shedynge,
> And thorugh fuire is fullyng and that is ferme bileue;
> *Aduenit ignis diuinus, non comburens sed illuminans, etc.*
>
> [B 12. 282–83] [14]

Nevertheless, there is something singular about Imagination's argument. The B poet makes the very "mistake" any unwarned modern reader would make: he associates Imagination with the writing of poe-

12. For a useful bibliography on this subject, see the notes to Bloomfield's appendix, "The Problem of Imaginatif," *Apocalypse.* The appendix itself provides an illuminating discussion of how unusual the poet's conception of the faculty is and some suggestions as to how the B poet could have arrived at it without resorting to a time machine, on the basis of hints in scholastic psychology.

13. Compare Keats's eventual realization that his scientific training, far from being a damaging "Bias," is enriching to him: "An extensive knowledge is needful to thinking people—it takes away the heat and fever; and helps, by widening speculation, to ease the Burden of the Mystery . . . The difference of high Sensations with and without knowledge appears to me this—in the latter case we are falling continually ten thousand fathoms deep and being blown up again without wings and with all [the] horror of a ⟨bare⟩ shouldered Creature—in the former case, our shoulders are fledge⟨d⟩, and we go thro' the same air and space without fear" (to J. H. Reynolds, 3 May 1818, *Letters,* vol. I, p. 277).

14. "The divine fire comes, not burning but illuminating" (see Skeat's note).

try. In fact, this is Imagination's first concern; his proper intellectual function comes second. Imagination begins by describing himself as the one activity which has remained, indefatigably, a part of the Dreamer's life during the "fyue and fourty wyntre" of his apostasy,[15] reminding him in elegiac terms of human limitation and the coming of death, the very elements which, as we recall, ultimately brought the Dreamer out of his oblivion:

> I am Ymagynatyf," quod he, "idel was I neuere,
> Thouȝe I sitte by my-self in sikenesse ne in helthe.
> I haue folwed the in feith this fyue and fourty wyntre,
> And many tymes haue moeued the to [mynne] on thine ende,
> And how fele fernȝeres are faren and so fewe to come.
>
> [B 12. 1–5]

Then he attacks the Dreamer for writing poetry:

> And thow medlest the with makynges and myȝtest go sey thi sauter
> And bidde for hem that ȝiueth the bred; for there ar bokes ynowe
> To telle men who Dowel is, Dobet and Dobe[s]t bothe,
> And prechoures to preue what it is of many a peyre freres.
>
> [B 12. 16–19]

This goading speech, with its ironic suggestion that the Dreamer need only take the friars' word for his rule of life, drives the Dreamer first to the comically lame excuse that his writing is mere recreation and then, in desperation, to his first direct defense of his way of life:

> . . . if there were any wight that wolde me telle
> What were Dowel and Dobet and Dobest atte laste,
> Wolde I neuere do werke but wende to holicherche,
> And there bydde my bedes but whan ich eet or slepe.
>
> [B 12. 26–29]

Writing the poem is his "werke," not his play, his only means of finding out what he has to know. His defense is not that his way of life is defensible—every attempt to reconcile it with traditional morality has failed—but that it is essential to him, that no other experience will

15. Cf. B 11. 46.

bring him "kynde knowynge." As he put it before, in the words which conjured Imagination himself into the action, "slepyng had I grace / To wite what dowel is, but wakyng neuere." It is this affirmation of the poem—of the very "makyng" as such—as a mode of discovery, that unleashes Imagination's more strictly philosophical forces.

Could the B poet possibly mean literally what he has the Dreamer say here? Certainly medieval *artes poeticae* do not speak in these terms, and even when such theologians as Saint Thomas Aquinas went far beyond the didactic aesthetics associated with Saint Augustine they did so not in this way but by praising qualities like consonance and radiance as good in themselves. But let us look more closely at what the Dreamer actually said. He is no romantic urging the primacy of feeling over reason, nor does he assert that a work of art as such creates a resolution between elements unreconciled in reality.[16] The Dreamer's remarks are the prologue to an explicitly intellectional resolution of specifically intellectual problems; he justifies the writing of "makyngs," not in emotional or mystical terms, but in terms of mental and moral discovery. This is radically unusual, if not unique, in formal medieval discussion of art. But is it so obviously incompatible with its historical context that it must mean something else?

For the medieval poet, whose milieu tended not to dignify his function beyond that of other craftsmen, as surely as for the Virgilian poet turning a prose draft into verse, the act of writing was still in a very basic sense a process of discovery. Quite apart from each age's theories about the nature of art, literary history confirms that the act of writing, when it involves deliberately extrapolating one's development into the objective and extremely selective medium of verbal expression, may be consciously as well as unconsciously undertaken as a catalyst in that development. In the form of diary and autobiography, it has produced some of the great classics of the spiritual life, medieval and modern, as well as some secular equivalents. Poetry, too, has served this purpose: for example, the poems of Saint John of the Cross; the lyrics—and in some sense the prose—of the *Vita Nuova*; and much seventeenth-century English metaphysical poetry, most explicitly Herbert's. More

16. See Robertson's warning against such anachronistic assertions about medieval aesthetic theory in *A Preface to Chaucer*, pp. 31–32.

immediately illuminating are works like *The Prelude, The Anatomy of Melancholy,* and the *Essays* of Montaigne. All of these are works of artistic stature; yet they were, in a very specific sense, necessary to the stability and development of their creators, who continually revised and expanded them throughout a lifetime, sometimes drastically altering themes, sometimes replacing "good" with "bad." Two of these are the work of essentially "one-work" artists; Wordsworth, while a prolific writer, considered that his very capacity to become a poet was inextricably entwined with *The Prelude*—first, with its being written at all and, subsequently, with its cumulative reflection of his consciousness, a view of its catalytic function shared by most modern criticism.

Perhaps the most illuminating instance of the symbiotic relationship between the writing process and intellectual and artistic development is to be found in the poet who seems at first glance least to resemble Langland: John Keats, noted rather for the completeness with which he outgrew his early efforts than for continuing to rewrite them, whose suspicions of Wordsworth's methods led him to call such poetry the "egotistical sublime." Nevertheless, the role of his letter writing in his artistic growth is major. The letters record a process of interaction between the Keats of "real life" and the Keats of the verse whose intellectual and emotional development was not only reflected in but at least partially achieved by means of the dialectic and self-examination the letters provide. Keats's consciousness of the problem of becoming a poet under conditions which rendered the tradition in which he understood his vocation hard to apply to his own life is equally illuminating, as is his attempt to resolve the problem by writing poetry about his attempt to write poetry. Most illuminating of all is the fact that Keats, after an interval equivalent to several years in any other poet's chronology and after a stylistic evolution far more drastic than that which separates the A, B, and C texts, returned to the unfinished *Hyperion,* a poem he had abandoned at least partly because its assumptions and structure did not allow it to resolve the questions with which it found itself confronted. He attempted to deal with this problem by building the question of his own development into the poem through the format of the dream vision. Within this later *Hyperion* we find a figure of the poet confronting the personification of poetry, who goads him into a defense of his vocation; and this personification, in an almost exact parallel with the B poet's term "Ymagynatyf," is Moneta: Memory, the mother of the Muses.[17]

The emphasis on the first-person narrator in medieval poetry, particularly in genres like the religious lyric and the dream vision, which have an image of the poet as subject and object within his own creation built into the demands of the form, would certainly lend itself at least as well as the diary, the essay, the letter, and the autobiographical novel to developments of this kind, as Keats's revival of the dream-vision genre confirms. But in all the cases we have discussed, we are dealing with a more or less conscious intention to use the act of writing in this way. Can we assert this of *Piers Plowman*? The character of the A text itself, including its ultimate disintegration, the attitude to entertainment and art expressed in it, and the contrast between Piers and the Dreamer so basic to its structure, makes it very difficult to believe that the A poet began with any such intention. Even when the poem began to take on this function, the first effects were largely destructive; and later, when they were not, the process of acknowledging what had happened seems to have been extraordinarily difficult, and the B poet's resistance to it is portrayed as having been overcome only painfully and by degrees—as we might expect if the aesthetics and philosophy of his own day worked against it but which would otherwise be incomprehensible. Even the view of the poem the Dreamer presents to Imagination does not seem to have overcome his doubts enough to allay the remarkable self-conscious-

17. Compare Walter Jackson Bate's account of *Endymion* as a precursor of the "symbolic debate" that "moves actively toward drama" in the Great Odes: "One use of the poem was confessional: it was used partly for self-expression in the hope of making a step in self-understanding. . . . Endymion was . . . reflecting uncertainties in Keats himself—uncertainties that were to remain with him until the end. No quick, doctrinaire solution to them could satisfy Keats' honesty. The mind, as he said much later, should be 'a thoroughfare for all thoughts'; and his friend Charles Dilke, who 'cannot feel he has a personal identity unless he has made up his Mind about everything,' will 'never come at a truth because he is always trying at it.' But how does one attain this openness—more especially how does one keep it—when the heart seeks immediacy and neatness of formula? Can this honesty be preserved in poetry unless uncertainties are dramatized, and unless arguments are seen as human persuasions or hopes, presented in interaction with each other?" (*John Keats* [Cambridge, Mass., 1963], pp. 191–92).

ness and guilt the A, B, and C poets all display about their vocations. To see the poem functioning precisely as the B Dreamer describes it has not only his authority but that of the very features of *Piers Plowman* that make it, artistically speaking, most fascinating and intractable: the tentative, circular character of its argument, with its sympathetic inclusion of conflicting attitudes; the vivid success of the total action in spite of—even through—uneven achievement and imperfect, often amateur means; the "errors" which, when clung to with sufficient tenacity, work their way into self-correcting insights; the way in which the author's self-consciousness about his role as creator, actor, and audience is intrinsic to the drama throughout, with a consistency worthy of *Tristram Shandy*. If the breakdown of the A text is the clearest single instance of the process at work, it is even more significant that the B poet's final step in clarifying and synthesizing the A poet's poem and making it the basis for a more objective drama was to face and formulate its nature clearly for the first time. Indeed, one may feel that the view of the poem's function which B's Ymagynatyf elicits is almost a retrospective defense, since from this point on the poem, for all its difficulties, seems much more publicly and objectively constructed.

THE BANQUET: THE FIRST STEP FORWARD

With the beginning of passus 13, the B poet begins to create new action about DoWell that carries the larger argument of the poem forward. The argument still derives from the A *Vita*, but it is no longer remedial. The B poet's long detour brings him back to the argument of the *Visio*, and he marks the convergence of the two poems by reintroducing Piers for the first time. After a waking interval which carries the portrayal of the Dreamer further toward madness, the kind of action shifts drastically. For the first time since the B additions to the Prologue, we have an emblem action inset into the argument in order to consolidate it and to analyze the relative roles of the different factors involved. And for the first time since the *Vita* began, we have a sharply and realistically observed group scene in which a variety of characters interact with each other. The Dreamer is only one among them; though he is more actively involved than in the Meed story or the pardon scene, he is essentially an observer instead of constituting the plot himself.

The banquet is one of the high points of the B text. On the simplest level, it is as fine an instance of social observation and the shrewd exploitation of characteristic behavior as the poem has to offer. The concrete detail is as acutely selected as Envy's "bolle and . . . broke schete" or his looking out of the corner of his eye at mass to notice Eleyne's new coat. The doctor's menu of "mortrewes and puddynges, / Wombecloutes, and wylde braune & egges yfryed with grece" (B 13. 62–63) is as convincing as the "genuine badger hair shaving brush" that overcomes the prosecuting attorney's scruples in *The Tin Drum*. The details of behavior are even better. When the Dreamer seems about to attack the doctor, Patience "perceyued what I thouȝt and [preynte] on me to be stille." When the Dreamer asks the doctor what DoWell is, " 'Dowel?,' quod this doctour—and [dranke after]— / 'Do non yuel to thine euenecrytene nouȝt bi thi powere' " (B 13. 103–4). The gesture reveals more about the doctor than the answer itself. The same is true of the doctor's reaction when he finds Patience stealing the scene:

> "It is but a *Dido*," quod this doctour, "a dysoures tale.
> All the witt of this worlde and wiȝte mennes strengthe
> Can nouȝt confourmen a pees bytwene the pope and his enemys,
> Ne bitwene two Cristene kynges can no wiȝte pees make,
> Profitable to ayther peple," and put the table from hym,
> And toke Clergye and Conscience to conseille, as it were,
> That Pacience tho moste passe for pilgrimes kunne wel lye.
>
> [B 13. 172–78]

The characteristic rebuttal of idealism with "it can't be done" and a reiteration of the cautionary motive ("profitable to either") are just right, but the irritated superiority of the gesture—he pushes back the table and tries to collect his immediate neighbors with a glance into an in-group that excludes Patience—is even better. The same shrewd observation is at work when the Dreamer has made an unpleasantness by attacking the doctor directly and Conscience becomes the perfect host smoothing over the gaffe:

> Thanne Conscience curteisliche a contenaunce he made,
> And preynte vpon Patience to preie me to be stille,
> And seyde hym-self, "sire doctour and it be ȝowre wille,
> What is Dowel and Dobet? ȝe deuynours knoweth."
>
> [B 13. 111–14]

Familiar indeed is this reaction of the hostess at a precariously balanced formal occasion when things are livening up unsettlingly: the grimace of mingled complicity and rebuke to the offender, the glance at the reliable guest that says "*Do* something"; and the flattering inquiry addressed to the offended party. Still another kind of psychological shrewdness is seen in the way Clergy and Conscience (each in a sense the host here) treat each other. The kind of close friendship and respect that expresses itself through sharp banter and conscious independence is perfectly reflected in their manner to each other at the end of the scene. In contrast to his formal farewell to the guest of honor, Conscience's goodbye to Clergy is oblique:

> Thus curteislich Conscience congeyde fyrst the frere,
> And sithen softliche he seyde in Clergyes ere,
> "Me were leuer, by owre lorde, and I lyue shulde,
> Haue pacience perfitlich than half thy pakke of bokes!"
> Clergye to Conscience no congeye wolde take,
> But seide ful sobreliche "throw shalt se the tyme,
> When thow art wery for-walked wilne me to consaille."
> "That is soth," quod Conscience. . . .
>
> [B 13. 198–205]

He pictures eloquently the world he and Clergy could create if they would combine forces with Patience. Clergy replies with characteristically judicious commitment, made convincing by wry self-mockery:

> "That is soth," [seide] Clergye, "I se what thow menest,
> I shal dwelle as I do my deuore to shewen,
> And conformen fauntekynes [other] folke ylered
> Tyl Pacience haue preued the and parfite the maked."
>
> [B 13. 211–14]

This Jane Austen eye for behavior (as distinct from the Ben Jonson–Dickens one so characteristic of the *Visio*) is the more remarkable since this social realism, unlike the *Visio*'s is only a means to an end that has little to do with sociological values. The scene is allegorical analysis at its most sophisticated. Just as the coronation procession in the B Prologue analyzes the factors in an ordered social structure, the banquet juxtaposes, to differentiate and correlate, the elements that make up the religious structure of that society, the Church as we actually see it present in time, not in its transcendence. These are all elements that have been under discussion individually at one time or another, so the cast is a familiar one. Conscience was an important character in the earlier *Visio,* although he has dropped out of sight since. He is the main character in one sense, the master of ceremonies, and his decision to come down from the high table and join the second-class citizens at the side table gives the scene its plot. The B poet seems to be bringing him back in to take over some of the Dreamer's functions without his pejorative connotations, a development that will culminate in his replacing the Dreamer at the end of passus 20 as the central quester. The rest of the cast is even more familiar. Clergy and Scripture have been crucial to the Dreamer's development. Patience is new as a character, but both Scripture and Imagination have singled him out as what nurtures grace and the development of the human spirit. The doctor is not only the walking image of the friars referred to throughout the text—he is called both "maistre" and "frere"—but the summation of all the arguments against learning and the Church advanced to date.

The cast is grouped and regrouped in varying ways throughout the scene. At first, position distinguishes the different figures: Scripture waits on the guests; Conscience, Clergy, and the doctor are on the dais, at the high table; Patience and the Dreamer are below at the side table. They are further subdivided by their food and its source. The doctor eats real food, actual dainties which he appears to conjure out of the air. Clergy and Conscience, like well-brought-up people, eat what is set before them, sound intellectual sustenance "of Austyn, of Ambrose, of alle the foure euangelistes" (B 13. 239). They are consumers, not originators or synthesizers, temperamentally opposed by the nature of their activities but complementary and nourished by the same traditional wisdom of the Church. Patience and the Dreamer, on the other hand, are served interiorized, ethical and psychological fare, an unappetizing-looking loaf of "agite penitenciam" and a draft of "diu perseuerans," with which they declare themselves delighted, at least when improved with such condiments as "miserere mei deus" and "Beati . . . quorum tecta sunt peccata." [18] Patience is sustained not by the knowledge of tradition but by an inwardly embraced process of remedial discipline.

The relation between the characters becomes clearer when they embark on the game of defining the three Do's, a game for the reader as well, since these drastically different characters produce definitions that are bafflingly similar, and the argument becomes increasingly difficult until it culminates in an actual riddle. The doctor goes first, and the disintegration of his body through gluttony, as Patience describes it, is paralleled by the disintegration of his mind. Like the friars of passus 8, he is almost right; his definition has the right elements but in the wrong order:

> "Dowel," quod this doctour, "do as clerkes techeth,
> [Þat trauailleþ to teche oþer I holde it for a dobet.]
> And Dobest doth hym-self so as he seith and precheth:—
> *Qui facit et docuerit, magnus vocabitur in regno celorum."*
>
> [B 13. 115–17]

Submission as the meaning of DoWell is not exactly wrong, but the doctor is evading the problem that managing to do everything that clerks teach is remarkably difficult; for him, "what clerks teach" needs no defense, and he seems more interested in claiming such obedience than in explaining how people can achieve it. And clerks don't have to live up to anything unless they are DoBest. His DoBet and DoBest reverse the order established elsewhere, notably by Clergy, as the very quotation the doctor so injudiciously selects actually proves. If Conscience were not the perfect host, he would treat the doctor the way he once treated Lady Meed when she was so ill advised as to cite a text

18. "Do penitence," "long lasting," "Lord have mercy on me." Ps. 32:1, "Blessed . . . whose sins are covered."

whose very next clause disproved her argument (an incident added by the B poet).[19]

Where the doctor garbles everything, Clergy can transmit more than he claims to understand. He does not reaffirm his earlier definitions (passus 10) but suspends judgment pending clarification of a new definition he has heard but which he finds it beyond his competence to evaluate unaided. With this new definition, we hear from the vanished Piers Plowman for the first time since the pardon:

> For one Pieres the Ploughman hath inpugned vs alle,
> And sette alle sciences at a soppe saue loue one,
> And no tixte ne taketh to meyntene his cause,
> But *dilige deum* and *domine, quis habitabit &c.*
> And [demeþ] that Dowel and Dobet aren two infinites,
> Whiche infinites, with a feith, fynden oute Dobest,
> Which shal saue mannes soule thus seith Piers the Ploughman.
>
> [B 13. 123–29]

This does not sound at all like the *Visio* Piers, even after the pardon. On the other hand, it corresponds fairly well, in outline if not in atmosphere, with Wit's castle, in which DoWell and DoBet are two coexistent and continuing states that will in time be superseded by DoBest, in which the evil will itself is eradicated. Study's discussion of love and her cryptic picture of the teleological interpendence between the three Do's are even closer to the spirit of Piers's remarks. Above all, in Piers's Do's, DoWell is no longer a "passing grade," a minimum

19. B 3. 333–39. Meed quotes *"omnia probate,"* and Conscience points out that "quod bonum est tenete" follows. As Skeat notes, the doctor's quotation is from Matt. 5:19–20: "Qui ergo solverit unum de mandatis istis minimis, et docuerit sic homines, minimus vocabitur in regno caelorum; Qui autem fecerit et docuerit: hic magnus vocabitur in regno caelorum. Dico enim vobis, quia nisi abundaverit justitia vestra plus quam scribarum et pharisaeorum, non intrabitis in regnum caelorum." This in itself rebukes the doctor; even more significant, for the pardon and everything since, are the immediately preceding lines: "Nolite putare quoniam veni solvere legem, aut prophetas: non veni solvere sed adimplere. Amen quippe dico vobis, donec transeat caelum et terra, iota unum, aut unus apex non praeterbit a lege, donec omnia fiant" (Matt. 5:17–18).

justification that settles a man's status safely, but an organic part of a process which is only complete in DoBest or through his agency.

Compared to Clergy's responsible conservatism, Conscience is volatile, and unstable. But he can see and respond to qualities of life, establish priorities, and express his caring in commitment even when he does not yet understand; his contribution is the opposite of Clergy's "holding operation." He cannot comprehend Piers, but he goes further than Clergy, on the basis, not of intellect, but of trust in what he has already known directly:

> "I can nouȝt her-on," quod Conscience, "ac I knowe Pieres;
> He wil nouȝt aȝein holy writ speken I dar wel undertake."
>
> [B 13. 130–31]

Neither Clergy nor Conscience has a definition of his own. Where Clergy quoted a text, Conscience appeals to Patience for the kind of knowledge "that no clerke ne can." Patience begins with a definition, "Learn, teach, love," which, since he says love taught it to him, must represent the science Piers does *not* "set at a soppe." [20] The climax of Patience's speech, however, is the announcement that he has DoWell with him wrapped up in his "poke," his pilgrim's bundle. It is a sovereign talisman against all material disasters and is clearly related to what he said about love, since he quotes *"Caritas nichil timet"* in support of its miraculous properties. The reader surely relaxes here, as he did when Piers unfolded his pardon, in expectation that the mysteri-

20. This, and the fact that the definition is clearly one by interior stages, makes his definition yet another of the complements to the basic perspective provided by Piers and by Wit's castle. To learn, like the earlier belief, dread, shame, and so on, is a way to express the acceptance of another reality's fundamental ascendancy over one's own. To teach is to extend this acceptance beyond one's own consciousness into sharing with others; teaching in that sense, like translating the Bible, has been a recurrent element in thinking about DoBet. To love is to achieve the orientation of spirit in which what one does comes no longer from dutiful enactment but is a matter of direct volition, the flowering of a healed spirit. In spite of the superficial resemblance to the doctor's Do's, the motivation and the meaning of the learning and teaching are altogether different; the doctor's "teaching" is revealed to be hypocritical because of his definition of DoBest. The fact that Piers's "infinites" of love come between the doctor and Patience is essential.

ous DoWell is to be displayed before him at last. But instead, Patience describes DoWell in a riddle. Attempting to solve it is one of the pleasures of the scene,[21] but the main point is that the riddle is supposed to be a riddle; it is a formula that, without being intrinsically meaningless, is incomprehensible to someone who cannot supply the clew that will reduce apparent gibberish to lucidity. Gibberish it remains to its immediate listeners and to the poem's audience, who are thus forced to share the diners' sense that Patience's words are going over their heads and that all their intellectual abilities are powerless to deal with the words natural to an inner, psychological wisdom.[22] Suddenly, then, we can no longer identify with Patience's inside knowledge. For the same reason, the poet chose to express Piers's new perspective in enigmatic terms that completely baffle Clergy and Conscience and to couch the scene's three definitions in terms that make them sound as puzzlingly alike as is compatible with some distinction of meaning. The impact of the scene does not depend on anyone's solving either the smaller riddle or these larger ones at the time. In direct contrast to the brilliant lucidity of the scene on its first level, as a comedy of manners, it is meant to bring the enigmas of the preceding action to a focus. It makes its main impression through the contrasting character and approach of the different speakers, while dazzling the reader with a kaleidoscope of shifting elements, all of which he rightly feels must somehow belong in the definition, if he could only manage to approach it from the right perspective. This is essentially the same dramatic strategy as the A pardon scene; there, too, there was an obvious aenigma. But the B poet does not need to put off the explanation for five more passūs. In the very next scene we will see Patience open his poke to offer Hawkin the talisman, and we will be told what it is in so many words; the scene as a whole, with its confrontation between Patience and

21. See the Skeat-Cooke "solution" given in Skeat's notes; and R. E. Kaske, " 'Ex vi transicionis and Its Passage in *Piers Plowman*," *Journal of English and Germanic Philology* 62 (1963): 32–60.

22. The C poet seems to have agreed that a riddle was dramatically necessary here. He seems to have felt the scene was much too difficult and took out B's riddle; on the other hand, he gave Patience a new riddle about carrying his talisman "In the corner of a cart-whel with a crowe croune" (C 16. 162).

Hawkin, will be the B poet's final emblem-definition of DoWell and his resolution of all previous ones.

The major achievement of the scene is not merely this gathering of forces for an intellectual resolution of the *Vita de Dowel* but its integration of intellectual awareness into fuller experience in precisely the way allegory should permit but so seldom achieves. We have the sharpness and density of texture we associate with "realism"; the humor, detachment, and psychological shrewdness of high comedy; the counterpoint between realistic and symbolic detail characteristic of satire and of absurd art, each depending on the juxtaposition of logically incompatible levels of action; the enlisting of the reader as an active participant through the very sense of bafflement that forces him to live the scene as action, unprotected by intellectual security, and to try on his own to solve the puzzles instead of relying on empathy with the characters. This is not a comedy or satire or novel, however, but a rigorous algebraic equation that gathers up the disparate elements in the intellectual-religious life and sets them in their intrinsic relationship to each other. Finally, just as the language of the B poet's additions has come to include, more and more overtly, basic archetypal images from common human and religious experience, the very action itself has now become such an image and acquires a power and resonance unaccounted for by the details in themselves. This convincing dinner party is a banquet and as such ties together the cluster of images the B poet has been working with back as far as the words he gave to Repentance at the end of passus 5, in which sin and pardon come together in the Atonement, the "mele tyme of seintes" (B 5. 500), the polar opposite of Glutton's parody. Such an image brings together, and at the same time distinguishes, the material feeding so basic to the *Visio* and the "nourishing" of each man's own growth that has been the subject of the *Vita*. Above all, the banquet is the mysterious "maungerie" Scripture preached about, which separates the "many" from the "few," and the feeding of the hungry and thirsty on which the Dreamer's capitulation speech turned. Both in theme and in imagery, the linear, picaresque A *Vita* has been given a three-dimensional structure and becomes fully cumulative.

HAWKIN AND THE FINAL DEFINITION OF DoWELL

The banquet scene has sifted out Patience, Conscience, and the Dreamer, the seeker who has finally achieved shame, and defined them as the qualities which can reach the synthesizing perception of DoWell. As they go off together looking for DoWell, what they find is "Haukyn the actyf man." Activity is his basic characteristic, and like Imagination he introduces himself as hating idleness. This activity is defined in so conflicting a manner that we clearly have to do, not with a character, even in the sense that the Dreamer is one, but with an emblem figure that brings together elements previously investigated separately. First Hawkin is a minstrel: as such he subsumes the Dreamer himself. At the same time, Hawkin is a "waferer," the supplier of sustenance to all the different vocations needed to carry out the functions of society: in this, he takes over from the Piers of the *Visio,* the Dreamer's antiself. In yet another perspective, Hawkin provides the "bread" that the priest offers at the mass and prays for mankind in a basic human commitment to yearning and hope for healing. And Hawkin has a pardon, but, like most fourteenth-century pardons, it is only a parody of Piers's. Finally, in one of the central images of the whole poem to date, Hawkin's identity is marked by his "contenaunce of clothyng," a "cote of Crysten-dome." But a closer look at Hawkin's coat shows that merely acknowl-edging the ascendancy of God does not resolve the problem of human finitude any more than did the Dreamer's baptism. When the three pilgrims politely call this to Hawkin's attention, it turns out that he knows it perfectly well himself:

> "I haue but one hool hatere," quod Haukyn, "I am the lasse to blame
> Though it be soiled and selde clene, I slepe thereinne on niȝtes;
> And also I haue an houswyf, hewen and children."
>
> [B 14. 1–3]

Hawkin tries to keep the coat clean, but he has never been able to maintain even for an hour the integration between will and actuality which a clean coat symbolizes. This image of the man for whom con-sciousness can only mean consciousness of the impossible is the ultimate expression of a whole line of development throughout the poem. The attempt to see in the basic conditions of well-meaning, ordinary human life some sanction for its own existence can lead only to the image of a man who must live out his life in one garment. Conscience and Patience respond differently to this dilemma, though each takes Hawkin's very consciousness of himself as a basis for hope. Conscience, the practical activist, sees it as an awareness that can be made deliberate and exteriorized into actions that integrate a man into a larger pattern of fallible men, all building, through positive action, a remedial way of life for themselves. For him, contrition is DoWell, confession is DoBet, satisfaction is DoBest. But Patience, on the other hand, takes Hawkin's self-knowledge as the point where the finite creature encounters reality, the revelation of justice and love together as the meaning of God's ascendancy over man; he promises Hawkin the support that makes all else possible: "lo! here lyflode ynough if owre byleue be trewe!" (B 14. 38). God who made the creature in his finiteness made the support for him as well.

Patience puts the dependence of man on God in terms that tie it to Kynde's vision of Middle Earth, to Piers's *ne solliciti* speech, and to Holy Church's original picture of man:

> "I shal purueye the paste," quod Pacyence, "though no plow erie,
> And floure to fede folke with as best be for the soule,
> Though neuere greyne growed ne grape vpon vyne.
> Alle that lyueth and loketh lyflode wolde I fynde,
> And that ynough shal none faille of thinge that hem nedeth.
> We shulde nouȝt be to busy a-bouten owre lyflode.
> > *Ne solliciti sitis, etc.: volucres celi deus pascit, etc.: pacientes vincunt, etc.*"
> > > [B 14. 28–33] [23]

Significantly, two of these quotations come from Piers's *ne solliciti sitis* speech and the third from Patience's own speech at the banquet, in which he explained that he had DoWell in his poke. The "lyflode" he offers Hawkin is thus linked at one and the same time with the pardon

23. Matt. 6:25, "Be not solicitous . . ."; Matt. 6:26, "God feeds the birds of the sky . . ."; "the patient shall conquer. . . ." See Skeat's notes.

and with DoWell, those two elements which the A Dreamer tried to link prematurely with such disastrous results. With all these associations evoked, Patience prepares to unwrap his bundle, and the Dreamer, who so long ago peered over Piers's and the priest's shoulders to see the pardon, peers again to see what Patience has unwrapped:

> But I [listnede and] lokede what liflode it was
> That Pacience so preysed [and of his poke hente
> A pece of the *pater-noster* and profrede vs alle
> And then was it *fiat voluntas tua* sholde fynde vs alle.]
>
> [B 14. 47–48] [24]

Like the pardon itself, DoWell is the simplest piece of the common heritage, but this time it is not an enigma. The lyric speech in which Patience explains this revelation, echoing his and Piers's earlier speeches, associates *fiat voluntas tua* with the first "infinite of love" from which the flowering of the human spirit can come, as Clergy at the banquet credited Piers with saying, and with the pardon itself, which so paradoxically affirmed that love and justice are simultaneously fulfilled in God. The disparate definitions of DoWell throughout the *Vita*—belief, dread, penance, thirst, contrition, suffrance, and shame, each the first stage in some trilogy of human development—come together in this formula for man's acceptance of a reality beyond his own as the assent of a person to a Person, rather than that of a mind to a proposition. Defining DoWell as *fiat voluntas tua* is the polar opposite of defining it, in the spirit of the prepardon *Visio* (and of the Dreamer's first musings in the *Vita*), as *voluntas tua facta est*.[25] The justification for human nature does not lie in its capacity to give itself value by having conformed to some minimal objective standard that will entitle it to a "good credit reference." Man, as such, has no such capacity; and even if he did, that is not, as tragedy itself asserts at least as emphatically as Revelation, what is valuable about him. He can achieve even the appearance of such sufficiency only when he limits the circumstances of which he permits himself to be aware and simplifies the problems

24. "A piece of the Lord's Prayer . . . thy will be done.
25. "Thy will has been done."

whose existence he will face, and the good for which he will yearn, to such an extent that he is even more dangerous and tragic in his narrowness than in his fallibility. What distinguishes man from the more satisfactory animals and gods is a capacity, infinitely variable but intrinsic, for deliberate vulnerability, self-knowledge and yearning. That, not the splendor Hamlet sees in man's "god-like . . . reason" or his "form and moving . . . express and admirable," gives meaning to this "quintessence of dust."

Fiat voluntas tua thus becomes the new definition of Hawkin's "cote of Crystendome" and the fulfillment of the new conception of baptism that has been developing since the Dreamer's capitulation speech. It is also food, the "lyflode" that will sustain Hawkin instead of the "wafer" he has relied on up to the present; it is the fulfillment of the cycle of hunger and nourishment so central to the poem and the mark of man's intrinsic dependency on realities beyond himself. It is the answer to Hawkin's dirty coat, the culmination of the pervasive clothing image. Finally, it is the central phrase in Christ's acceptance of the Crucifixion, three times repeated in the Garden of Gethsemane. "Lyflode," baptism, and the "wafer" of the mass are linked in the Atonement and point toward the centrality of the life of Christ to the later B text, especially toward B's great drama of the Passion and the Harrowing of Hell.

The force and conciseness of this image at the thematic level are somewhat dissipated at the dramatic level by the presence of three discursive pieces that intervene to explore its implications (at the expense of vivid pacing): Hawkin's account of the seven deadly sins; Conscience's account of contrition, confession, and satisfaction as parallel with the stages in Wit's castle; and Patience's long discourse on poverty, which provides a culmination to the analysis throughout A and B of the relationship between a life of outward deprivation and a life of inward asceticism. But nothing weakens the final lines in which the poet subsumes the whole drama of the poem in a final image of man faced with his own nature. The Dreamer, "wery forwandred," found his hopeless quest caught up into the deeper quest of his dream; Robert the Robber wept as he realized his own incapacity to provide the prerequisites of repentance and in that very awareness provided them; Piers accepted the pardon with the words "Fuerunt michi lacrime mee

panes die ac nocte";[26] the Dreamer's "wo," as he realized that his own
recalcitrance had cut him off from the dream that was his only hope
of knowledge, brought him at last to the acceptance of shame; Conscience preferred the pilgrimage that "moeued my mode to mourne
for my synnes" over Clergy's "pakke of bokes." All these come together in Hawkin's final response:

> "Allas!" quod Haukyn the actyf man tho, "that after my Crysten-
> dome,
> I ne hadde ben den and doluen for Doweles sake!
> So harde it is," quod Haukyn, "to lyue and to do synne.
> Synne suweth vs euer," quod he and sori gan wexe,
> And wepte water with his eyghen and weyled the tyme.
> . . . .
> "I were nouȝt worthy, wote god," quod Haukyn, "to were any
> clothes,
> Ne noyther sherte ne shone saue for shame one,
> To keure my caroigne," quod he and cryde mercye faste,
> And wept and weyled and there-with I awaked.
>
> [B 14. 320–24, 329–32]

The uncensored awareness that makes such grief possible is "the leste
degre that longeth to Dowel," the moment of *fiat voluntas tua*. It can
come only when the remorseless, self-contained logic of man's tragic
vision has been taken up into cathartic awareness that a larger reality
surrounds and redefines it. Hawkin's grief marks the point at which the
human spirit makes the most fundamental of all shifts, from an an-
thropocentric to a theocentric understanding of his own good and evil.
The B poet's final definition of DoWell is not a formula but an image:
Hawkin weeping in his dirty coat.

26. "My tears have been my bread day and night."

6

Will and Act: The Three Do's in the Drama of the B Text

THE EXPANSION OF THE POEM

With passus 15, the third great segment of *Piers Plowman,* the drama peculiarly B's own, begins, expanding A's basic image of man on the fair field outward both in space and in time, as B's additions to the Prologue itself began to do, until it achieves the scope and the momentum Bloomfield has so rightly called "apocalyptic." We have the sensation one has in climbing that, as the view widens, the very geography of the climb itself becomes clear for the first time only when it is seen in retrospect. This opening-out comes, as in climbing, gradually. The Dreamer meets the colorless yet chameleonlike Anima in an interview aptly termed transitional—"finit dowel et incipit dobet"—since it keeps the basic format of the *Dowel* scenes while synthesizing the argument of *Dowel* in terms of the action to come. The subsequent Tree of Charity scene is also transitional, synthesizing *Dowel* through a visual image instead of an argument, and remains enigmatic and intellectually taxing in a way that has affinities with *Dowel*'s riddles. From there on we are, poetically speaking, in a new world. Analytical emblem merges into the drama of history as the Holy Ghost speaks to the Virgin Mary and God enters the world of time. The Dreamer's meeting with Abraham-Faith, Moses-Hope and the Good Samaritan-Charity spans human history from man's first recognition of one transcendent God to the coming of that God in his immanence. The great drama of the Passion unrolls from Christ's entry into Jerusalem to his Ascension and the coming of the Holy Ghost at Pentecost, in poetry which, idiosyncratically powerful as it seems in the larger context of English literature, is perhaps the most classically splendid in *Piers Plowman*. From here on, the desperate attempts of mankind to actualize this revelation in a Christian society move ineluctably toward disaster.

ANIMA: THE PROLOGUE TO A NEW DRAMA

If we are to establish what the later B text contributes to an understanding of the three Do's, we must begin with the role of Anima, who provides the conclusion to *Dowel* and the beginning of *Dobet,* and who stands in much the same relation to the later *Dowel* as Imagination to the earlier and Holy Church to the landscape of the Prologue.

Anima begins, in a fulfillment of the promise of Fortune's mirror, by revealing to the Dreamer where he comes from, where he is going, and what his nature is and introduces himself by his nine names, the nine functions or personae of the soul. This list resolves single-handedly one of *Dowel*'s most confusing features, the variety of apparently conflicting definitions proposed by the different faculties. Anima's names show us that the faculties we met in *Dowel* are only manifestations of the same essence, differentiations of its function rather than conflicting norms. The human spirit, fragmented into a cast of competing characters by *Dowel*'s intensive analysis, is thus resynthesized, and the gains of the analysis are refocused. The different definitions fall into place: they are all attempts to define the same central act of acceptance as it manifests itself in each of the roles the human spirit plays. Anima then reiterates Study's warning against the dangers in the Dreamer's omnivorous desire for knowledge. Knowledge is a means of, not an alternative to, man's acceptance of his place in a hierarchical universe.

This brings Anima to his main contribution to the ensuing drama, his discourse on charity. Anima's portrait of Charity, whose "lyflode" is *fiat voluntas tua* and whose motto is "pacientes vincunt," is as vivid, in a more Herbert-like way, as the sins in passus 5. But what is crucial is Anima's definition of charity, which is, intellectually speaking, the key line in the whole later B text:

> "What is Charite?" quod I tho; "a childissh thinge," he seide;
> *Nisi efficiamini sicut paruuli, non intrabitis in regnum celorum;*

With-outen fauntlete or foly a fre liberal wille."

[B 15. 145–46] [1]

This remarkably bold summation of the Bernardine view of the will, already suggested by the pardon scene, Wit's three Do's, and the Dreamer's name, sheers away in one stroke all sentimental conceptions of love. How can love be defined as a "childlike but not childish" condition of the will (not of the feelings or appetites), in which the will is "fre"—generous—and "liberal"—the opposite of servile, mechanical, or utilitarian?

If all being is act, from that of matter to that of God, to be is in some sense to will. The will of God, his act of being, by which he creates the world and sustains it in existence, is love; and his will is the great chain of love that binds the universe. For man, *to be* is in a very special sense *to will,* since man alone within the creation was created to imitate God's nature through a free choice, to be "I am" in a sense that has special autonomy vis-à-vis omnipotence. To will is to be conscious of the integrity of one's own being over against all else that is and to create one's own relationship with that reality. Yet reality does not give way before the individual will. It remains what it is, and God, not the individual man, remains the will that makes reality be. A man's will can only see itself as the maker of his own universe by total self-deception, in which he impresses his identity on all things until he can see only himself wherever he looks. The autonomy of the will, which is man's distinguishing mark among the creatures, does not in fact exist in any empirical sense, since he is not in actuality autonomous, either in his outward relationship to the world or in any inner inviolability of identity. Nor is he immune from shaping by heredity and habit. For man, freedom of will can only be a matter of willing the relationship that in fact exists between his own self and all that is. That is, the true freeing of the human will comes only in love; and that complete and unconditional affirmation of another person's identity that individuals can feel for given other individuals is, as so many poets

1. Matt. 18:3, "Unless you become like little children, you will not enter the kingdom of heaven.

have found it, the best image of what the condition of caritas toward the universe is like.

This condition Anima presents as supported by DoWell, *fiat voluntas tua,* and by the event with which the phrase is associated (which will be the key event of *Dobet*), the Passion. The relation between the three thus suggests Piers's enigmatic "definition":

> . . . Dowel and Dobet aren two infinites,
> Whiche infinites, with a feith, fynden oute Dobest,
> Which shal saue mannes soule, thus seith Piers the Ploughman.
>
> [B 13. 127–29]

Only through two processes, each marked in its own way by stoicism and docility, does the will reach a stage in which, along with greed, servility is left behind. As Augustine puts it, in a phrase as widely misunderstood as it is often quoted, "Love, and do as you like."

Indeed, Anima himself prepares us for Piers's first appearance on the stage of the poem since the *Visio* by tying the whole subject of charity explicitly to Piers. The Dreamer is greatly impressed by Anima's portrait of Charity:

> "By Cryst, I wolde that I knewe hym," quod I, "no creature leuere!"
> "With-outen helpe of Piers Plowman," quod he, "his persone see-
>   stow neuere."
> "Where clerkes knowen hym," quod I, "that kepen holykirke?"
> "Clerkes have no knowyng," quod he, "but by werkes and bi wordes.
> Ac Piers the Plowman parceyueth more depper
> What is the wille, and wherfor that many wyȝte suffreth,
>   *Et vidit deus cogitaciones eorum.*
>
> [B 15. 189–94] [2]

A few lines later Anima adds:

> There-fore by coloure ne by clergye knowe shaltow hym neuere,
> Noyther thorw wordes ne werkes, but thorw wille one.
> And that knoweth no clerke ne creature in erthe,
> But Piers the Plowman, *Petrus, id est, Christus.*
>
> [B 15. 203–6]

2. "And God saw their thoughts.

This shocking-looking equation between Piers and Christ, which has produced so much controversy, can mean a number of things. Anima can mean that Piers has reached the point at which he exercises the function to which "vidit deus cogitaciones eorum" refers, one which Christ exercised during his ministry when—as Conscience will point out later—he was DoBet and when he was not even performing a miracle but recognizing a questioner's motive.[3] Anima may be referring to Piers as the illuminated man who exercises the authority of the Church —that is, as DoBest—by evoking the scene[4] in which Christ gave Peter his name and delegated authority to him to an even more drastic extent than anything Anima himself is talking about here. We will see Piers in just this role in the Tree of Charity scene which follows. Anima may be talking about the ultimate redemption of man—DoBest again —as the restoration of a perfect likeness between God and man, a renewal of the *imago dei* which man was created to embody and which was disfigured by the Fall; in this respect, Christ is "the first-born of many brothers." [5] Anima may be doing no more than what any typological exegete does when he says that anything in the Bible "is" Christ in the sense that it foreshadows or embodies some aspect of the reality fulfilled in Christ.[6] Perhaps Anima is simply informing the Dreamer,

3. Skeat cites two instances where almost these words are used of Christ: Matt. 9:4, "vidisset Iesus cogitationes eorum"; and Luke 11:17, "Ipse . . . vidit cogitationes eorum." On the other hand, closely parallel sentiments are common in the Psalms (10:13–14, 19:14, 44:21, 90:8, 139:3, and especially 94:11—"Dominus scit cogitationes hominum") and elsewhere (1 Chron. 28:9, 1 Cor. 3:20, and Heb. 4:2).

4. Matt. 16:15–20.

5. Rom. 8:29, "Primogenitus in multis fratribus."

6. It has been suggested that we ought to associate this line, not with "Tu es Petrus," but with "petra autem erat Christus," Paul's gloss on Moses' bringing forth water from the rock for the Israelites in the wilderness (see Donaldson, *C-Text,* p. 185, for this argument and a summary of previous discussions). Such a reading associates this Christ-like function of Piers with Moses, and Moses will soon appear (passus 17) as the incarnation of Hope, that is, as DoBet. Therefore we might be able to acquit Piers of the charge of being the wrong Do at the wrong time. Unfortunately, however, when we actually see Piers in the next passus, in the tree-of-charity scene, no ingenuity can evade the fact that he is not DoBet, at least not exclusively, but the authoritative gardener-farmer who dominates the action of *Dobest* and directs the defense of mankind against evil.

like a responsible allegorist, that he is using the name Piers metaphorically to represent Christ. None of these possibilities, all of which are
probably involved, makes any pantheistic equation between man and
God. In fact, if this line occurred in *Dobest,* it would never have caused
any problems at all. The important thing about the passage is that,
whatever it means, it refers to stages which do not fit the passus title,
as, indeed, the very subject of charity does not. Piers is clearly being
stated to be in the wrong Do at the wrong time, and the poet has
chosen to climax his introduction to the later B text by stressing this
as ostentatiously as possible. He does so, and does so at exactly this
point, because from now on he is changing the function of the three
Do's in the poem and their relation to its structure, as becomes clear
as soon as the first scene of *Dobet* proper begins. From now on there
are to be no more formal definitions. The very names of the Do's disappear from the text; with one exception, Conscience's account of the
life of Christ, the terms will be confined to the passus titles. Instead,
the kind of analysis provided by *Dowel* is superseded by a series of
master images, some emblematic and some historical, within which
DoWell, DoBet, and DoBest, along with a myriad of other factors, may
be seen in action and interaction.

THE THREE DO'S IN THE B TEXT

To understand this development, we must think about why Langland
has been defining the Do's in the first place and how the development
of the poem has superseded some of the functions the definitions provided and modified others. The first reason for defining DoWell was
a product of the pardon: it was an attempt to isolate the "one thing
needful" for man in an almost polemical desire to find some minimum
requirement in terms of which man could find himself justified; or to
isolate some absolute starting point, one that does not already presuppose some earlier starting point, from which man can take hold of
himself and begin a development toward the good life. *Dowel* has replied that there is no such point except the recognition that there is
none. Langland's second purpose was to write an anatomy of social
man. This purpose has been drastically redefined by an awareness that
even social man cannot be understood by any analysis which confines

itself to exterior manifestations. Furthermore, the Do's are not an out-
standingly good tool for such analysis, since the obvious way to use such
a format to rank the professions is to show various professions, or the
faculties on which professions are based, defining the Do's in conflicting ways, so we can judge their relative excellence. But such a strategy
is effective only if the reader already has a clear enough idea of the
"right" answer that he can watch the characteristic distortion of each
speaker emerge. Consequently, this second purpose does not combine
well with serious and taxing analysis where the right answer is anything but clear.

On the other hand, two of the original purposes have actually increased in importance. First, to define the three Do's is to analyze the
nature of human growth by seeing its order and interrelationships.
Second, the Do's are a means of formulating the relative roles of God
and man and offer an approach to the questions of free will and the
nature of human merit. But, precisely because these problems remain
central, they have outgrown the constricting format provided by the
formula of the "three lives" as such. The very success of the definitions
is manifested by the fact that they have brought the analysis of human nature to the point where it must be released from this rigid
parallelism. Once the whole man in his historical actuality, rather than
the integers of an individual psyche, becomes the subject, the Do's must
recede in importance. Indeed, it now becomes clear that the poet's
strategy all along has been one of retrospective definition, in which
nothing can be defined until it has been bracketed with elements that
belong to later stages. (One thinks of Jung's dictum that no problem
of real importance can be solved except by being outgrown.)

Not only have both texts refused to define any Do outside the context of the other two; B's structure all along has been an overlapping
one. This is not only desirable but inevitable in a dramatic structure
concerned with defining the stages in man's gradual acclimatization to
reality, since in any but the most rigidly stylized plot different characters
will necessarily be at different stages at any given moment. The DoWell
stage reached by Hawkin in the climactic scene of *Dowel,* where for the
first time DoWell is clearly defined, was achieved earlier in its essentials
by the Dreamer, in the scenes from his capitulation to his acceptance of

shame, and even earlier by Piers after he tore the pardon. That these three experiences cannot be hastily equated is essential to their function in defining the essence of DoWell. In the case of Piers the moment of *fiat voluntas tua* is being reached by an ethically virtuous man, the man of law; in the case of Hawkin, by Piers's opposite, an overt sinner, a breaker of law; and in the case of the Dreamer, by a seeker who, in a life based on empathy and acrimonious struggle, fits neatly into neither category. By the time Piers is introduced into *Dowel,* when Clergy quotes him at the banquet, he represents a stage beyond it. Piers, then, does embody DoWell, but not in *Dowel,* except in the sense that it is only in the light of *Dowel*'s argument that we can look back on Piers in the *Visio* and see that it was not in his exterior virtues that he was DoWell but in his inward recognition of his intrinsic insufficiency in the face of God: "Therefore I abhor myself and repent in dust and ashes," as the equally righteous Job said when his questions were answered not with answers but with a revelation of the divine nature. The Do's cannot disappear, after all that has been invested in them, but they must be transmuted into metaphors, whose function is to remind the reader to stand back from the new and more mimetic action of the poem to see how it relates to the formal analysis of the earlier stages.

Not only have the Do's become metaphors, but the force of the metaphor no longer emphasizes analysis. Instead, it illustrates, whatever the immediate subject, that all being is act and all act is process, even that of the eternal, immutable God. All productivity is sequential and involves interrelationships. Furthermore, all being, even the most active, must be understood in part as response, creative receptivity, even apparently passive sufferance. The polarity—even the antagonism—between God and man seemed, in the earlier stages of the poem, to turn on the fact that God, as the creator and ruler who gives the universe its reality by his sheer act-of-being, is pure autocrat, forcing man into a dependent and subservient status that seems to deny the very qualities which distinguish man from the animals. But occasional remarks throughout *Dowel* about the "suffrance" of God culminate in Anima's presenting a new perspective on the whole problem. Not only does the list of Anima's names put man's ostensibly "active" and ostensibly "passive" qualities on a footing of parallelism, but Anima goes so far as to define God's own nature—his sheer act—as involving a mode of response to man that man can only call passivity. If the first step in man's reacquisition of his true identity is to say "fiat voluntas tua," the very act of God on which that whole process depends was an act marked by the same phrase. Both the problem of power and the problem of suffering are thus completely redefined:

> . . . god suffred for vs more,
> In ensample we shulde do so and take no veniaunce
> Of owre foes that doth vs falsenesse, that is owre fadres wille.
> For wel may euery man wite, if god hadde wolde hymselue,
> Sholde neuere Iudas ne Iuwe haue Iesus don on rode,
> Ne han martired Peter ne Poule ne in prisoun holden.
> Ac he suffred in ensample that we shulde suffre also.
>
> [B 15. 255–61]

Or, as Reason put it in defining sufferance as a fundamental principle of the universe, "Who suffreth more than god?" (B 11. 371). The difference between the man who takes action to improve the world (or prevent evil) and the man who abstains from confrontation with it (either through withdrawal or through collaboration with the status quo) seemed self-evident in the *Visio* and in most of *Dowel*. The very polarity between Piers and the Dreamer, and much of the Dreamer's guilt about his vocation, was a function of this distinction. Now it becomes clear that such a common-sense division into active and passive has been superseded as completely as the law of the conservation of energy is in atomic physics or as Euclidian geometry is outside Tellurian conditions.

Hence, it is the natural outgrowth of the poem's development that its structure should ultimately come to turn on three contrasting interventions by God in the affairs of men, three distinctly dramatized events that are three modes of the same essential act: the sending of the pardon, the Crucifixion, and Pentecost. And from here on the poem becomes increasingly concerned with triads which no ingenuity can twist into illustrations of the three Do's, triads whose essential characteristic is that they are nonethical and nonhierarchical. Some are sequential whereas others are cumulative, but all illustrate the fact that any essence manifests itself in different modes.[7] The most important of these non-hierarchical triads is, of course, the Trinity itself, and the importance of this concept to the argument of *Dobet* and *Dobest* is clear from the space the poet devotes to explaining it and to illustrating it through the images of the three "props," the lighted candle and the human hand, each intimately connected with a major metaphor of the poem: farming, light, and man as *homo faber*. The poem's action from passus 15 no longer attempts to polarize the human situation in order to set its factors in sharp distinction from each other. Instead, it provides events and images which draw these factors together into patterns that define their interrelationship and cumulative effects. The B poet's decision to draw together the main cast of *Dowel* into a single banquet hall and a single conversation was a foreshadowing of his strategy for the rest of the poem.

MASTER IMAGES OF THE THREE DO'S

The first of B's master images, the Tree of Charity, is by long odds the most difficult, and its contribution to defining the three Do's is its least important function. Like Anima's discourse, of which it is the continuation, it is a prologue to the entire subsequent drama. Like the *Troilus* prologue, which "gives away the plot" in order to deflect our curiosity about the events from their outcome to their character and causality, this scene presents a capsule version of B's story, the interaction between God and man during the different stages of history. The scene is difficult because it attempts to present, in one concise visual image, a group of events—most of which will be portrayed mimetically in the ensuing passūs—that are closely related causally but are widely separated from each other in time. The scene begins in the present: the Dreamer still does not understand charity, and Anima shows him an analytical diagram of the human heart which shows how, under the cultivation of a man's own free will directed by Piers Plowman, the human heart may ultimately produce charity by going

7. For instance, J. B. Adams has proposed that we see the three sections of the *Vita* in terms of the three ages of man ("*Piers Plowman* and the Three Ages of Man," *Journal of English and Germanic Philology* 61 [1962]: 23–41.

through a series of stages subsequent to the acceptance of its position vis-à-vis transcendence which constitutes DoWell. Here Piers, in contrast to his earlier role on the Half Acre, clearly represents DoBest, illuminated man, and the Church, which bears the responsibility for guiding other men in their growth toward DoBest. But then the Dreamer is plunged into a deeper dream in which the forces that hinder man in his growth—the world, the flesh, and the devil—are portrayed as well as those that help him. Here the time dimension of the scene is expanded along with its spatial and thematic scope. Piers continues his authoritative role by explaining the situation to the Dreamer, and at the same time he transforms the image of the garden from a static, analytical one into a dynamic one in which we see enacted the stages of human history. Piers plays, first, the role of Adam, knocking down an apple in response to human curiosity and thus bringing death and the devil into the world; then he enacts the role of man contributing, in the fullness of time, to the action of the Logos, who initiates the Incarnation to recover what was lost in the Fall (here mere docility on the part of the individual man is not enough, and free will bears the crucial responsibility).

In this scene, then, Piers plays all three of man's archetypal roles. He sins, he participates in the Atonement, and, as post-Pentecostal man, he acts in the authority of God (just as Anima indicated earlier). The scene might be considered a portrayal of the paradox summed up in the proper preface for mass in Passiontide: "Qui salutem humani generis in ligno Crucis constituisti: ut, unde mors oriebatur, inde vita resurgeret: et, qui in ligno vincebat, in ligno quoque vinceretur: per Christum, Dominum nostrum." [8] The scene with the apple tree in the garden superimposes two distinct moments: the moment when man,

8. "Who didst set the salvation of mankind upon the tree of the Cross, so that whence came death, thence also life might rise again: and that he who overcame by the tree, on the tree also might be overcome: through Christ, our Lord." Passiontide is the period leading up to the celebration of the Easter days proper—Good Friday, Holy Saturday, and Easter Sunday—and its proper preface is first used on Passion Sunday, the Sunday before Palm Sunday. It thus marks the transition from the Sundays of Lent proper to those in the entourage of Easter itself and is compatible with the term "a Mydlenten Sundaye," which the Dreamer uses in the subsequent waking interval.

who was set in the garden to till and keep it, picked the apple in the desire for knowledge and became subject to death; and the moment when man, having come the full circle, stands before a second tree where life and death are at stake. Just as the choice of man before the first tree has been expressed in the paradox "O felix culpa!" so the second tree is paradoxical. It marks at one and the same time the second rebellion of man, the murder of God which is a second fall (Piers reacts, as he did when he tore the pardon, in "pure tene" [9]), and the triumphant victory in which, as Christ's human nature accepts death, man becomes—in the snake's words but not as he meant them—"as the gods." In the words so familiar to us through Handel's exuberant music, "Since by man came death, by man came also the resurrection of the dead. For as in Adam all die, even so in Christ shall all be made alive." Such scenes juxtaposing in space moments widely separated in time are common in medieval painting (for instance, in the *Très riches heures du duc de Berry,* the artist chose to portray the stages of the Fall, not in separate miniatures, but as occurring simultaneously in different parts of an orblike garden in the center of a page). It is only because words are the medium, and because of the comic portrayal of farmer Piers chasing the devil with his pike like the irate foreman of the half acre at the very moment that he foreshadows Christ leveling his lance against the fiend, that the scene is a riddle too difficult to be a completely successful prologue. Nevertheless, it effects a transition between the timeless world of the human psyche (Anima's world, the world of *Dowel*) to the world of human history, the theater of *Dobet* and *Dobest.*

The Tree of Charity is the only one of B's master images for the Do's to be confined to one scene, but it participates in all the others by containing within itself elements of each. Two of these images are characters in the poem, Piers and Christ, and because of Piers's major role in the garden scene, we must consider him next. Piers spans the whole poem and shows us man as the orderer of his environment, man as he responds to potentiality and disorder by imposing pattern, both to draw potential good into actuality and to defend potentiality against

9. Donaldson, *C-Text,* p. 184.

damage and evil. He is man as the maker of civilization. When we saw him first, he exemplified this capacity literally and in its purest natural form, that of the honest farmer. In spite of his ultimate "epiphany" as Petrus, the "rock" on which the Church is built, he is never seen as the fisherman, although this is the dominant image for the apostolate in the Gospels and is still the image used of the pope. The poet is undoubtedly influenced by the familiarity and immediacy of farmers for his audience, but, besides that, the relationship of the fisherman to his world is completely different.

The greatest single force holding the poem together, other than the Dreamer, is the sequence of expansions this image undergoes. Stage by stage, we see the forms through which Piers's capacity is developed and transformed, as the greater reality of God acts upon it, until it achieves its fullest expression when man, acting in the authority of God, orders and transforms society through the Church and is the farmer of souls instead of plants. First we are shown the healthy state of an honest craftsman who works in his own medium in accordance with reality as his own experience manifests it to him. Then his horizons widen to include a sense of responsibility for other men whose life has no such self-defining basis. As he tries to work in this new medium, the fact of his own fundamental dependence becomes conscious and then, as revulsion becomes recognition of reality, willed. Because Piers needs no remedial discipline, since he has never represented corrupt man, the process by which his assent to his own nature becomes actualized in every faculty of his personality, the DoBet stage, will bear little outward resemblance to the process any ordinary man undergoes and is not portrayed. Instead, Piers serves as a landmark by which others measure their movement. Our only glimpse of him at this second stage is the moment when his nature has achieved such perfect plasticity and subordination to the activity of God that he is the human medium in which Christ carries out the crucial action of history, the Atonement. As DoBest, Piers finally emerges to manifest the enlightened will acting directly in the authority of God, having undergone the transformation Wit described, in which even docility disappears because there is no evil left in the will, and radiant authority over his world is the perfectly spontaneous expression of his nature.

Insofar as Piers shows the different postures open to the uncorrupted human mind vis-à-vis the will of God, he is, among other things, a definition of the Do's. As such he moves from self-contained, childlike acceptance of the world as he finds it, across the great gulf into willing the fact of his own subordination, then into willing whatever manifestations of his nature the superior reality may use, and finally into free, generous, triumphant will that is a full and authoritative imitation of God's own; that is, from innocence into DoWell, then into DoBet, and at last, with DoBest, back to innocence. He becomes, in Anima's words, "a childissh thinge . . . withouten fauntelte or foly, a fre liberal wille" and the means through which others are helped toward this state.

The stages in the life of Christ, B's third master image, are obviously essential to the later passūs of the B text in a variety of ways. That one of these is as an image of the three Do's is a concept so difficult and so contradictory to our natural associations of ideas that the B poet had to realize no reader would be able to work out the correspondence himself. So here, as nowhere else in *Dobet* and *Dobest,* the labels actually occur within the text, in Conscience's account of the names of God in passus 19. It should be noted that Conscience's diagram does not appear until after the life of Christ has been presented in direct action and allowed to make its own impact independently and that even Conscience introduces the Do's only after a series of other plays on names. What Conscience tells the Dreamer is that from the birth of Jesus to the first miracle (the changing of water to wine at the wedding of Cana, a miracle which is essentially a theophany, not an act of service to mankind) he is associated with DoWell by the very act of revealing his being within the medium of human experience; this is DoWell in the sense that here human nature achieves recognition of his reality. Man through no virtue of his own recognizes the fact of God. Then during Jesus' ministry, with its teaching and healing, and in his suffering and death, he manifests DoBet. That is, in actual service to those in physical and psychological need and in total, active availability to the will of God, he enacts the complete docility as a tool of Divine Reality that is the essence of DoBet. Finally in the Harrowing of Hell, the Resurrection, the Ascension, and the sending of the Paraclete, the Comforter, at Pentecost, he is DoBest, both in manifesting the triumphant liberty of the will in total ascendancy over every limitation within and without and in bringing into being the new Adam: the transformed human creature who is a son, not a servant; who acts, not in docility, but in love and freedom; and who can bear, as God does, the burden of mankind yet in servitude.

We must remember that this speech of Conscience's is a response to a particular question from the Dreamer, who asks whether the figure he sees "al blody" after the Crucifixion is Jesus or Piers Plowman. That is, its function is to distinguish the human elements in Christ's life both from the transcendent and from the lives of ordinary men. To the extent that the Do's apply to Christ at all, they apply to the modes in which Christ's two natures are related, which Conscience sees as changing from one stage to the next. The life of Christ affords the only instance in which the changing relationship between God and man, which is the essence of the difference between the Do's, can be seen, not as varying modes of communication between subject and ruler, but as adjustments in the respective roles of factors within one living creature. In DoWell, humana natura is the totally passive medium upon which God's existence is revealed in sheer condescension. In DoBet, humana natura participates by fully active use of all its powers, but still in entire docility. In DoBest, a transformed humana natura loses its limitations and acts in a mode in which the difference between autonomy and subordination has disappeared. Here, for the first time, humana natura itself "is" Christ, because for the first time it is fully man.

There remains something forced and difficult about this idea, which conflicts with our sense that the Passion is the highest manifestation of charity and that the Incarnation is one sustainedly perfect act. It also conflicts with the dramatic structure of B, since the Crucifixion and Harrowing of Hell are, by literary standards, the high point of the poem, and the *Dobest* passūs with their terrifying pessimism are correspondingly bleak. The image has also been rendered difficult by the previous use of Christ to define the Do's, notably through the phrase *fiat voluntas tua*. This image is, consequently, the least successful of the four.

In his fourth master image, the one most important to the texture of his poem, the B poet again draws on elements already present in the earlier passūs and by his additions and his emphasis turns them into a powerful cohesive force in the action. This image is human history itself as it unrolls from the Creation to the coming of Antichrist. The B poet uses it in two distinct forms.

The simpler and more diagrammatic of B's two historical images is also the one whose relevance to the three Do's is the clearest. In B's long prologue to the events of Passion Week, the Dreamer meets three figures who embody the relationship between the stages of Old Testament history and the coming of Christ. The first is Abraham, who reveals himself to be Faith and who is later called a herald. The second is Moses, called Hope, and the bearer of Law, a scout. The third is the Good Samaritan, and in a brilliant though apparently traditional conceit, the three enact the parable of the Good Samaritan, with Faith and Hope passing by on the other side and with the further reversal that the Samaritan defends the conduct of the other two, saying that they could not have helped the man in the ditch and indeed only succeeded in getting past the robbers themselves because the latter saw the Samaritan following along after them "On my caple that hatte *Caro* (of mankynde I toke it)."

The major function of the image is to illuminate a central paradox of Christianity that has been a problem throughout the poem, the problem of priority among the different aspects of religion. This problem results from the apparent incommensurability between chronological priority and causal priority, or between the two meanings of "end," as last outgrowth and as *telos*. The image of the three travelers on the road shows how this paradox can be resolved. Faith and Law depend on an initial encounter with Caritas, and to find him again will bring that initial but abortive experience to fruition. He appeared to Abraham, bearing the blazon of the Trinity and promising lordship and "lyf with-outen ende" to him and his heirs; now Abraham has heard that John the Baptist is proclaiming the knight's return to rescue his people. Hope is seeking the knight because he gave him "a maundement vpon the mounte of Synay / To reule alle rewmes with" (B 17. 2–3), which is engraved on "a pece of an harde roche" and reads, like Piers's "tixte" at the banquet and like the very commandment the Good Samaritan parable itself is expounding, "dilige deum et proximum tuum." This "patent" has yet to be sealed and will not be until the Crucifixion. Both the herald and the scout are journeying to Jerusalem at the very time that the Samaritan himself is going there after them to fight Death and find the salve that can heal the man in the ditch. In one sense, Faith and Hope-Law are the forerunners, and Caritas follows them in the fullness of time. In another sense, Caritas was the initiator, the knight who started Faith and Law on their way, for whom they are seeking and who, alone, makes their journey possible. The resolution of the paradox lies in the convergence of all times, places, and sequences on the one historical moment that is the key to them all, the Redemption. In terms of the parable-plot, the Crucifixion is the battle in which the robber will be fettered and the medicine for the wounded man obtained. Not only will the Samaritan return and make possible what Faith and Law could not do, but he will affirm them, giving them their functions: Faith will become "forester" of this wilderness and guide to travelers, while Hope-Law will become "the hostelleres man . . . there the man lith an helynge": "For the barne was born in Bethleem that with his blode shal saue / Alle that liueth in faith, and folweth his felawes techynge" (B 17. 122–23). In short, this scene is an embodiment of the very idea put so paradoxically in the pardon scene. Only those who believe and commit themselves to right action will be saved, but those very people do have to be "saved," that is, rescued from a situation which their own qualities are simply not enough to resolve. "Qui bona egerunt ibunt in vitam eternum" is not a mere observation of fact, no quid pro quo formulation of justice, but a deed of rescue, an enactment—in fact, a pardon.

The intellectual counterpart to this emblematic solution of the paradox is provided by the Samaritan in his subsequent discourse on the Trinity, which is a response to the Dreamer's pessimistic comment: "It is ful harde for any man on Abraham byleue / And welawey worse ʒit for to loue a shrewe!" (B 17. 41–42). The point of the Samaritan's discourse is the relationship between the distinct factors in God's act of being—the Trinity—and the stages, necessarily sequential though interdependent, of man's coming-to-be within history and within individual life. This the Samaritan explicates by comparing the Trinity to a burning candle and to the movement of the human hand. These in their completeness illustrate the coexistent factors in the nature of God, but in their separable and sequential character, as man uses them, they analyze the stages of man's growth. The interrelation between wax, wick, and flame and between fist, palm, and fingers shows how there is a fulfillment of each part in the activity of the whole, which no single part itself can achieve. The test of the goodness of the part is not whether it can work itself up into doing what the whole alone can do but what it is in itself. The part alone is helpless: it must despair. Within the totality, the part is "rewarded" for what is already is. In ethical terms, the demands of belief and obedience, which seem nonsense or impossible when approached in their own terms, become perfectly accessible from the perspective of Charity; yet without the earlier attempts to struggle with the demands of Faith and Hope, the resolution of these struggles will never come; the very vulnerability implicit in the struggle is the DoWell of Faith and the DoBet of Hope and Law and, indeed, explains why the B poet insists on linking Law with Hope.

The drama becomes more rich and gripping when the field widens to include the whole panorama of human history, which is divided, in keeping with tradition, into three stages: Old Testament history, Israel in the time of Christ, and Christian history from Pentecost to the present. This pattern emerges gradually, drawing the vignettes and references to biblical events that have been scattered through the poem into a coherent pattern, and illustrates the process by which the very fact-of-being of a transcendent God is faced by a whole people, through an elaborate counterpoint of rebellion and allegiance, providing a panorama of the attitudes a human consciousness may take up when it conceives of its existence as separate from and over against that of a God who, since he is "I am," has the ascendancy. The first stage, in which man grapples with the existence and exigency of the transcendent God, has been pretty well covered in the earlier B text, since the gamut of incidents hitherto noted amounts to a recounting of the major incidents in Old Testament history and needs only the increased historical consciousness and the few specific events of the later passūs to become perceived as cumulative. B's main addition is the picture passus 17 gives us of Abraham and Moses: the one bowing before God—"thre men to my siȝte"—and allowing their demands to supersede his own desires and sense of logic to such an extent that he is willing to sacrifice his only son for the sake of a promise which depends on that son for its meaning; the other bearing with him an impossible demand that is also a promise of future dominion. This tension between hope and despair, between acceptance and incompleteness, between obedience and an autonomy that continues to set terms and conditions, is the DoWell stage in human evolution, *fiat voluntas tua,* in which the two wills are over against each other and man's commitment is expressed in the subjunctive.

The second stage is presented in the brief account of Christ's birth and ministry and in the close-up of Passion Week. Here both man's rebellion and his allegiance are intensified as the immediacy of God's presence and the stringency of his demands increase: we see outright hatred and resentment that issue in murder and, at the same time, a completely new intimacy between God and man in which Christ can joust in the armor of Piers Plowman. Then comes the third stage: with the Resurrection, the freeing of the devil's prisoners, and the coming of the Holy Spirit begins man's era of grace and charity. Even here the flowering of man is accompanied by the intensification of his capacity for rebellion. Now, instead of a blind knight stabbing the cru-cified Christ with a spear in a terrible parody of Christ's "joust" with the devil, we have the countermarching of great armies across the fair field, as first the forces of Pride and then Antichrist himself with all his train ravage Piers's newly plowed fields and leave but a tiny remnant of mankind besieged within the walls of Piers's barn, Unity. Among those for whom the new era of grace is a reality, we see the coming of age of man, whose new shouldering of responsibility for his world is marked by his return to reiteration of the simplest standards of ethics with which the *Visio* was preoccupied. The phrase which reechoes through *Dobest* is addressed, not to God, but to man: "redde quod debes"—pay what you owe.

The principal characteristic of this historical image is that each stage in the sequence it presents has both a positive and a negative form and that both are intensified as it progresses. Man's climb upward from stage to stage and from Do to Do is also a series of falls, the kind of movement with countermovement that we have seen before in the confession scene but that is now revealed on a cosmic scale. The progress of mankind is the polarization of mankind. Every step that opens up the possibility of greater perfection simultaneously opens the gates to new dimensions of chaos and disaster, as the movement of the poem, ever since the Meed verdict, has implied. Until man's will can know itself in the perception and commitment that is love, it can only manifest itself negatively, as a sort of futile veto power on the universe, destructive primarily to the user himself. It can be tamed by contract, quid pro quo, or counteracted if another will controls the objects on which it can exercise itself—appealing to its desires (Meed) or associating distasteful results with the satisfaction of those desires (dread). But neither process is any better than a remedial one, and the more God's free and loving will toward man removes such checks in order to make more than dread (or at best docility) possible, the more man's will is unleashed in rebellion against all that denies him total autonomy, above all against God himself, directly or indirectly. The ultimate vulnerability of God before man in the Passion is the moment where experience can transform the one will into the other, rebellion into love; but if man's capacity to "veto" God does not remain even here, his love is not "fre," "liberal," and willed. The coming of age of man through the Passion is the beginning for man not only of complete love but of complete evil: "I came not to bring peace but a sword," or, as Dante sees over the gates of Hell, "Divine Love set me here." The inexorable movement of the poem toward the further and further polarization of man is the inevitable expression of that sense of human nature which led Langland to give his everyman-protagonists the name of Will.

7

The *Visio* Revisited

THE STRUCTURE OF THE B TEXT

We emerge from surveying the way in which larger and larger portions of *Dobet* and *Dobest* answer the questions raised by *Dowel* with a sense of how far any concern with defining the Do's has receded as a new drama emerges, whose structure is as different from that of the earlier passūs as the A poet's *Dowel* was from his *Visio*. When we look back and forth across B's twenty-one passūs, we see that it turns upon three confrontations between God's will and man's, in terms of three comings of God into the world of the fair field: the pardon scene, the Crucifixion, and Pentecost. Since the first is contemporary and fictional and the other two are historical, these three are not presented as having the continuity of temporal sequence or of cause and effect, the two kinds of cohesion we associate with the plot of a long fiction. Rather, the three moments are three completementary versions of the same reality, which together add up to an image of the convergence of the divine and human wills, in which time itself is only the dimension within which the confrontation takes place. The three moments are nearly antithetical in character. In the pardon scene, the polarity and antithesis between God and man is thrown into the highest relief. Our empathy is with man's desire to be responsible for himself, and God's attitude is felt keenly to be stern, autocratic, intransigent, patronizing, and nearly—if not wholly—incomprehensible. Whatever understanding our intellects can bring us to, that is how it feels, and Piers's ultimate submission leaves the audience totally disoriented. In the Crucifixion scene, the opposite impression is just as carefully cultivated. Where God accused man, he now attacks the devil. Where man's efforts were once found wanting, man judges and God dies. Where the pardon was associated with the "valley of the shadow of death," the Crucifixion ends in a blaze of light and in the triumph of Life over Death. Where the pardon was couched in the most intransigent and repellent terms available to the poet, the drama of the Crucifixion has built into it the debate of the Four Daughters of God who resolve its riddles at last. Yet, this new mode of enacting the drama of God's response to man is not a denial but a fulfillment of the earlier action. The third coming, which differs in that the actual moment of intervention recedes in dramatic prominence and the working out of its implications comes to the fore, is Pentecost, in which man's will itself becomes the theater of action. All three actions are presented through narration which provides an essentially literal, if highly stylized, mimesis. The first is the most intimate and realistic, as well as the most enigmatic; the second is epic; the third is abstracted and apocalyptic and, with its battles and its barns under siege, approaches the nearest of any part of *Piers Plowman* to the purely metaphorical action of allegory proper. In the first, man is acted upon; in the second, he is a participant; in the third, he becomes the actor. In the first, God is revealed in judgment; in the second, in compassion; in the third, in illumination. In the first, the issues appear as paradox; in the second, they are clarified by enactment and by debate; in the last, they appear in terms of their application by man to man. No one of them suffices alone to define the action they cumulatively present, but they converge on the climactic scene of the poem, the Passion, that action of the three which, for Christianity, is the resolution of human history.

To structure a poem in such a way creates great technical problems for the artist along with great possibilities—and raises a number of difficulties for any reader who is used to sensing cohesion in a work of art primarily in terms of causal sequence or at least of the centrifugal force exercised by a single consciousness which is itself the subject of the work. For the B poet the central continuity comes through incident itself, as later stages and actions incorporate and redefine earlier ones, including those he took over from the A text, and become as much their fulfillment as their complement. Much of what the B poet does in the later passūs comes to seem, retrospectively, as if it had been essential to the poem all along as, in a sense, it was. This is what makes

Piers Plowman the most dreamlike of all the medieval dream visions
(which are generally anything but dreamlike), by exploiting to the
full the possibilities of the dream for letting images melt into complementary images and figures melt out into many manifestations, coalesce
into more inclusive ones, or reappear in new meanings whose continuity with the old ones is a matter of pure connotation almost devoid
of denotation.[1] In places this method succeeds in transmitting to the
reader the vivid immediacy and almost intolerable pressure of actual
dream, in which we are taken possession of by something we can recognize as our own experience but stripped of the controls and modulations
consciousness can always impose on empathy. In such states, complete
intimacy and total strangeness coexist.

Above all, it is in the later B text (and in the effect it has retro-
actively on the earlier) that we see an artist taking the modes of thought
characteristic of medieval biblical exegesis and, instead of merely regarding them as a treasury of accepted images and symbols, creating a
genuine artistic equivalent for them in his poem, thus giving it a new
kind of structure. Medieval exegesis is heavily (though by no means
exclusively) typological, but rarely allegorical.[2] What the typological
exegete sees in the Bible is an actual and historical relationship between
real events, in which one event lays the groundwork for the other,
which will be its fruition and which it already resembles. The Bible
becomes, precisely because it is a literal account of God's interaction
with his creation throughout history, a vast network of motif and
reprise, in which image unfolds into fuller and richer image. This is
so because God is an artist working in the medium of history as the
poet does in the medium of words. The events of history, then, are
connected both by the cause-and-effect links of "plot" and by a pattern
of echo and response, of cumulative definition and redefinition. As suc-

1. See Constance B. Hieatt's discussion of this aspect of *Piers Plowman,* including
the "melting" of images and the splitting and transference of characters, *The Realism of Dream Visions* (The Hague, 1967), pp. 94–95.
2. The best analysis of the difference between the allegorical and the typological is
still Erich Auerbach's "Figura," reprinted in *Scenes from the Drama of European
Literature* (New York: Meridian Books, 1959), pp. 11–76. See also Bishop's distinction between the "allegory of the poets" and the "allegory of the theologians" in
Pearl in Its Setting.

cessive biblical commentators worked out a generally accepted exposition of this double linkage, a reservoir of symbols and associations of ideas was built up that played a highly significant role in medieval culture and art, on which poets could draw for various purposes, all in one way or another "allegorical"—that is, all providing a built-in explication or evaluation of experience from a communally accepted religious perspective. Of course, many of the events of the B poet's story are in themselves biblical and must, explicitly or implicitly, bring their associations with them. But he does something else as well. The *Piers Plowman Visio,* as we have argued earlier, is primarily a literal fiction, which has what J. R. R. Tolkien has called "applicability," [3] clearly expounded, and which employs the rhetorical shorthand of presenting some factors in the plot through personification. The A *Vita* introduces a major shift in dramatic level by interiorizing the issues of the *Visio.* Here personification becomes more dominant, but the action is still literally about what it overtly presents. Both the *Visio* and the *Vita* also include examples of allegory proper: the rat parliament, Piers's pilgrimage, Wit's castle, the banquet, the tree of charity, and other scenes. But these are all vignettes inserted into the main action to comment on it, and all come equipped with a commentator or his equivalent. What makes the B poet's dramatic structure, in its entirety, different from all these kinds of action (and distinctive in medieval narrative) is his creation of a pattern of echo, development, recapitulation, and resolution between the incidents of the poem itself analogous to that found within the Bible and his boldness in ultimately trusting the impact and continuity of his poem to the force of this pattern.

To see how he has created such a structure around the three comings of God, we will have to look not only at how he creates such a pattern of echo and response by juxtaposing key incidents that are not, like those of the Bible, part of one chronological sequence but also at how he devises patterns to give his drama the cumulative urgency and cohesion usually achieved through cause-and-effect plot. He does not, of course, eliminate the latter. In the *Visio,* a plot (a "what-if" plot, like that of so much science fiction) about the decision of a king to

3. In defending *The Lord of the Rings* from the charge of being allegorical, in the preface to the paperback edition (New York: Ballantine Books, 1965), 1:xi.

revitalize his kingdom provides the continuity which channels the force of each scene into the next. In the *Vita de Dowel,* the "plot" of the Dreamer's progress provides—with markedly less success—a basic cohesion, reinforced by the device of a common question in each scene. The B poet strengthened this element and did much to render the plot less episodic by including "recapitulation" scenes. But with passus 15 the action moves beyond the primary control of either device. The poet's answer lies, not simply in treating God's second and third interventions in such a way as to link them as closely as possible with the pardon scene, but in introducing a series of subsidiary sequences that, along with the continuity the Dreamer provides, establish cohesion between the units. The new "metaphorical" role of the three Do's and, to an even greater extent, the other, nonhierarchical triads, becomes one means of doing this, but such devices do not establish a pattern of fully consecutive development. The poet deals with this problem by imposing on the last passūs (exploiting in the process many details already present in the earlier sections of the poem) three sequences, all of which, in one way or another, merge the Dreamer's individual and idiosyncratic experience into a larger, corporate pattern.

THE UNITY OF LITURGY

The first of these patterns is provided by the Easter liturgy. This element has not been prominent in most of the poem, though there are important parallels between B's confession scene and the Confiteor; the pardon scene and the Dreamer's capitulation speech are linked through the proper of late Lenten masses; and the proper preface for Passion Sunday sheds light on the riddles of the Tree of Charity. With passus 16, the pattern becomes explicit and covers both "waking" and "dream" scenes, linking apparently disparate analyses and vignettes into a cumulative pattern. The first overt allusion to the liturgical sequence comes immediately after the Tree of Charity, when the Dreamer dates his encounter with Abraham on "a Mydlenten Sondaye," and the events of the Good Samaritan parable have been altered, as we noted earlier, to conform to a movement toward Jerusalem. In the next waking interval, the Dreamer tells us he wandered "lyke a lorel" until he ". . . wex wery of the worlde and wylned eft to slepe, / And lened me to a lenten and longe tyme I slepte" (B 18. 4–5). He "rutte faste tyl *ramis-palmarum*," when he begins to dream the events of Palm Sunday. These melt into Christ's trial before Pilate (Thursday) and into the Crucifixion (Friday) and the Harrowing of Hell, and the Dreamer is wakened by the bells of Sunday morning ringing for Easter. He calls his wife and daughter, and they go off rejoicing, dressed in their best, to Easter mass.

The next dream actually begins in the midst of this mass:

> In myddes of the masse tho men ʒede to offrynge,
> I fel eftsones a-slepe and sodeynly me mette,
> That Pieres the Plowman was paynted al blody,
> And come in with a crosse bifore the comune peple,
> And riʒte lyke in alle lymes to owre lorde Iesu;
> And thanne called I Conscience to kenne me the sothe.
> "Is this Iesus the Iuster?" quod I "that iuwes did to deth?
> Or is it Pieres the Plowman? Who paynted hym so rede?"
>
> [B 19. 4–11]

What the Dreamer is seeing in the sacrificed but triumphant figure that is somehow Christ and somehow Piers is the host, which is seen for the first time in the mass immediately after the "offrynge," when the priest, saying the Suscipe Sancte Pater, holds it up and then places it on the altar.[4] The Dreamer's question evokes Conscience and his discourse on the names of God. As this long speech ends, we seem still to be at the same point in the mass: "Thus Conscience of Crist and the crosse carped, / And conseilled me to knele ther-to . . ." (B 19.

4. For ways in which medieval English usage differed from the modern Roman Catholic missal, see William Maskell, *The Ancient Liturgy of the Church of England* (London, 1846), which prints the ordinary of the mass according to the uses of Sarum, Bangor, York, and Hereford, as well as the modern missal, in parallel columns. See also Frere, *The Use of Sarum,* which reprints the Sarum Consuetudinary and Customary (vol. 1) and the Ordinal and Tonal (vol. 2). None of the differences affects the argument below. For the evolution of the mass, see Jungmann, *The Mass of the Roman Rite.* Jungmann notes the fondness of late medieval artists for the subject of "St. Gregory's Mass"; while Gregory is at mass, the figure of Christ with the instruments of the Passion appears to him above the altar (1:116–17).

194–95). Not only do the Dreamer and Conscience still seem to be
looking at the same figure, but at this point in the mass, when the
offertory is complete, the congregation kneels and remains kneeling
through the action until those who are taking communion rise and
come forward.[5] But what the Dreamer sees next is the coming of the
Holy Ghost to "Piers and his felawes" in an enactment of Pentecost,
and Conscience, the Dreamer, and the congregation join in the singing
of the hymn *Veni Creator Spiritus.* Thus, at the very moment when
the Dreamer is present at the events of New Testament history, he is
also still at mass, and the mass is no longer that of Easter but of Pentecost, at which the biblical accounts of the coming of the Holy Ghost
are read,[6] separated by the singing of this very hymn.[7]

No striking parallel exists between the specific events of *Dobest* and
the specific liturgies of the Sundays after Pentecost, which span the
summer and early fall, at least in the missal itself. There is, however,
one more major liturgical affinity of great importance to B's structure,
and this concerns the last Sunday of the liturgical year, which always
completes the Easter sequence. Its gospel is Christ's prophecy of the
"abomination of desolation," the coming of false prophets and anti-
christs, of "signs in the heavens" that shall make "all the tribes of the
earth mourn," and of the coming of the "Son of Man" in "power and
majesty" to gather together his elect wherever they may be scattered
(Matt. 24:15–36). This is, of course, the basis for B's final passūs. Like
the Pentecost sequence, *Dobest* does not end with the Second Coming,
as an apocalypse proper would do, but ends with man's awareness that
it is the inevitable outcome of the remorseless process he sees occurring
around him: "Ita et uos, cum uideritis haec omnia, scitote quia prope
est in ianuis." [8] Together with this comes a promise: "Caelum et terra
transibunt: uerba uero mea non praeteribunt." [9] It is indeed in the

---

5. For the variations in posture at mass throughout the Middle Ages, see Jungmann,
Mass of the Roman Rite, 1:240.
6. Acts 2:1–11, from which the Communion also is drawn, and John 14.
7. The phrase "veni creator spiritus," though not the hymn, also occurs at the
beginning of mass in some medieval English rites (see Maskell, *Ancient Liturgy*).
8. Matt. 24:33, "So you also, when you shall see all these things, know ye that it
is nigh, even at the doors."
9. Matt. 24:35, "Heaven and earth shall pass away; my words shall not fail."

spirit of *Piers Plowman* that this formula should be simultaneously a promise of help and salvation and a remorseless reaffirmation of law.

By thus integrating the events of this poem with a familiar sequence of tightly connected events that were part of the familiar annual cycle, the B poet has given them a cumulative pattern that runs all the way from the early days of Lent to the culminating last Sunday after Pentecost, the final day before the new liturgical year begins with the first Sunday of Advent. Such a pattern of cohesion for *Dobet* and *Dobest* is based on a consciousness that the liturgical year is the very pulse of the annual cycle throughout all Christendom, the very calendar by which men reckoned, so that the most cynical date their very business ventures in terms of its landmarks. For the medieval Christian, whether he was a great scholar who also studied the Bible in its own right as a totality or an illiterate who never read anything, his central, dominant experience of the Bible came in the public worship of the Church. His primary association with any text or story was with the feast at which it was heard. We remember, for instance, the Pearl maiden's way of identifying Scripture passages for the Dreamer as an accommodation to his perspective; she introduces the parable of the vineyard with the words, "As Matthew meleʒ *in your messe* / In sothfol gospel of God almyʒte." [10] Even someone who did not know Latin probably had a consciousness imbued with snatches of meaningless words borne upon the Gregorian melody with which they were associated, which he could recognize though not understand when he heard them quoted and which seemed haunted by the significance of the feast and the season of the year at which they were heard. This was no semiprivate pattern of symbolism, like T. S. Eliot's quotations, but one which he knew he shared with his entire community, by a process as involuntary as the one by which the most recalcitrant modern mind finds itself pervaded with the words and tunes of common advertisements. If he knew Latin, his experience of the mass combined the intelligibility of one's own language with the primordial force of a "special" ritual tongue whose use affirms one's community with worshipers in all other places and at all times. The medieval man who knew Latin had the

10. *Pearl* 9. 497–98; italics mine.

experience which modern American society has, on a somewhat comparable scale, only with Handel's *Messiah,* where, even in the absence of belief, the mind's response to language, the spirit's response to beauty and ritual, and the psyche's response to a communal action inextricably associated with the rhythm of our own year and its activities, all reinforce one another. The medieval poet had a body of common and elemental knowledge and experience to count on in his readers, literate and even illiterate, for which we can find a modern analogy only in the idiom of "pop art" and which he could channel into his own dramatic structure by even comparatively slight allusions.

The Unity of History

The second sequential pattern that the poet uses to bind his poem together requires much less explanation and has already been largely covered in connection with the three Do's. It is provided by the events of human history itself, from Holy Church's first account of the creation and fall of the angels to the ominous immediacy of the Last Judgment at the end of *Dobest.* Allusions and vignettes scattered in no particular order throughout the earlier parts of the poems are affected, as scattered iron filings are affected when a magnet is brought near, by the firmly handled historical sequence of *Dobet* and the less sharp but equally urgent movement of *Dobest.* This pattern is obviously intimately related to the previous, liturgical one and is just as communal, but its effect on the cohesion of the poem is altogether distinct. The liturgical echoes make the action seem familiar, immemorial, timeless, and contemporary, an endlessly renewable common experience. Liturgy is a force toward a cyclic understanding of the human condition. It has affinities with allegory, in that it involves men corporately engaging in a rite which they know to be an artifice by comparison with daily living and which they perform partly in order to arrive at a capacity for, and conviction of, control over real life. The historical pattern has an opposite urgency. It affirms the ruthless reality of time and the irreversibility of human choice and its results. Where liturgy makes each moment seem recurrent, history makes it unique. If liturgy focuses man's awareness toward religion as edification, history focuses it toward religion as fact. The result of adding a historical dimension to the liturgical one is to modify man's consciousness of liturgy itself and to reaffirm that the mass is not primarily a pedagogical device but an action, and that it is not done *by* some men *to* others but is corporately engaged in. This historical urgency is the more important, since the fourteenth century was feeling the effects of strong tendencies toward making the liturgy more and more "magical" and meaninglessly elaborate and a concurrent tendency to use the mass not as a communal act but as a private one. One expression of this was the proliferation of masses offered for and financed by the dead; another was the high proportion of attenders at mass who did not take communion and saw themselves as spectators, edified or even merely protected and made lucky. We can see, in this dialogue of liturgy and history, affinities between *Piers Plowman* and poems as diverse as the Old English Advent lyrics of the *Exeter Book* and *Four Quartets,* in that all three involve the attempt to revitalize the language of the liturgy and quicken the "dead metaphors" into which religious imagery so remorselessly deteriorates as it becomes communal. In another sense, this dialogue reflects another tension in the poem. We can follow the story as focusing on the Dreamer, which makes its plot essentially interior and personal, contemporary with the reader, oriented toward the succession of psychological and religious states. Or we can see it as an objective drama, distanced by the arbitrariness of time, in which we see unroll man's corporate attempt to bring his world into conformity with the will of God. The first pulls the poem toward mysticism, convoluted analysis, psychological realism, autobiography. The second urges it equally strongly toward satire, tragedy, didacticism, and a psychology simplified and stylized toward the communal and away from the personal. It is a sign of the B poet's increasing sophistication and objectivity that this tension, implicit in Christianity itself and embodied in the contrast between the A *Visio* and *Vita,* moves toward a resolution in the later B text. One reason for this development in B is undoubtedly the release provided by a successful solution to the immediate problems of the A Dreamer, analogous to the role the composition of the first *Prelude* played in releasing Wordsworth to write more objective poetry. The other is that the counterpoint between these two tendencies is essential to any drama which tries to do justice to the way in which Christianity sees man as both individual and species, subject and object.

THE UNITY OF ECHO AND RESPONSE

Important as these two patterns are, and brilliant as the poet's exploitation of them sometimes is, they are not unique to him; the historical structure common to much of the Middle Ages' worst didactic verse and the role of the antiphons in the Advent lyrics testify to the possibilities liturgy and history presented to the artist. The third pattern is a pattern of his own creation, a pattern made up of his own incidents, and one in which we see him at last fully exploiting the two models for pattern in sequence available to him—the Bible, as understood typologically, and music. Drawing on the material that already made up the earlier passūs and shaping his new material in relation to it, he created a pattern of echo and response, motif and reprise, reorientation and recapitulation, which binds the disparate and often ungainly integers of the poem into a continuity beyond that provided by plot or allusion, by recurrent characters, or even by the narrator. The resulting system is of two sorts, a pattern of recurrence among scenes and one among figures.

The action of *Dobet* and *Dobest* is in a very obvious and straightforward sense the sequel and response to *Dowel*; much of the foregoing thematic analysis has been concerned with this particular continuity. In another sense altogether, *Dobet* and *Dobest* together can be seen as a formal sequence of scenes that correspond, but in reverse order, to those of the *Visio,* a sequence whose ultimate effect is to return us with new eyes to the poem's original point of departure. Readers of *Piers Plowman* have long been conscious of a fundamental parallel between the fair field of the Prologue and the great plain of the final passūs, and, indeed, the argument that comes full circle to its own starting point is highly characteristic of both A and B. The first consecutive speech, that of Holy Church, displays this sort of construction, and we noted an instance, however incomplete and abortive, of reverse matching of argument in the "unwinding" of the A text in its final passus. Only in the last five passūs of B, however, do we find this tendency raised to the status of a formal principle.

Because of the poem's passus titles, we think of it as falling into two parts, *Visio* and *Vita*; or four, *Visio* and three *Do's*; or five, if we consider the transitional Anima unit as a distinct component. But if we look at the poem, not simply to see how each section grows out of A's original schema, but to observe what the B poet's efforts finally amounted to, we find that a more striking feature of his poem than any of these divisions is the fact that it is made up of a dense block of consecutive intellectual analysis at the center of the poem, framed by blocks of objective action on either side, blocks which are built to correspond to and complement each other. The central block consists primarily of the *Vita de Dowel* but includes the scene with Anima and, to an extent, the Tree of Charity scene Anima introduces, scenes that are, as the poet's label suggests, transitional and that recapitulate *Dowel's* argument in a perspective that makes it a prologue to *Dobet* and *Dobest*. Indeed, the Tree of Charity scene, so structurally significant already as a nexus for all the major images of the later B text and as providing the one direct confrontation between Piers and the Dreamer, thus takes on an even greater significance. Its garden of the human heart links itself with the landscapes of both the Prologue and the ending to form a sequence of three increasingly metaphorical emblem-pictures of man in relation to his finite world which utilize the poem's basic image of farming. We recall that the opening picture of the fair field was followed by the Dreamer's encounter with Holy Church who "þi feiþ þe tauȝte," whereas Piers's garden is followed by the Dreamer's encounter with one who tells him "I am Feith" (B 16. 176).

To divide the poem into these three parts also corresponds with the division of the Dreamer's career into three stages, according to the three questions he asks in introductory waking interludes, each of which corresponds to the action of the ensuing part. The Prologue begins with the disreputable wanderer in a "somer sesoun" seeking "wondris to here." [11] *Dowel* begins with a parallel waking interlude in which the Dreamer changes his question:

11. At the beginning of passus 5 he merely hopes to "see more." The structure of the *Visio* has also been seen as turning on the Dreamer's question to Holy Church, "Kenne me by sum craft to know þe false" (A and B 2. 4); important as this is, a greater structural role is played by the three waking questions.

Thus, yrobid in rosset, I rombide aboute
Al a somer sesoun for to seke dowel,
And fraynide ful ofte of folk þat I mette
ʒif any wiʒt wiste where dowel was at Inne;
And what man he miʒte be of many man I askide.

[A 9. 4–5; also B 8. 4–5]

In *Dobet* the question does not change until after the transitional
Anima and Tree of Charity scene; in passus 15. 1–2, the issue is still
DoWell.[12] After this, we find a waking interval in which the Dreamer
describes himself, for the first time, as seeking Piers Plowman:

And I awaked there-with and wyped myne eyghen,
And after Piers the Plowman pryed and stared.
Estwarde and westwarde I awayted after faste,
And ʒede forth as an ydiote in contre to aspye
After Pieres the Plowman, many a place I souʒte.

[B 16. 167–72]

The importance of this division is further indicated by the fact that
from here on, as Vasta notes,[13] the Dreamer stops his continual reiteration that he lacks "kynde knowynge."

A central block of subjective experience and convoluted analysis,
reaching from passus 8 through the Tree of Charity scene, is thus
framed by two action sequences, one from the Prologue through the
pardon and one from Abraham through Conscience's departure to

12. The Dreamer's question to Anima about charity might be thought of as corresponding to the question within the first dream about the false, but whereas the
Dreamer's question to Holy Church was asked on his own initiative, the question
to Anima, important as it is, is merely in response to Anima's having already
brought up the subject. In any case, it corresponds to the division into Do's even
less well.

13. *Spiritual Basis,* p. 45. Note that from here on the waking interludes cease to
give general statements of purpose. Nevertheless the shift to a search for Piers
Plowman as the organizing device for the last part of the poem is confirmed by
the fact that two of the three remaining interludes move into the dreams they introduce through an image of Piers (B 18. 1–14, B 19. 1–7); the exception is the Need
dialogue (B 20.1–49), which is in many respects atypical. And the poem ends, of
course, with Conscience's departure to find Piers.

seek Piers Plowman at the end of the poem. These can be seen as unrolling in counterpoint to each other, not in the sense that the scenes duplicate or imitate each other or can be reduced to a common meaning, but in the "typological" sense that each scene in the second sequence is fundamentally the fulfillment—that is, the correction, clarification, completion, extrapolation, and the universalization—of a scene in the first. On either side of the central block is the bewildered waking Dreamer, preoccupied with thoughts of Piers Plowman. At the end of passus 7, he is "for Peres the plowman ful pensyf in herte" because of the pardon "And how the prest impugned it with two propre wordes," but he succeeds in shifting his attention from Piers to DoWell; in passus 16 he finally changes the object of his search from DoWell back to Piers. On either side of that are the two climactic scenes of the poem on whose complementary character we have already commented. The *Visio* has the sequence of the sending of the pardon, with the explication of how "helping Piers Plowman" qualifies a man to participate in it; the destruction of the pardon; and its effect. In the *Vita* we have the cumulative sequence from the meeting with Abraham, Moses, and the Good Samaritan (corresponding to the need of Piers and the analysis of how submission and ethics relate to salvation), the Crucifixion (corresponding to the tearing of the pardon), and the Harrowing of Hell and Easter (corresponding to the transformation of Piers).

Preceding the pardon sequence in the *Visio* is the half-acre sequence, which portrays the virtue of Piers by comparison with the folk, Piers's acceptance of responsibility for the folk's progress toward the good life, and the tragicomic plowing of the half acre; and succeeding the Atonement in the *Vita,* via the transition provided by Easter mass and Conscience's speech, is Grace's inspiration of Piers, the delegation of jobs and vocations to the people, and Piers's "plowing" of Christendom. Preceding the plowing of the half acre in the *Visio* is the confession scene, in which Conscience—or in B, Conscience and Reason—plays such a crucial role. There the relationship between sin, repentance, and restitution are analyzed, and we see the paralysis that results when man only knows himself and cannot translate that knowledge into act. The scene culminates in the helplessness of Robert the Robber who

". . . on *reddite* lokede, / And for ther was nouȝte wher-of he wepe swithe sore" (B 5. 469–70). Following Piers's plowing in the *Vita* is the coming of Pride, the capital sin with which the confession scene's portrait of human degeneration began, against which Conscience tries to marshall a defense by inviting into Unity whoever will pay "to Pieres pardoun the Plowman *redde quod debes*" (B 19. 387–88), only to encounter the increasing cynicism of the people, expressed by the brewer, the lord, and the king and so tartly analyzed by the "lewed vicory." Just as, in the *Visio,* the efforts of Conscience and Reason could not mobilize the folk at a sufficiently fundamental level to produce lasting results, so the virtues stressed in passus 19—*spiritus iusticie, spiritus prudencie, spiritus intellectus,* and *spiritus fortitudinis,* the natural as opposed to the theological virtues—and the leadership of Conscience cannot provide more than a temporary holding action against the forces of degeneration.

This brings us to the principal division in each sequence, marked in both cases by the only waking interlude within the action. In the *Visio* it is a brief one which does not divide the confession scene sharply from the preceding action to which it is the sequel: the Meed debate with its analysis of the relationship between material need, reward, and law. In the *Vita,* Conscience's defense of Unity is followed by the Dreamer's complex and enigmatic waking encounter with Need, who analyzes necessity (which "hath no lawe") and temperance and contrasts a vocation for living in privation as Christ did with the standards of the natural virtues. The first scene of the *Visio* was the great set piece of the fair field with its coming and going "as the worlde asketh"; the analysis of the institutions that attempt to impose some minimum order and protection upon it; the Dreamer's catechism by Holy Church, who analyzes the factors that govern the world; and her insistence that "loue is leche of lyf." To the Dreamer's anxious inquiries about Truth— "ȝe mote kenne me better / By what craft in my cors it comseth and where"—she replied that "kynde knowyng" teaches it, and it is love:

"It is a kynde knowyng," quod he "that kenneth in thine herte
For to louye thi lorde leuer than thi-selue;
No dedly synne to do, dey thouȝ thow sholdest:

> This I trowe be treuthe; who can teche the better,
> Loke thow suffre hym to sey and sithen lere it after.
> For thus witnesseth his worde, worch thow there-after;
> For trewthe telleth that loue is triacle of heuene. . . .
>
> [B 1. 140–46]

The last titanic scene in the *Vita* is the confrontation between the forces of Conscience and those of Antichrist, a cosmic battle across the fair field, and the defense of Unity, the remnant of the Church. In this conflict the Dreamer, under the assault of Old Age and Death, changes sides and joins in the defense of Unity after a catechism by Kynde:

> "Conseille me, Kynde," quod I, "what crafte is best to lerne?"
> "Lerne to loue," quod Kynde, "and leue of alle othre."
> "How shal I come to catel so, to clothe me and to fede?"
> "And thow loue lelly," quod he, "lakke shal the neure
> [Weede] ne worldly [mete] whil thi lyf lasteth."
> And [I], by conseille of Kynde, comsed to rowme
> Thorw Contricioun and Confessioun tyl I cam to Vnite.
>
> [B 20. 206–12]

Even Contrition himself is ultimately drugged by the friars under the direction of Envy and Sloth until he forgets to weep:

> "He lith [adreynt] and dremeth," seyde Pees, "and so do many other;
> The frere with his physik this folke hath enchaunted,
> And [doþ men drynke dwale] thei drede no synne."
>
> [B 20. 375–77]

The final acquiescence in corruption, out of a desire to be relieved of fear, which was first portrayed in the folk's gifts to the Pardoner in the Prologue and carried further in the portrait of the sins culminating in Sloth, has come about. Finally, at each end of the poem we have the figure of a pilgrim at the end of his resources, who nevertheless embarks on a new pilgrimage: it begins with the ambiguously clothed Dreamer "wery forwandrit" from having walked "wyde in þis world" and ends with Conscience:

"Bi Cryste," quod Conscience tho, "I wil bicome a pilgryme,
And [wenden] as wyde as al the world [renneþ],
To seke Piers the Plowman that Pryde [miȝte] destruye,
And that freres hadde a fyndyng that for nede flateren,
And contrepleteth me, Conscience; now Kynde me auenge,
And sende me happe and hele til I haue Piers the Plowman!"
And sitthe he gradde after grace til I gan awake.

[B 20. 378–84]

Such a pattern does not entirely account for the events of the *Visio*
and the later *Vita*. If the poet was to develop each sequence with any
dramatic integrity of its own, he had to let it acquire its own momentum and autonomy, and the reversal of order means that certain incidents necessary to the continuity of one sequence are unnecessary to
the other. For instance, the B poet does not include at the end of
Piers's plowing in passus 19 any equivalent to the threat of famine at
the end of his plowing of the half acre in the *Visio,* since the next block
of action, Conscience's first defense of Unity and his enunciation of
"redde quod debes" as the principle on which resistance to Pride depends
(which corresponds primarily to the confession scene), exercises the
same function. Similarly, the *Visio* has no equivalent to the scene of
communal rejoicing at Easter mass that leads into the coming of Grace
to supervise the division of labor on the field, because the relation of
each scene to its neighbors is quite different. The equivalent scene in
passus 6, the arrangements for plowing the half acre, functions as a
transition out of a highly pessimistic situation, in which the repentant
folk "blustreden forth as bestes ouer bankes and hilles" and can find
no guide but a palmer, into one of apparent (though, as it turns out,
false) security. In the *Vita,* on the contrary, the transition must go
in the opposite direction and head from the high point of triumphant
regeneration to its increasingly desperate danger. A further problem
for the reader in applying the reverse matching too rigidly is that it
may prevent his being sufficiently conscious of other less formal affinities
between *Visio* and *Vita.* For instance, though the content of the
Dreamer's interview with Need ties it in significant ways to the Meed
debate, the Dreamer's own role in that scene has affinities with his role

in the confession scene, and the dialogue stands in somewhat the same relationship to his subsequent appeal to Kynde as his confession in passus 5 does to his earlier dialogue with Holy Church. Similarly, the roles of Conscience and the king in the defense against Pride have significant affinities with the roles of king and Conscience in the Meed debate, over and above the parallelism of the scene as a whole with passus 5. The debate of the Four Daughters of God at the Harrowing of Hell has no equivalent in the pardon scene, because the whole strategy of the pardon scene depends on the exclusion of any intellectual resolution for its paradoxes. Instead, this debate recalls and resolves the debate so much earlier between Meed and Conscience over the relationship between justice and reward. Nevertheless, the total effect of unwinding the poem in the same order in which it was originally wound up is fundamental to the coherence of B as a whole.

But what gives this rather formal construct the living quality of musical structure is a second kind of echoing between parts, much less systematic and in the long run more rich, a pattern which includes the poem's middle third as well as its extremities. This is an echoing of image rather than of scene and involves the reappearance of the known in stranger and more complex contexts, in which its meaning is expanded and made more and more metaphorical without ever losing touch with the simple integrity it had at first. The most obvious and straightforward example of this is the recurrence of specific characters, not with the continuity of "characters" in a novel (Mr. Micawber is Mr. Micawber every time he turns up), but with the expanding and evolving reality of characters in a dream. This is most obvious, of course, in the two main instances, Piers and the Dreamer, but it is true of many lesser characters as well, such as Conscience, Reason, and Kynde. Conscience at the banquet (or at Easter mass or in the war with Antichrist) is not the same character who vilified Lady Meed in the sense in which the Pip who narrates *Great Expectations* "is" the Pip who once stole a pork pie. All the same, these successive Consciences are in continuity with each other, and this continuity makes the poet's successive analyses part of the unfolding of one reality through a multiplicity of manifestations. Among these "characters" should be included the crowd: again and again we see flocks of people streaming across the fields of the poem—the milling crowds of the Prologue; the followers of Meed pressing toward London; the folk crowding to hear Reason's sermon, straggling forth in search for Truth, then working in orderly disorder on the half acre; the crowds pouring into Jerusalem on Palm Sunday, shouting at Pilate and the soldiers on Good Friday, converging on the church dressed in their best for Easter mass and going forward at the offertory, clamoring around Piers and Grace as vocations are dispensed, melting away from Unity when Conscience demands "redde quod debes," and ultimately polarizing into two armies in the final war.

A second kind of expanding image has affinities with the recurrent imagery of other narrative poems, but in most long poetic structures the basic continuity is that of plot, which gives the imagery its cumulative character rather than vice versa. In *Piers Plowman,* the continuity through images becomes central and plot an intermittent reinforcing factor. Some of the simpler images involve the recurrence of familiar material things in a pattern that begins with realistic sociological detail and widens to include major theological and liturgical associations. Clothing is such an image. There are the realistic details of clothing in the *Visio* and the clothes-swapping game in Glutton's tavern; the emblematic finery of Lady Meed; the squalid garments of the sinners; the disguises like the Dreamer's "shroud," the "cuntenance of clothing" of the proud in the Prologue, and the robes of "Frere Flatterer," the doctor in passus 20; the clean clothes that mark renewal, like the promised cleansing of Hawkin's coat and the Dreamer's new garments on Easter morning. Food and drink is another such image, which at its realistic pole is essential to the poem's analysis of the economic structure and at the liturgical pole suggests the mass. The Prologue begins with the food raised by the plowman, consumed by the wasters, crammed into bags by the "bidderis and beggeris," proclaimed from their doorways by cooks and taverners. Meed defends corrupt food purveyors: Avarice and his wife water the wine and ale; Glutton and his fellows carouse at an anticommunion; Piers and the folk feed Hunger into torpor. The pardon comes when famine is imminent. The Dreamer and Patience attend Clergy's banquet. Hawkin is a "waferer" who feeds the people and makes the Host for mass and is ultimately given his "liflode" by Patience. The Crucifixion, which Repentance described earlier as "mele-tyme of seintes" and which the Dreamer saw as Isaiah's "wine and milk, without money and without price," dispensed to all who thirst, is a joust in which the price is "Piers fruit the Plowman"; and Christ tells Lucifer:

> For I, that am lorde of lyf, loue is my drynke,
> And for that drynke today I deyde upon erthe.
> I fauȝte so me threstes ȝet for mannes soule sake,
>
> [B 18. 363–65]

and commands him: "That are doctour of deth, drynke that thou madest!" (B 18. 362). And the raising of food returns to dominance as the central image in the last great passūs.

The very action of the poem is patterned around three fundamental human activities which become metaphors for human life: farming; search or questing; and war. Although one is dominant in each third of the poem—farming in the *Visio,* search in *Dowel,* and combat by single champion and by armies in *Dobet* and *Dobest*—all recur and become increasingly interwoven as the poem progresses, until the final scene belongs to all three sequences. The images of farming demonstrate most clearly the expansion from realistic action into metaphor. The Prologue description of the world begins with the good plowmen who support the social and economic structure, and Piers describes his service to Truth in realistic farming terms. When he directs the folk in the plowing of the half acre, the farm has become a metaphorical world, but the action is still highly realistic. The farm recedes in importance in *Dowel,* though it remains a rather escapist ideal for the Dreamer and crops up in that character in the tirade, and Wit uses the imagery of growing things. In passus 15 the human heart is a farm under the care of Piers Plowman, a garden lost to the devil through the sin of Adam. Finally, Piers plows the fields of all Middle Earth with a biblical and patristic team, plants the seed of virtue, and builds the barn of Holy Church to store the harvest; even the Last Judgment itself is called "the vendage . . . in the vale of Iosephath" (B 16. 367).

The second image, search, includes the curiosity of the human mind, the journey of the pilgrim and the quest of the knight-errant, and thus is inextricably intertwined with the poem's economic and philosophical analysis and its image of knighthood and war. The Dreamer of course is central here; his search, though continually redefined, extends unbroken from his first steps on a May morning until he finally abandons the isolation that is the mark of his quest and enters Unity at the end, giving the poem its nearest equivalent to a cumulative plot. Quest is not confined to the Dreamer: Piers, Patience, Conscience, Faith, Hope, and the Good Samaritan all become questers, and the poem ends as it began, with pilgrimage. War, both as conquest and as defense, dominates the last passūs, and even the barn, Unity, becomes a castle under siege, but the metaphor is not new. There have been towers and castles melting into each other ever since the "tour on a toft" and the "dungeoun" in the dale which dominated the field of the Prologue. There is war in heaven when God creates the angels, the first "knights," and the rebellious ones are put to flight; King David creates the order of knighthood; the castle of Truth at the end of Piers's "pilgrimage" is guarded by a gate ward who will only unbar the gates for someone who can show the right token; the castle of Wit's Anima is under siege, defended by DoWell and his knights; Piers's "herber" of the human heart is attacked by the devil and defended by Piers with the pike "Filius"; the Crucifixion is a joust between knights in armor; and the gates of Hell are battered down at the coming of the Lord of Light.

Perhaps the most important sequence of all is a sequence of parallel moments in the response of separate characters. This is, in fact, the kind of echoing between biblical figures on which typological patterns are primarily based. These figures are not to be equated with each other after the manner of allegory; rather, each, in addition to carrying out his function in the particular dramatic and intellectual sequence in which he is found, contributes to a total emblem which takes on richer and richer meaning as the poem progresses and gives greater and greater urgency and intensity to each successive scene in which it occurs. These moments, as they echo and define each other, provide the poem's central continuity, its image of finite man before the infinite. If the closest analogue to the recurrences of character and metaphor we have been discussing before is music, here one must think of ballet, which John Cranko has described as an art based, not on "metaphor" (the explicit or implicit comparison he epitomizes as "the moon is *like* green cheese"), but on "image," a created moment of experience that speaks for itself but whose relation to meaning and to other experience the audience must supply for itself by working with the image.[14] Ballet, when it does not allow itself to be trapped in pantomime and reduced to mimesis, is the ultimate in the art of sequence of image, where the coherence is inherent in the images as such and the meaning is a function of the sequence. Since the integers of the image are human movments, it renders human experience accessible, but here "meaning" is not limited to, and may have no connection with, intellectual content, let alone plot.

It may seem paradoxical to suggest that the meaning of *Piers Plowman* is of that kind, since in no other poem is intellectual content and intellectual experience so much in the foreground, demanding the most concentrated attention; and this invites us to find the poem's meaning and continuity in that content. But our difficulties with the poem's argument stem less from its admittedly taxing character than from the fact that it does not lead us to the release from anxiety and bewilderment we expect of intellectual analysis. We seek continually in the argument for a stability and satisfaction it does not provide. *Piers Plowman* is not a poem that is best understood in terms of the classical process of medieval philosophy, that of *fides quaerens intellectum*. This is the poem of *intellectus quaerens fidem,* understanding seeking reconciliation with faith, or even *intellectus quaerens caritatem*. Learned as it is, it reminds us not of Saint Anselm but of the epileptic's father in the Gospel: "I believe; help thou mine unbelief" (Mark 9:24). The poem's continuity is not in the argument, contentious and authoritarian as it so often is, but in its unfolding from human image to human image. Perhaps the poem which most resembles *Piers Plowman* in this respect is a poem as rich and craftsmanly as *Piers Plowman* is gnarled and uneven, *The Faerie Queene*. Like the Great Dance to which C. S. Lewis compares it, the coherence and splendor of Spenser's structure lies above all in just such a pattern of echo and response between images that define and enrich each other almost apart from their dependence

14. In a documentary film on his work with the Stuttgart Ballet, entitled "Cranko's Castle" and aired on National Educational Television in 1969–70.

on the continuities of plot, or the precise and lucid intellectual structure of philosophy.

This is why the elements that make the B structure so much more difficult and so much less "rational" than C—the elements that the C poet tends to eliminate or diminish—are essential to his purpose. The overlapping structure, for example, in which his analysis of any given stage or problem is complicated by the presence of characters and themes proper to another stage, makes the intellectual development much more difficult to follow; and his increasing tendency to make a line of argument culminate not in verbal formulation of the answer but in a dramatic image forces us to provide intellectual knowledge and intellectual effort in order to participate in a process in which both are to be superseded by another sort of awareness altogether. The price of such a strategy is obvious, but the gain is twofold. On the one hand, by playing more stages and factors against each other at each stage than the C poet was to do and by forcing the intellectual and psychological cost of such a theological structure into the foreground, the B poet's analysis is greatly enriched, both implicitly and explicitly, and is much fairer to the inherent difficulties of the problem. The C poet's lucidity is a function of his having drastically reduced the scope of his subject, both in his explicit content and with respect to his portrayal of search and human development. The B drama, like that of A, is a defense of the faith precisely because of the complete unsentimentality with which it faces the very elements of which one might say, as the Dreamer did on first hearing Scripture's sermon,

> . . . the matere that she meued, if lewed men it knewe,
> The lasse as I leue louyen [thei wolde
> The bileue of our lord þat lettred men techeþ].

> [B 11. 104-5]

But even beyond that, Christianity has always had implicit in it a tension, accentuated by conflicts throughout Christian history between its Judaic and Greco-Roman heritages but not limited to that element alone. Is the "good news" of Revelation the fulfillment of actual life, the flowering of the created world in its very createdness into the splendor of the New Jerusalem? Or is it rather the call to freedom from the material, the finite, the particular, the mixed, the conflicting, the individual? Is man *imago dei* in his creatureliness or in his spirituality? Christianity has somehow managed, in spite of leaning far in one direction or the other at different stages in its history, to go on answering, "both." But the price has been interim contradiction, paradox, the painful process of struggling to keep faith with many realities at the cost of self-doubt and conflicting loyalties. One might argue that as soon as *Piers Plowman* diminishes too sharply this element of conflict and struggle with diversity, it loses the one quality that gives it a stature, either as poetry or as a formulation of Christian belief, that goes beyond that conferred by the presence of brilliant individual passages. For many readers, the paradox of the C text is that while its larger structure and much of its line-by-line revision seem to diminish this essential quality, its new passages display it in the purest form of any version.

In *Piers Plowman,* the greatest of these sequences of images is in portrayals of the moment in which a consciousness grasps its finitude in the face of reality and, in the very moment of its despair and rebellion, breaks through to a new level of being. Many of these we have already noted in connection with DoWell. Together they define a pattern that emerges more and more clearly: consciousness of helplessness before impossible standards, one's own weakness, recalcitrant reality, or an overawing presence; despairing collapse or rebellion; breakthrough; and only then weeping. The first, most low-key, and incomplete instance is the Dreamer at the beginning, when his first search ends, leaving him "wery forwandrit" before the second, the dream, can begin. The first full emblem is the confession of Robert the Robber, whose tears mark his awareness that he is incapable of restitution and his hope in Christ's forgiveness of the repentant thief. The next, and the key one for the poem as a whole, is the pardon scene. Here Piers, confronted with the simultaneous revelation of God's standards and his compassion, tears the pardon and in that moment is transformed, saying:

> Þe prophet his payn eet in penaunce & wepying
> Be þat þe sauter vs seiþ, & so dede manye oþere.

Þat louiþ god lelly, his liflode is þe more:
Fuerunt michi lacrime mee panes die ac nocte.

[A 8. 108–11]

For the Dreamer, the stages in the same process are separated. When his whole search for DoWell seems to have brought him only to despair, and Scripture scorns him with "Multi multa sciunt et seipsos nesciunt," he weeps "for wo and wratth," and is plunged into the deeper dream that is his greatest sin and yet also the beginning of true self-knowledge. Later, when he comes back to Scripture, who preaches on predestination, he despairs again: "Al for tene of her tyxte trembled myn herte / And in a were gan I waxe . . ." (B 11. 110–11). As he recognizes that the whole affair is in a sense out of his hands anyhow, he hears the voice of Trajan, who answers the central question of his earlier tirade; and the story of Trajan is another image of the same kind. Again, when the Dreamer has interrupted the dream by his refusal to listen to Kynde, he becomes capable for the first time of shame, and with the "wo" he feels, there materializes Ymagynatyf. Conscience at the banquet decides to leave all the activities that others have found useful and to go off, mourning his sins, in search of Piers Plowman. Perhaps the clearest instance is the despair of Hawkin who manages to stand up for himself until the moment when he knows himself to be taken care of out of pure charity; then for the first time he breaks down and weeps, and this grief is the final definition of DoWell. The poet's decision to treat the Crucifixion as a joust precludes his making the Garden of Gethsemane part of this pattern, as he might well have done. Instead he uses the experience of the blind knight Longeus, who gives Christ the wound in the side:

But this blynde bacheler thanne bar him thorugh the herte;
The blode spronge down by the spere and vnspered the kniȝtes
    eyen.
Thanne fel the kniȝte vpon knees and cryed [Iesu] mercy—
"Aȝeyne my wille it was, lorde, to wownde ȝow so sore!"
He seighed and sayde "sore it me athynketh;

For the dede that I haue done I do me in ȝowre grace;
Have on me reuth, riȝtful Iesu!" and right with that he wept.

[B 18. 85–91]

The poem ends at the moment when things are so desperate that even Contrition "lith and dremeth" and has lost the capacity for grief. Then Conscience begins a new pilgrimage: "And sitthe he gradde after grace til I gan awake."

The ultimate manifestation of this image does not come within the B text at all, a fact which illustrates most poignantly how the three versions of the poem play the game of echo and completion among themselves. This is the confession of the C Dreamer. Reason and Conscience force him out of one defense of his life after another until in desperation there is nothing for him to do but acknowledge the truth:

". . . and so ich by-knowe,
That ich haue tynt tyme and tyme mysspended;
But ȝut, ich hope, as he that ofte haueth chaffared,
That ay hath lost and lost and atte laste hym happed
He bouhte suche a bargayn he was the bet euere,
And sette hus lost at a lef at the laste ende,
Suche a wynnynge hym warth thorw wordes of hus grace;
     *Simile est regnum celorum thesauro abscondito in agro, &
       cetera:*
     Mulier qui inuenit dragmam vnam, et cetera;
So hope ich to haue of hym that is al-myghty
A gobet of hus grace and bygynne a tyme,
That alle tymes of my tyme to profit shal turne."
    "Ich rede the," quath Reson tho "rape the to by-gynne
The lyf that ys lowable and leel to the soule"—
"Ȝe, and continue;" quath Conscience and to the kirke ich wente.
    And to the kirke gan ich go god to honourie,
By-for the crois on my knees knocked ich my brest,
Sykinge for my synnes seggynge my *pater-noster,*
Wepyng and wailinge tyl ich was a slepe.

[C 6. 92–108]

Here the poem's most urgent thread of imagery becomes identified with its very character: a tentative, imperfect, and agonized unfolding of perception toward an awareness of man himself. It is an image of consciousness struggling for identity and meaning within the concentric pattern of all the greater and greater realities that surround it, beginning with the economic and social compulsions which man has brought into being and reaching all the way to the ultimate Presence, the God who is "a circle whose center is everywhere and whose circumference is nowhere." For Dante the journey leads to the supreme vision of love expressed in a majestic geometry for which the *Comedy* itself, in its perfection of exquisite control, is a human equivalent. For Langland it leads, by the way of "a thousand visions and revisions," to the image of the single man crying out for grace.

Index

The index does not note *Piers Plowman,* the Dreamer, Langland, A text, and B text, except when a major point is being made about them, since they recur on almost every page. Biblical passages are not indexed. Material in the notes is not indexed unless the note contains substantive discussion distinct from that of the corresponding argument in the main text, except for frequently cited *Piers Plowman* scholars. Where a character or scene is frequently referred to, the main discussion is indicated by italics.